RUSSELL ON RELIGION

Russell on Religion contains a selection of writings designed to give the reader representative material on all aspects of his thinking on this subject.

Russell contends with religion in every genre of his writing from mathematical treatises to his ventures in fiction; as a philosopher, historian, social critic and private individual.

Students at all levels will find *Russell on Religion* a valuable presentation of the development and diversity of Bertrand Russell's thinking about religion.

Louis Greenspan is Professor Emeritus, Department of Religious Studies, McMaster University and former Director of the Bertrand Russell Editorial Project.

Stefan Andersson is a research scholar at the Bertrand Russell Archives, McMaster University.

RUSSELL ON...
General editor's introduction
A. C. Grayling

Russell achieved public fame – often enough, notoriety – because of his engagement in social and political debates, becoming known to a wide audience as a philosopher in the popular sense of the term. But his chief contributions, the ones that have made a permanent difference to the history of thought, lie in logic and philosophy; and they are such that his influence both on the matter and style of twentieth-century philosophy, principally in its Anglophone form, is pervasive. Elsewhere I have described his contribution as constituting the 'wall-paper' of analytic philosophy, in the sense that his successors 'use techniques and ideas developed from his work without feeling the need – sometimes without recognizing the need – to mention his name; which is influence indeed'.

Russell devoted much attention to central technical questions in philosophical logic, epistemology and metaphysics. He also wrote extensively and forcefully about moral, religious and political questions in ways not merely journalistic. Much of his work in all these areas took the form of essays. Some have of course been famously collected, constituting a fundamental part of the canon of twentieth-century analytic philosophy. But there are many more riches in his copious output, their value to some degree lost because they have not hitherto been collected and edited in such a way as to do justice to the development and weight of his thinking about these subjects. This series, in bringing together Russell's chief writings on major subject areas in an editorial frame that locates and interprets them fully, aims to remedy that lack and thereby to make a major contribution both to Russell scholarship and to contemporary analytic philosophy.

RUSSELL ON RELIGION

Selections from the writings of
Bertrand Russell

*Edited by Louis Greenspan and
Stefan Andersson*

Routledge
Taylor & Francis Group

LONDON AND NEW YORK

First published 1999
by Routledge
2 Park Square, Milton Park, Abingdon, Oxon OX14 4RN

Simultaneously published in the USA and Canada
by Routledge
270 Madison Avenue, New York, NY 10016

Reprinted 2001, 2002, 2003, 2004, 2006

Routledge is an imprint of the Taylor & Francis Group

Typeset in Garamond by Taylor & Francis Books Ltd
Printed and bound in Great Britain by Biddles Ltd, King's Lynn, Norfolk

British Library Cataloguing in Publication Data
A catalogue record for this book is available from the British Library.

Library of Congress Cataloguing in Publication Data
Russell, Bertrand, 1872–1970.
Russell on religion: selections from the writings of Bertrand Russell /
edited by Louis Greenspan and Stefan Andersson. p. cm. Includes
bibliographical references and index.
1. Religion–Philosophy. I. Greenspan, Louis I., 1934– .
II. Andersson, Stefan, 1953–. III. Title.
81649.R91G74 1999   210–dc21   98–30931

ISBN 0–415–18091–0 (hbk)
ISBN 0–415–18092–9 (pbk)

CONTENTS

CONTENTS

ACKNOWLEDGEMENTS

The research for this volume has, in the case of Dr Andersson, been supported by The Wenner-Gren Foundation in Stockholm, The Hultengren Foundation for Philosophy in Lund and The Anders Karitz Foundation in Uppsala. For information concerning the papers published here we have relied heavily on *The Bibliography of Bertrand Russell* by Kenneth Blackwell and Harry Ruja, and the introductions and headnotes supplied by the editors of *The Collected Papers of Bertrand Russell*. We are grateful to Dr John G. Slater for his help and for giving us access to Volumes 10 and 11 before they were published, to Dr Richard Rempel and Dr Andrew Brink for access to Volume 12 and to Dr Rempel and Dr Beryl Haslam for access to Volume 15 prior to its publication. In addition we would like to thank McMaster University and Dr Richard Rempel as Director of the Russell Project for their generosity in allowing us to draw on the facilities of this Project. We are especially indebted to Arlene Duncan, Office Manager of the Project, for her good cheer and hard work in putting out this volume. We are grateful to series editor Anthony Grayling for his learned counsel and unfailing support. We are also grateful to our editor at Routledge, Richard Stoneman and his assistant, Coco Stevenson, as well as Dr John Slater, Dr Kenneth Blackwell at The Bertrand Russell Archives, Dr Nicholas Griffin, Dr Richard Rempel and Dr Andrew Bone for stimulating discussions concerning Russell on religion.

INTRODUCTION

Bertrand Russell belonged to that company of freethinkers who wrote continually about religion. Religion is the subject of one of his earliest writings, the secret diary that he started to keep when he was sixteen years old, it is the theme of well-known essays such as 'The Free Man's Worship', and figures prominently in the mature treatises on sociology and politics such as *Prospects of Industrial Civilization*. Even some of his treatises on mathematics and philosophy of science contain speculations about the reality of a spiritual realm independent of the senses. Religion is prominent in the unpublished fiction that he wrote early in the century as well as the fiction that he published at a great old age. Throughout much of his life Russell contended with religion as philosopher, as historian, as social critic and as private individual. In one of his memoirs he declared that he overcame religion when he was an adolescent during a struggle recorded in his secret diary when 'I rejected successively, free will, immortality and belief in God'. But the record of a lifetime of writing suggests that the struggle continued for many years, and on several fronts.

In this volume we have presented only a small selection from Russell's vast corpus of writings on religion. We have chosen material from diverse genres of literature, omitting only his most technical work and his fiction. We have included his most important philosophical and literary articles, his personal statements and selections from his surveys of world history as well as his books on science and society. We have been selective, but we have endeavoured to cast as wide a net as Russell's so that the reader will be exposed to all aspects of his work on this subject.

Freethinkers and humanists cherish Russell as revealed in essays such as 'Why I Am Not a Christian' and 'Has Religion Made Useful Contributions to Civilization?' and in passages such as 'my own

1

view of religion is that of Lucretius. I regard it as a disease born of fear and as a source of untold misery to the human race.'[1] Such passages remain an important part of the canon of sacrilege. Russell argued the case against religion in public debates with eminent theologians and took delight in making anti-religious jibes, such as his retort that when he made his appearance before the Heavenly Throne, he would reprimand his Maker for not providing sufficient evidence of His existence. Though, supposedly, he lived in an age of declining faith, religious authorities found the energy to pour wrath upon him and his works. His enemies spread rumours that the school he established at Beacon Hill was a nest of atheism, nudity and free love. In 1940 a coalition led by the Bishop of New York succeeded in having him stripped of the position of a visiting professorship at City College, New York, and issued an indictment (that Russell often repeated with relish) in which he was cited as 'lecherous, lustful, venerous, erotomaniac, aphrodisiac, irreverent'.

Yet many students of Russell's life and works agree with Russell's daughter Katherine Tait, who in her splendid memoir says, 'He was by temperament a profoundly religious man, the sort of passionate moralist who would have been a saint in a more believing age.'[2] Anthony Grayling affirms that 'Although Russell was hostile to religion he was nevertheless a religious man.'[3] An English bishop called him a 'natural Christian' except for his views on sex and marriage, and the Quaker war resisters with whom he formed an alliance during the First World War treated him as a comrade, a Christian in spirit if not by confession. Ray Monk, Russell's biographer, maintains that Russell's search to break out of personal isolation into love, friendship and ultimately into union with the cosmos[4] is one of the dominant motifs of his life, and Russell himself confessed that 'human affection is to me at bottom an attempt to escape from the vain search for God'. The thousands of ordinary men and women who wrote to him about their spiritual and personal problems[5] thought of him as a colleague of other saintly figures such as Tagore, Albert Schweitzer and other spiritual mentors for our time. The great sociologist Max Weber, who wrote volumes about religion, could plausibly describe himself as 'religiously unmusical', but few would have believed this of Russell.

How then are we to treat Russell as both secular and religious? One approach is to consider his religious and his anti-religious writings separately, each characteristic of a different period in his life. Students of Russell's work know that Russell's development as a thinker was not a smooth one and that he was prone to change his mind on a number of important subjects. When he was exposed for having different views on different subjects he solemnly pleaded guilty. Russell held different views about the ontological status of mathematics at different times in his life and there is no reason to suppose that he could not hold different views of religion.

The argument that Russell simply changed his mind about religion is given substance by Griffin's insight[6] that Russell took two different approaches to religion during two different periods of his life. His writings before 1920 were apologia of the life of the spirit, intended 'to preserve religion without any dependence on dogmas to which an intellectually honest assent becomes daily more difficult'.[7] From the 1920s, beginning with the passages on religion in *Prospects of Industrial Civilization*, however, his writing on religion became more polemical. He simply abandoned one set of views and adopted another.

But the evidence shows that Russell did not intend his later polemical writings as disavowals of his earlier ones. While Russell has provided us with autobiographical writings that give evidence that he became critical of some of his earlier essays, notably 'The Free Man's Worship' and 'The Essence of Religion', there are none in which he renounces his early calls for a 'life in the spirit'. In his 'Reply to Criticisms' in *The Philosophy of Bertrand Russell* edited by Paul Arthur Schilpp,[8] Russell admits that his attitude to religion is 'somewhat complex'. He admits that 'I consider some form of personal religion highly desirable and feel that many people are unsatisfactory through lack of it.'[9] In that same excerpt he cites the chapter 'Religion and the Churches' from his World War I volume *Principles of Social Reconstruction* (reprinted in this volume) as the statement on religion that he was able to endorse as the 'least unsatisfactory' of his pronouncements on religion. But this statement contains Russell's most passionate call for a life which is aware of 'a mystery half revealed, of a hidden wisdom and glory, of a transfiguring vision in which common things lose their solid importance and become a thin veil behind which the ultimate truth of the world is dimly seen'. Thus, the problem remains of finding a formula that will embrace Russell's admiration for the atheism of Lucretius as well as the Russell who can write apologetically about religious dogmas, arguing that

> they were believed to facilitate a certain attitude towards the world, an habitual direction to our thoughts, a life in the whole, free from the finiteness of the self and providing an escape from the tyranny of desire and daily cares.[10]

The history of philosophy suggests another solution to this puzzle. Since Socrates was put on trial for promoting his own piety while acting with impiety towards the gods of the city, philosophers have, from time to time, declared a distinction between the Divine Order that was disclosed to philosophers and the religious beliefs upheld by the public. Students of the history of philosophy can provide evidence of this distinction in every age. As early as the Ancient Greeks there were philosophers who distinguished between this Divine Order accessible to philosophy, and the phantasms and imaginings of the unreflective. Xenophanes[11] complained that the multitude invent gods after their own image, while philosophers seek the true logos. Over the centuries different philosophers gave different evaluations of these different forms of piety. According to Pascal, who was sympathetic to the revealed truths of the Bible, we must shun the 'gods of wise men and philosophers and embrace the God of Abraham, Isaac and Jacob'. According to Gibbon, while such a distinction was prevalent in the Roman Empire, and while philosophers thought that public order demanded that all pay homage to the gods of the populace, they still 'approached with the same inward contempt and the same external reverence the altars of the Libyan, the Olympian or the Capitoline Jupiter'.[12] Gibbon's solution appealed to the eighteenth-century Enlightenment, of which Russell is commonly thought to be a twentieth-century embodiment. Thus, the combination of scepticism and devotion in Russell's approach to religion seems traditional and, from the evidence of the history of philosophy, not exceptional.

But the reader cannot fail to observe that though Russell is thought of as an heir to the Age of Reason as it has been understood throughout the history of philosophy, much of his critique of religion is, in fact, a critique of the religion of reason. His polemic against 'the argument from design' in 'Why I Am Not a Christian' as well as in other essays is directed against the followers of Newton as much as against the Mediaevals. Much of his critical acumen is directed against theologically minded physicists. Yet the paradox of Russell as a writer on religion is that while he championed the rationalism of the eighteenth century in his writings on religion, he is that tradition's most energetic critic. He would have agreed readily with Tertullian and Kierkegaard that religion concerns the absurd rather than that it discloses a rational structure to the universe. But for all this, as we shall suggest, religion and the spiritual life is, for Russell, an ally in the pursuit of scientific truth.

Russell and the religion of reason

In the autobiographical sketches included in this volume Russell presents a portrait of a youngster whose early religious struggles centred on his family's version of the 'religion of reason'. He was raised by his grandmother, who professed a modern, rational religion in harmony with the sciences rather than the traditional religion of revealed dogma. Lady Russell was a Scotch Presbyterian who gradually became a Unitarian. Though she took the young Russell to the local parish church and to the Presbyterian church on alternate Sundays, 'at home I was taught the tenets of Unitarianism...on most topics the atmosphere was liberal....Darwinism was taught as a matter of course.'[13] Russell was taught to revere the Bible as a source of moral instruction rather than as a source of scientific truth. He tells us in his memoirs that many of its injunctions, such as 'Thou shalt not follow a multitude to do evil' (EX 25:2), remained personal mottoes for life. But he was never troubled by questions such as whether the sun stood still or whether Genesis is literally true.

Religious fundamentalists today would regard such a religion with scorn as wishy-washy and lacking in moral fibre. But Russell's grandmother, though liberal in her theological views, was intensely religious and a very strict Puritan. Russell was raised in a regime so severe and in a discipline so relentless that his early life can be compared to that of novices in a rigorously ascetic monastic order. Russell concluded early in life that uncompromising moral austerity does not need the stimulus of religious threats or dogmas. Russell could have been used as an illustration of Weber's thesis that the house of reason is an iron cage.

One might have expected that Russell's teenage revolt against his grandmother's rationalist religion would have been a revolt in the direction of romanticism or a version of hedonistic *carpe diem* or even religious fundamentalism. This is not the case. This revolt, as recorded in the secret diary that he started to keep when he was sixteen years old, emphasized the illusory hopes and comforts that this religion still maintained. Russell insisted in this diary (as he did for the rest of his life) on a religion that was consistent with science. He conceded that belief in a deity passed this test but that the doctrines of immortality and freedom of the will did not. Russell's first revolt against the religion of reason sought consistency with his moral asceticism rather than any romantic urge (these came later). He came to believe in a deity who was in his heaven but cared little for what happened below. Later he gave up his conviction that there was rational basis for the idea of a deity.

Throughout the early years of his life he flirted with some version of a religion of reason, one in which mathematics or science or philosophy disclosed a stable universal order. In his thesis, Stefan Andersson[14] has argued that there was a religious dimension in Russell's search for mathematical certainty. For a time he was held by Plato's argument that mathematics revealed a realm of eternal ideas above the flux of everyday things, a realm that provided a stable superstructure for our own world of ceaseless change. Russell was intermittently held by philosophical proofs of the deity, such as the famous episode when he believed in the ontological proof. At Cambridge he was exposed to McTaggart's defence of the Hegelian version of the God of reason. He writes: 'I had gone out to buy a tin of tobacco; on my way back, I suddenly threw it up in the air and exclaimed as I caught it: "Great God in boots, the ontological argument is sound." '[15]

Eventually Russell rejected the religion of reason. He came to stand firm in his scepticism concerning whether reason could direct us to any sort of Divinity. He began his argument against the God of wise men and philosophy before he began his polemic against the God of the Bible because, unlike most, he had been tempted by the former.

Russell's argument against the religion of reason and indeed the tradition of natural theology can be divided into three themes, all of which are intimately related, and all of which make an appearance in his seminal essay 'Why I Am Not a Christian'. The first is his argument against the traditional proofs of the existence of God that had been elaborated by the Mediaevals, especially by Anselm and Aquinas. The second, especially prominent in the eighteenth century, is the argument of the Deists concerning the Divine Order of the universe. The arguments of the Deists of the eighteenth century can be distinguished from similar views in previous ages because they were inspired by the discoveries of the Newtonian mechanics. The third is his critique of the claims by scientists that the scientific revolution of the twentieth century had restored the alliance between science and religion, albeit on new foundations. Among the traditional proofs that Russell discusses in his texts are the ontological proof, the cosmological proof and the proof from design. Sometimes he devotes sustained argument to these proofs and at others he seems casually dismissive. The ontological proof is the one that is often of greatest interest to mathematicians as it is put forward on the basis of logic without any empirical component. It maintains that the idea of a perfect being implies the existence of a perfect being. This proof suits the mathematician who believes that mathematical ideas have an independent existence. Once Russell gave up this latter idea the attractions of the ontological proof vanished. Russell tells us that for a time he was convinced of the validity of the cosmological argument. This argument states that every effect must have a cause which is itself the effect of some other cause. It states further that there cannot be an infinite regress, so that we must come at last to a First Cause, which we call God. Russell's refutation of this proof seems casual and is certainly unoriginal. He writes: 'In John Stuart Mill's autobiography, I found that James Mill had taught him the refutation of that argument, namely that it gives no answer to the question, "Who Made God?" ' Russell concludes that this simple insight compelled him to give up this proof.

Russell treats the proof from design as the pivotal proof for the existence of God, one that he turns to again and again. Russell's judgment on its centre life can be supported by its popularity in every genre of literature. The proof from design is declared by poets as well as logicians. The poet declares that 'The heavens declare the glory of Thy handiwork.' Logicians have maintained that the evidence of an orderly functioning of the universe is so impressive and overwhelming that the inference of a Divine Maker is inescapable. The argument is also the favourite among those put forward by those who look to the discoveries of modern science. Russell remarks that

> In the eighteenth century, under the influence of Newton, the alliance between theology and natural law became very close. It was held that God had created the world in accordance with a plan, and the natural law was the embodiment of that plan.[16]

As a proof, the design argument is *primus inter pares*.

Much of Russell's polemic against the argument from design is either satirical or a *cri de cœur*. In one passage he enlists Voltaire, recalling his satirical remark on the order of the universe that 'obviously the nose was designed to be such as to fit the spectacles'.

In other passages Russell registers his own version of Ivan Karamazou's outrage concerning the absence of a just order in the universe where innocent children died needlessly. Such a universe could not have been designed by a good God. Russell protests: 'If indeed the world in which we live has been produced according to a plan, we shall have to reckon Nero a saint in comparison with the author of that plan.'[17]

In the 1920s Russell felt compelled to affirm his scepticism concerning the possibility of a religion of reason because 'In recent times the bulk of eminent physicists and a number of eminent biologists have made pronouncements stating that recent advances in science have disproved the older materialism, and have tended to reestablish the truths of religion'.[18] He was thinking of scientists such as Eddington, the pre-eminent atomic scientist in Britain, who in assessing the results of the revolution in microphysics concluded that 'religion first became possible for a reasonable scientific man about the year 1927'.[19]

The reviews and essays in ' Religion and Science ' (Part III of this volume) present Russell's rebuttals of the argument of Eddington and Jeans, the leading scientific writers who argued for a rapprochement between science and religion. These selections provide fine examples of Russell's skill as an expositor of modern scientific theories. The science of the eighteenth century was said to support religion because it demonstrated a regularity in nature that provided decisive evidence in support of the argument from design. The physics of the twentieth century was said to support theology, because it showed the universe to be chaotic. The science of the twentieth century unveiled a reality where particles might at one time be heat and another time be light, where the determinism of the older generation of scientists no longer obtained and where the situation of the observer had to be factored into the reality of the observed, a reality which, like that described by Hegel, is one in which 'not a soul is sober'. Eddington argued that the new physics opened the door to the freedom of the will and Jeans to the possibility of a spiritual universe created by mathematical thought. A new wave of speculation explored, and continues to explore, the new physics as a gateway to a spiritual realm.

Russell's response is rhetorically vigorous but philosophically cautious. Unlike the anti-religious writers of the late nineteenth century he does not confront the theological certainties of his adversaries with atheistic certainties of his own: rather, he seeks to situate himself between dogmatism and utter scepticism. He admits that the new scientific theories have opened gaps in the older determinism and the older materialism and that he cannot provide the argument that will serve as a 'knockout blow' against the new religious apologetic. But he accuses the theologians of making the old fallacy of trying to cram God in the temporary gaps in the sciences. He acknowledges that the iron laws of physics might reflect the ingenuity of physicists rather than immutable order of nature, but urges that determinism is still the basis of scientific enquiry. Finally he calls on the reader to perform his version of the famous Pascalian wager, to focus on the important question which is 'not whether matter consists of hard little lumps or of something else, but whether the course of nature is determined by the law of physics'.[20]

Russell's critique of the alliance between science and religion extends to biology. He rejects the view that had been propounded by Bergson and that has survived as the view of Teilhard de Chardin (and now the Creationists) that evolution is guided by an inner logos.

> Nor does the process of scientific investigation afford any evidence that the behaviour of living matter is governed by anything other than the laws of physics and chemistry. Babies suck not only their mothers' breasts, but everything physically capable of being sucked: they endeavour to extract food out of shoulders and hands and arms. It is only after months of experience that they learn to confine their efforts after nourishment to the breasts. Sucking in infants is at first an unconditioned reflex, and by no means an intelligent one.[21]

Russell's intended *coup de grâce* against the argument from design is derived from the evidence of physics. It is a version of an observation about science that he made as early as 'The Free Man's Worship' where he declared that modern physics proclaims the opposite of a universe designed for the perfectibility of the human race. He wrote:

> If you accept the ordinary laws of science, you have to suppose that human life in general will die out in due course. You see in the moon the sort of thing towards which the earth is tending, something dead, cold and lifeless.[22]

In summary, Russell rejected the view that reason in general and especially science provided evidence for any path whatever to a spiritual realm. Nonetheless, we shall find that Russell did advocate a piety which was in its own way a handmaiden to science. First, however, we will examine Russell's view of popular or revealed religion.

Russell and popular religion

This collection contains a number of examples of the uncompromising polemics against religion that Russell wrote beginning in the late 1920s. The cultural historian of the twentieth century should be puzzled by the vehemence and frequency of Russell's polemic. These essays were composed during a period of unmistakable religious decline. Russell acknowledged this in the excerpt from *Prospects of Industrial Civilization*. Nonetheless, his anti-religious polemic remains vigorous, urgent and never seems to lose its energy. It is as though he had anticipated the fundamentalism that has erupted with such force in many parts of the world.

In these writings he rejected the compromise of the philosophers cited earlier by Gibbon, which held that while the myths of popular religion cannot be directly attributed by reason, philosophers must nonetheless acknowledge their importance, participate in the appropriate rituals and revere the appropriate gods because popular religion offers the masses solace and maintains public morality. Russell's family, he tells us, concealed their enlightened religious views from the servants for similar reasons. In these essays Russell maintained the opposite. He denied that public religion sustains public morality. On the contrary, he argued that public religion is a source of strife, disorder and persecution. His writings suggest a number of theories of popular religion. According to one it is possible to distinguish between the religious ideas of founders and those promoted by self-serving and fanatical priesthoods. According to this:

> There is nothing accidental about the difference between a Church and its Founder. As soon as absolute truth is supposed to be contained in the sayings of a certain man, there is a body of experts to interpret his sayings, and these experts infallibly acquire power, since they hold the key to truth. Like any privileged caste they use their power to their own advantage.[23]

But Russell is uneasy with this as he is also critical of the founders. Thus, in his account of Jesus in 'Why I Am Not a Christian', he
makes the familiar point that those who declare the maxims of Jesus
never live by them, but he also stresses the shortcomings of Jesus
himself, whose angry assurances that sinners will burn in hell are
inconsistent with his calls for universal love.[24]

Russell's critique of the role of religion in civilization gained
strength in the 1920s, as did Freud's. Freud's famous last works on
this subject, beginning with *The Future of an Illusion*, are also dated
from this period. Russell is in one sense more uncompromising than
Freud. Freud described religion as an illusion; he conceded that
religion was, at one time, necessary for civilization, but maintained
that it has now lost its power to maintain order against anarchy.
Russell never made even this concession. He considered that
religion was always harmful.

Both Russell and Freud, however, shared a belief that the civilization of post-World War I was descending into anarchy and
disorder and needed some new vision to bind peoples together, and
that this vision was given in reason and intelligence. Russell and
Freud opposed the revivals of traditional religion that appeared
among the intelligentsia during this period, and sometimes called
for a new secular religion. Much of Russell's criticism of the old
religion was in the spirit of the criticisms of Freud.

Like Freud, Russell sought the roots of popular religion in
psychology: 'the three impulses embedded in religion are fear,
conceit and hatred. The purpose of religion one might say, is to
give an air of respectability to these passions, provided that they
run through certain channels.'[25]

The three are usually so artfully combined that it is often impossible to separate them. Fear is often the simple fear of nature and of
the unknown. Christianity, Russell finds, combines these motifs in
a poisonous way. Fear of the outside and of the body has led to the
separation of the soul and the body, allowing the soul to be a retreat
or hiding place from the body's engagements with the world:

> the body represents the social and public part of man
> whereas the soul represents the private part. I think it clear
> that the net result of all the centuries of Christianity has
> been to make men more egoistic, more shut up in them-
> selves, than nature made them.[26]

Sexual repression is as central to Russell's negative assessment of religion as it is to Nietzsche and Freud. He writes: 'Almost every adult in a Christian Community is more or less diseased as a result of the Taboo on sexual knowledge when he or she was young.' Indeed, sexual ignorance allows the other psychological motif, righteousness, which gives licence to persecution.

The impulse of self-esteem creates the illusion that the human race has some central importance in the universe. This illusion is fostered by biblical religions which teach that God had an overwhelming interest in that speck of the universe which is situated on the eastern Mediterranean. Denial of this is one of the persistent themes in Russell's account of religion. The vision of a universe of blind matter haunted him since youth and is poetically expressed in his youthful 'The Free Man's Worship'. Russell never changed his view. He pours scorn equally on the biblical and secular evolutionary view that the universe was designed for the fulfilment of human purposes.

Russell utterly rejects the view that religion is a source of consolation and meaning. The vehemence of his views is sometimes puzzling because he was for the most part addressing an age when religion was in retreat. It is important, however, to remember that from the end of the First World War, in the mid 1930s and in the mid 1940s there were a series of religious revivals among the intelligentsia. Paul Edward's collection of Russell's writings, 'Why I Am Not a Christian', was issued as a response to religious revivals among the intelligentsia in the post-war period.

The writings included in this volume provide ample evidence of Russell's uncompromising opposition to religion. The volume cannot, however, provide the complete content of Russell's views. This context does not suggest that Russell believed that religion was the only or even the most important obstacle to the attainment of a rational society. Russell, again like Freud, did not believe that once religion was rooted out of modern society its inherent rationality would emerge full blown. He believed that the modern world itself had produced its own sources of anarchy – for example, nationalism, Bolshevism, Fascism and even Pragmatism – sources, connected in his philosophy to the 'power philosophies' that he has described in his writing. It is the proliferation of these power philosophies and the will to power that they manifest that must be countered by a piety that is in harmony with scientific observation as a way of life.

Russellian piety

It is likely that Russell's views on religion were influenced by those of William James. William James delivered the Gifford lectures in 1901–1902 which were the basis of his classical book *The Varieties of Religious Experience*, published in 1902. Russell read the book shortly thereafter with approval. He was influenced by James' approach to religion as a psychologist who announced that he would 'ignore the institutional branch entirely to say nothing of the ecclesiastical organization, to consider as little as possible about systematic theology, and the ideas of the gods, and to confine myself to personal religion pure and simple'.[27] Uncannily, some of James' descriptions of types of religious experience, that of the 'sick soul', the twice-born type whose experiences provided instances of 'conversions experience' and 'mystical experience', could have been comments on parts of Russell's life. James offered an account of the spiritual life and religion as an expression of being human rather than as an outcome of dogma and creed.

In one of his books, *Religion and Science*,[28] written in 1935, Russell, echoing James' programme, offers three different senses of religion. He distinguishes between Church, creed and religious feeling. He finds the Church to be a source of mischief and the creed to be a source of dogma. Religious feelings, however, can be valid because they are 'independent of scientific discoveries'. Russell's emphasis on feeling can be interpreted as calling for 'privatization' of religion, on the grounds that religion can be valid for the individual providing that it does not offer the public realm any cognitive claims.

But does the term 'feeling' adequately convey Russell's or James' account of personal religion? James defines personal religion: 'The feelings, acts and experiences of individual men in their solitude, so far as they apprehend themselves to stand in relation to whatever they consider Divine'.[29] In 'The Essence of Religion', Russell defined religion as 'that quality of infinity that makes religion, the selfless, untrammelled life in the whole which frees men from the prison house of eager wishes and thoughts'.[30] Thus, in his descriptions of religion, Russell refers to feelings, but very complex ones of resignation and liberation. He uses terms such as the 'infinite' and tries to persuade the reader of the value of the spiritual experience that he is describing. Even in *Religion and Science* he offers the following as an example of feeling.

The man who feels deeply the problems of human destiny, the desire to diminish the sufferings of mankind, and the hope that the future will realize the best possibilities of our species, is nowadays said to have a religious outlook....In so far as religion consists in a way of feeling, rather than in a set of beliefs, science cannot touch it.[31]

Such feelings are in some sense private, but are also put forward to make claim on all of us.

Russell's 'personal religion', then, flourishes in a domain which is bounded on one side by purely private feelings of pain and on the other by the universal and verifiable statements of science and philosophy. It is very similar to the domain that Russell identifies as the legitimate domain of philosophical speculation. Russell uses terms such as 'infinite' and 'finite', terms that any theologian would feel comfortable with, and describes experiences of transcendence in language that mystics would endorse. Brightman,[32] Jaeger[33] and others have written philosophical works on Russell's piety and exposed it to philosophical assessment. It is a piety that consists in a religion without God and an ethic of self-enlargement, both interpreted through echoes of Spinoza's 'Amor Dei Intellectualis'.

In 'The Essence of Religion' Russell called for a new spirituality, arguing that the impartial worship that he advocated 'has been thought, wrongly, to require belief in God'. Russell's readiness to speak of religion without God is an accepted approach to spirituality in contemporary religious studies. Traditionally the study of religion meant the interpretation of sacred scripture and sacred sacrament. By the seventeenth century, during the age of exploration, religion came to mean any system of spiritual beings. By the twentieth century the definition of religion has become open-ended, and can apply to a wide variety of phenomena, including the possibilities of religions, such as forms of Buddhism, without God. Since the nineteenth century there have been a large number of definitions of religion that do not rely on theology. For example, the nineteenth-century theologian Schleiermacher defined religion as 'The feeling of total Dependence', Rudoph Otto defines it as the experience of mysterium tremendum, and Paul Tillich as the 'expression of ultimate concern'.[34] In 'The Essence of Religion' Russell has insisted that we come to a definition that does not require a belief in God. If Russell were to be asked for the basis of religiosity, his writings suggest that his answer would be that religious feeling could be identified as 'a striving for self-enlargement'.

Blackwell has coined the term 'self-enlargement' to describe Russell's regard for and affinity with Spinoza.[35] Blackwell suggests that Russell takes Spinoza's 'Amor Dei Intellectualis', removes the Dei, much of the 'intellectualis', but leaves the 'love'. By this Russell means to recover Spinoza's union with the universe, but not one that can be demonstrated by Spinoza's geometric method nor through any other series of proofs. Russell's religion, then, is Spinozism treated as personal mysticism and feeling, rather than as cosmology accessible to geometric demonstration. Blackwell observes that: 'There is a similarity between Russell's concept derived from Spinoza, of impersonal self-enlargement and the Buddhist concept of egolessness.'[36]

The most famous of Russell's conversion experiences is his moment of union with Evelyn Whitehead, while she was suffering with angina. In a letter to Lady Ottoline Morrell he wrote:

> The moment of my first conversion was this way: I came to know suddenly (what it was intended I should know) that a woman I liked greatly had a life of utter loneliness, filled with intense tragedy and pain of which she could never speak. I was not free to tell my sympathy, which was so intense as to change my life. I turned to all the ways there might be to alleviate her trouble without seeming to know it, and so I went on in thought to loneliness in general, and how love bridges the chasm, how force is the evil thing, and strife is the root of all evil and gentleness the only balm. I became infinitely gentle for a time. I turned against the South African war and imperialism (I was an imperialist till then) and found that I loved children and they loved me. I resolved to bring some good and some hope into her life. All this happened in about five minutes. In spite of many faults and many backslidings I succeeded on the whole in what I undertook then. When I told her of you, she bade me remember that she is permanently better and happier owing to me. But it took me rather more than a year to acquiesce in her pain and to learn to love the cause of it, though he deserves much love. It was during that year that I learned whatever wisdom I possessed before meeting you.[37]

In this account Russell describes 'mystical illumination' as impelled by love, an outreach rather than an upreach, an outreach which expands in various stages. In the first stage he escaped from the 'chasm' of the self by identifying with the suffering of another being, then he identified with other people and their 'inmost thoughts' and finally with children. In the second stage there were inner changes in himself. He became gentler, which turned him against imperialism and caused him to seek a philosophy that would make life more endurable. This inner revolution of outreach was impelled by love, which in each succeeding stage embraces more and more of the universe.

Self-enlargement for Russell includes an element of disinterested acceptance. In this experience he emphasizes the final stage as one of impartiality and submission in which he learned to 'acquiesce in her pain' and even 'love the cause of it', in this case Whitehead himself, not as a responsible human being but as a metaphor for the causality that obtains in the universe.

This description offers a Russellian account of religious experience. It is one in which the self breaks out of its prison, embracing more and more in the universe, an approach to ethics and politics wherein such an experience ends one's interest in strife and domination. Finally – and this is of the highest importance – an attitude of lofty austerity, impartiality and of acceptance, 'which allowed me to love the cause' of the pain that he witnessed, is a decisive element in Russell's account of spirituality.

But it is this very attitude of impartiality that links the spiritual and the scientific. Russell combined his sense of spirituality with science in his essay on 'Religion and the Churches' in *Principles of Social Reconstruction*,[38] when he said, 'The life of the spirit centres around impersonal feeling, as the life of the mind centres around personal thought.'[39] This statement seems to suggest an affinity between the life of spirit and science, rather than either a logical connection or a complete separation. We have seen that he rejected the possibility of philosophy or science whose conclusions offered support to religious belief. In his call for a mystical religion based on feeling, he seemed to be calling for a type of spirituality that was in a separate compartment from science, and was careful to emphasize that it would not be a mysticism that had any cognitive content. 'Mysticism,' he argued, 'is, in essence, little more than a certain intensity and depth of feeling in regard to what is believed about the universe.'[40] But in the phrase quoted above he suggests a kind of affinity between the 'impartiality' of the cosmic vision, one that offers neither praise nor blame for things.

The link between science and religion that Russell sought was not to be found in the results of science and religion but rather in the affinity of outlook. In his essay 'The Place of Science in a Liberal Education' he had argued that 'the kernel of the scientific outlook is the refusal to regard our own desires and interest as affording the key to the understanding of the world'.[41] Scientific objectivity, then, was not simply a way of controlling the universe, as contemporary critics have argued, but was rather connected to the impartiality of the mystic, who saw all things without blame with what the Buddhists revere as detachment.

Russell's spirituality offers support to those who argue that the religions of the east have more in common with science than the religions of the west. Such a view of the relationship between religion and science is not merely a matter of private feeling, but rather for Russell one of great spiritual and ethical importance. For Russell believed that science had become enmeshed in the intoxication with power that had been generated by modern technology. From his earliest youth, Russell was aware of the fact that science had fallen into the hands of those who sought power. This is a constant theme in his writings and is behind his call for a reverential attitude towards the universe. In his *History of Western Philosophy*, Russell warns that 'modern technique...has revived the sense of the collective power of human communities....In all this I feel a grave danger, the danger of what might be called *cosmic impiety* [our italics]...this intoxication is the greatest danger of our time.'[42] The feelings that Russell calls private and without cognitive content are in fact urgent and universal. In *The Impact of Science on Society* Russell declared:

> The root of the matter is a very simple and old fashioned thing, a thing so simple that I am almost ashamed to mention it, for fear of the derisive smile with which wise cynics will greet my words. The thing I mean – please forgive me for mentioning it – is love, Christian love, or compassion....If you feel this, you have all that anybody should need in the way of religion.[43]

General note

This selection of Bertrand Russell's writings on religion and related topics has been made to provide the reader with an overview of the development of his thinking about religion from the turn of the century to the end of his life. We have not included any of his writings on religion prior to 1900: this means we have omitted his first diary 'Greek Exercises' (1888–1889), 'A Locked Diary' (1890–1894), the papers he wrote as a graduate student, and his writings for the Apostles. These and other documents are published in *Cambridge Essays, 1888–99* (1983), the first volume of *The Collected Papers of Bertrand Russell*, edited by Kenneth Blackwell and others. Twelve more volumes have been published since its appearance, plus a three-volume bibliography by Kenneth Blackwell and Harry Ruja, but there are still more than a dozen volumes to come before the series is complete.

The writings in this volume are mostly concerned with Russell's views on religion rather than with his own personal religion or his philosophy of life. The distinction might be a clear one, but it does not give us distinct sets of writings, since Russell often writes as a critic of religion and expounds his own personal religion at the same time.

We have partitioned his writings on religion into five sections, but it must be said that our decisions are not as clear-cut as one could wish, since Russell often discusses more than one topic at a time. Within each section except the first one, the papers are chronologically ordered, in order that the reader can acquire an appreciation of the development of his thinking and the various ways in which he expressed his thoughts. All endnotes in the Introduction and headnotes are ours; others, except where otherwise stated, are Russell's.

Part I

PERSONAL
STATEMENTS

This first section contains two kinds of statements: the first
(Chapters 1 and 3) is mainly autobiographical, the second (Chapters
2 and 4) expresses his views at the time they were written.

As Russell grew old, he became more candid concerning the role
that religion played in his search for certainty in mathematics and
philosophy. As late as 1923 he wrote an essay called 'Logical
Atomism', which was published the following year in *Contemporary
British Philosophy: Personal Statements*, where he remarks that he
'came to philosophy through mathematics, or rather through the
wish to find some reason to believe in the truth of mathematics'
(*CPBR*, vol. 9, 1988).

Four years later, he wrote an essay called 'Things That Have
Moulded Me', where he says that his passion for mathematics goes
back to his introduction to Euclid at the age of eleven. He
continues:

> At the same time, I found myself increasingly attracted to
> philosophy, not, as is often the case, by the hope of ethical
> or theological comfort, but by the wish to discover whether
> we possess anything that can be called knowledge.
>
> (*The Dial*, 1927 and in *CPBR*, vol. 10, 1996)

But in 1956, in an essay called 'An Autobiographical Epitome',
he claims:

> When I first became interested in philosophy, I hoped that
> I should find in it some satisfaction for my thwarted desire
> for a religion. For a time, I found a sort of comfort in Plato's
> eternal world of ideas. But in the end I thought this was
> nonsense and I have found in philosophy no satisfaction

whatever for the impulse towards religious belief. In this sense I have found philosophy disappointing, but as a clarifier I have found it quite the opposite.

(*Portraits From Memory*, 1969)

The first paper, 'My Mental Development' (1944), was written when Russell was in his eighties, for the volume on his philosophy in *The Library of Living Philosophers* series, edited by Paul Arthur Schilpp. Both his autobiographical essay and his reply to Mr Brightman, who had written about Russell's 'personal religion' and his views on religion, are essential for understanding the development of Russell's thinking about religion from his earliest years until 1945. In 'Reply to Criticisms' Russell distinguishes three aspects of religion and accepts Mr Brightman's description of his 'personal religion'.

The second paper, 'The Free Man's Worship', is Russell's most famous, most frequently anthologized, and most widely translated essay. The title is almost certainly inspired by his reading of Spinoza's *Ethics*, in which the idea of 'the free man' is of crucial importance. It was written around the same time (1902–1903) as he was working on 'The Pilgrimage of Life', which he never completed, and is a natural companion to 'The Education of the Emotions', 'On History' and 'The Study of Mathematics'.

The writing of the essay had two major sources: his conversion experience of 'mystic illumination' in February 1901, and the realization, in the early months of 1902, that he no longer loved his wife. If he had written an essay on this topic after his 'conversion' but before he fell out of love with Alys, it probably would have emphasized the power and importance of universal love.

But his mystic insights concerning the power of love were not enough to maintain his feelings for Alys. As was typical of Russell, he claimed that the realization that he no longer loved Alys came to him quite suddenly without any forewarnings. It left him in a state of cosmic despair, and made him realize that the only way to cope with this feeling was to adopt the stoic attitude of acceptance of the brute facts of reality that is so evident in this essay.

When he wrote the essay, he still believed in the objective nature of good and evil, but this was of little comfort considering the ultimate destiny of the universe, which, according to the laws of physics, was bound to disintegrate sooner or later. The only way to liberation from human suffering, he argued, was to abandon our hopes for private happiness and to burn with passion for eternal things that were not affected by the ruin of the physical universe.

Russell began writing the essay at the end of 1902 while staying with Alys' brother-in-law, Bernard Berenson, at his villa, I Tatti, near Florence. Berenson liked the essay, as did George Trevelyan, who claimed it was the best thing he had ever read. It was he, with Goldworthy Lowes Dickinson's support, who arranged its first publication in *The Independent Review*.

However, not everyone was as impressed. Gilbert Murray did not find it convincing; neither did Theodore Davies, and T.S. Eliot, reviewing it fifteen years later, criticized the style.

Russell came to think less well of this essay. Around 1914 Russell changed his mind concerning the objectivity of good and evil, due, he tells us, to the criticism of George Santayana. In its place he adopted a subjectivistic understanding of ethics, a view he was to hold for the rest of his life. With this change much of the argument of 'The Free Man's Worship' is undermined.

In spite of this, the essay reflects Russell's pessimistic view of life at the time, a view that in turn reflects a permanent element in Russell's thought, namely that the scientific point of view has no regard for human hopes and interest; life in the universe started without any reason and it will necessarily end one day, regardless of our hopes for justice and dreams of eternal life.

When the essay was reprinted in *Philosophical Essays* in 1910 and in *Mysticism and Logic* in 1918, Russell changed the title from 'The Free Man's Worship' to 'A Free Man's Worship' and deleted two passages that he probably found too optimistic due to his re-evaluation of the importance of his experience of 'mystic illumination'. Talking about the inspiration that comes from the contemplation of music, art and the beauty of nature, he omitted the last two sentences of that paragraph:

> At times of such inspiration, we seem to hear the strange, deep music of an invisible sea beating ceaselessly upon an unknown shore. Could we but stand on that shore, we feel, another vision of life might be ours, wider, freer, than the narrow valley in which our private life is prisoned.

On the following page he deleted:

> Those who have passed through that valley of darkness emerge at last into a country of unearthly beauty, where the

air is calm, and the pale sun coldly illumines a frosty land-
scape; and there the deep-toned paean of freedom vibrates
in the soul that has conquered fear.
(Ibid., Paper 4, see also the textual notes on pages 524–525)

This talk about passing through the valley of darkness might
have sounded too much like what many mystics have referred to as
'the dark night of the soul', which is a crucial part of the path to
final illumination according to some Christian mystics.

The third paper is taken from the first part of Russell's *Autobiography*, which was published in 1967, but which he started to work
on in the summer of 1931 by dictating it to a secretary. The passage
is a description of the experience he went through in February 1901,
an experience he later referred to as his first conversion or mystical
experience. The second took place ten years later, but is not
mentioned in his *Autobiography* or in any of his other published
writings.

It was an important event at the time and it remained with him
as a secret that he shared with Lady Ottoline and some other close
friends ten years later, but officially didn't say anything about until
he mentioned it in a series of radio talks broadcast on the BBC's
General Overseas Service in 1954 and 1955. These talks were later
published in *Portraits From Memory* (1956).

In an essay called 'From Logic to Politics' he writes: 'Early in
1901 I had an experience not unlike what religious people call
"conversion". I became suddenly and vividly aware of the loneliness
in which most people live, and passionately desirous of finding ways
of diminishing this tragic isolation.'

'What Is an Agnostic?' was published in *Look* in November 1953
and later reprinted in several books. The paper consists of answers to
twenty questions concerning agnosticism, atheism and religion,
which were prepared by the editors of the magazine. Although the
paper is only seven pages in length, Russell succeeds in explaining
the difference between an agnostic and an atheist and in clarifying
several other relevant issues.

1

FROM 'MY MENTAL DEVELOPMENT' AND 'REPLY TO CRITICISMS'

From 'My Mental Development'

In 1876, when, after my father's death, I was brought to the house of my grandparents, my grandfather was eighty-three and had become very feeble. I remember him sometimes being wheeled about out-of-doors in a bath chair, sometimes in his room reading Hansard (the official report of debates in Parliament). He was invariably kind to me, and seemed never to object to childish noise. But he was too old to influence me directly. He died in 1878, and my knowledge of him came through his widow, my grandmother, who revered his memory. She was a more powerful influence upon my general outlook than any one else, although, from adolescence onward, I disagreed with very many of her opinions.

My grandmother was a Scotch Presbyterian, of the border family of the Elliots. Her maternal grandfather suffered obloquy for declaring, on the basis of the thickness of the lava on the slopes of Etna, that the world must have been created before 4004 BC. One of her great-grandfathers was Robertson, the historian of Charles V. She was a Puritan, with the moral rigidity of the Covenanters, despising comfort, indifferent to food, hating wine, and regarding tobacco as sinful. Although she had lived her whole life in the great world until my grandfather's retirement in 1866, she was completely unworldly. She had that indifference to money which is only possible to those who have always had enough of it. She wished her children and grandchildren to live useful and virtuous lives, but had no desire that they should achieve what others would regard as success, or that they should marry 'well'. She had the Protestant belief in private judgment and the supremacy of the individual conscience. On my twelfth birthday she gave me a Bible (which I still possess), and wrote her favourite texts on the fly-leaf. One of them was 'Thou shalt not follow a multitude to do evil'; another, 'Be strong, and of a good courage; be not afraid, neither be thou dismayed; for the Lord thy God is with thee whithersoever thou goest.' These texts have profoundly influenced my life, and still seemed to retain some meaning after I had ceased to believe in God.

At the age of seventy, my grandmother became a Unitarian; at the same time, she supported Home Rule for Ireland, and made friends with Irish Members of Parliament, who were being publicly accused of complicity in murder. This shocked people more than now seems imaginable. She was passionately opposed to imperialism, and taught me to think ill of the Afghan and Zulu wars, which occurred when I was about seven. Concerning the occupation of Egypt, however, she said little, as it was due to Mr Gladstone, whom she admired. I remember an argument I had with my German governess, who said that the English, having once gone into Egypt, would never come out, whatever they might promise; whereas I maintained, with much patriotic passion, that the English never broke promises. That was sixty years ago, and they are there still....A great event in my life, at the age of eleven, was the beginning of Euclid, which was still the accepted textbook of geometry. When I had got over my disappointment in finding that he began with axioms, which had to be accepted without proof, I found great delight in him. Throughout the rest of my boyhood, mathematics absorbed a very large part of my interest. This interest was complex: partly mere pleasure in discovering that I possessed a certain kind of skill, partly delight in the power of deductive reasoning, partly the restfulness of mathematical certainty; but more than any of these (while I was still a boy) the belief that nature operates according to mathematical laws, and that human actions, like planetary motions, could be calculated if we had sufficient skill. By the time I was fifteen, I had arrived at a theory very similar to that of the Cartesians. The movements of living bodies, I felt convinced, were wholly regulated by the laws of dynamics; therefore free will must be an illusion. But, since I accepted consciousness as an indubitable datum, I could not accept materialism, though I had a certain hankering after it on account of its intellectual simplicity and its rejection of 'nonsense'. I still believed in God, because the First-Cause argument seemed irrefutable.

Until I went to Cambridge at the age of eighteen, my life was a very solitary one. I was brought up at home, by German nurses, German and Swiss governesses, and finally by English tutors; I saw little of other children, and when I did they were not important to me. At fourteen or fifteen I became passionately interested in religion, and set to work to examine successively the arguments for free will, immortality, and God. For a few months I had an agnostic tutor with whom I could talk about these problems; but he was sent away, presumably because he was thought to be undermining my faith. Except during these months, I kept my thoughts to myself, writing them out in a journal in Greek letters to prevent others from reading them. I was suffering the unhappiness natural to lonely adolescence, and I attributed my unhappiness to loss of religious belief. For three years I thought about religion, with a determination not to let my thoughts be influenced by my desires. I discarded first free will, then immortality; I believed in God until I was just eighteen, when I found in Mill's *Autobiography* the sentence: 'My father taught me that the question "Who made me?" cannot be answered, since it immediately suggests the further question "Who made God?" ' In that moment I decided that the First-Cause argument is fallacious.

During these years I read widely, but as my reading was not directed, much of it was futile. I read much bad poetry, especially Tennyson and Byron; at last, at the age of seventeen, I came upon Shelley, whom no one had told me about. He remained for many years the man I loved most among great men of the past. I read a great deal of Carlyle, and admired *Past and Present*, but not *Sartor Resartus*. 'The Everlasting Yea' seemed to me sentimental nonsense. The man with whom I most nearly agreed was Mill. His *Political Economy*, *Liberty*, and *Subjection of Women* influenced me profoundly. I made elaborate notes on the whole of his *Logic*, but could not accept his theory that mathematical propositions are empirical generalizations, though I did not know what else they could be.

All this was before I went to Cambridge. Except during the three months when I had the agnostic tutor mentioned above, I found no one to speak to about my thoughts. At home I concealed my religious doubts. Once I said that I was a utilitarian, but was met with such a blast of ridicule that I never again spoke of my opinions at home.

Cambridge opened to me a new world of infinite delight. For the first time, I found that, when I uttered my thoughts, they seemed to be accepted as worth considering. Whitehead, who had examined me for entrance scholarships, had mentioned me to various people a year or two senior to me, with the result that within a week I met a number who became my life-long friends. Whitehead, who was already a Fellow and Lecturer, was amazingly kind, but was too much my senior to be a close personal friend until some years later. I found a group of contemporaries, who were able, rather earnest, hard-working, but interested in many things outside their academic work – poetry, philosophy, politics, ethics, indeed the whole world of mental adventure. We used to stay up discussing till very late on Saturday nights, meet for a late breakfast on Sunday, and then go for an all-day walk. Able young men had not yet adopted the pose of cynical superiority which came in some years later, and was first made fashionable in Cambridge by Lytton Strachey. The world seemed hopeful and solid; we all felt convinced that nineteenth-century progress would continue, and that we ourselves should be able to contribute something of value. For those who have been young since 1914 it must be difficult to imagine the happiness of those days.

Among my friends at Cambridge were McTaggart, the Hegelian philosopher; Lowes Dickinson, whose gentle charm made him loved by all who knew him; Charles Sanger, a brilliant mathematician at College, afterwards a barrister, known in legal circles as the editor of Jarman on Wills; two brothers, Crompton and Theodore Llewelyn Davies, sons of a Broad Church clergyman most widely known as one of 'Davies and Vaughan', who translated Plato's *Republic*. These two brothers were the youngest and ablest of a family of seven, all remarkably able; they had also a quite unusual capacity for friendship, a deep desire to be of use to the world, and unrivalled wit. Theodore, the younger of the two, was still in the earlier stages of a brilliant career in the government service when he was drowned in a bathing accident. I have never known any two men so deeply loved by so many friends. Among those of whom I saw most were the three brothers Trevelyan, great-nephews of Macaulay. Of these the oldest became a Labour politician, and resigned from the Labour Government because it was not sufficiently socialistic; the second became a poet, and published, among other things, an admirable translation of Lucretius; the third, George, achieved fame as a historian. Somewhat junior to me was G.E. Moore, who, later, had a great influence upon my philosophy.

The set in which I lived was very much influenced by McTaggart, whose wit recommended his Hegelian philosophy. He taught me to consider British empiricism 'crude', and I was willing to believe that Hegel (and in a lesser degree Kant) had a profundity not to be found in Locke, Berkeley, and Hume, or in my former pope, Mill. My first three years at Cambridge I was too busy with mathematics to read Kant or Hegel, but in my fourth year I concentrated on philosophy. My teachers were Henry Sidgwick, James Ward, and G.F. Stout. Sidgwick represented the British point of view, which I believed myself to have seen through; I therefore thought less of him at that time than I did later. Ward, for whom I had a very great personal affection, set forth a Kantian system, and introduced me to Lotze and Sigwart. Stout, at that time, thought very highly of Bradley; when *Appearance and Reality* was published, he said it had done as much as is humanly possible in *ontology*. He and McTaggart between them caused me to become a Hegelian; I remember the precise moment, one day in 1894 as I was walking along Trinity Lane, when I saw in a flash (or thought I saw) that the ontological argument is valid. I had gone out to buy a tin of tobacco; on my way back, I suddenly threw it up in the air and exclaimed as I caught it: 'Great God in boots, the ontological argument is sound.' I read Bradley at this time with avidity, and admired him more than any other recent philosopher.

My intellectual journeys have been, in some respects, disappointing. When I was young I hoped to find religious satisfaction in philosophy; even after I had abandoned Hegel, the eternal Platonic world gave me something non-human to admire. I thought of mathematics with reverence, and suffered when Wittgenstein led me to regard it as nothing but tautologies. I have always ardently desired to find some justification for the emotions inspired by certain things that seemed to stand outside human life and to deserve feelings of awe. I am thinking in part of very obvious things, such as the starry heavens and a stormy sea on a rocky coast; in part of the vastness of the scientific universe, both in space and time, as compared to the life of mankind; in part of the edifice of impersonal truth, especially truth which, like that of mathematics, does not merely describe the world that happens to exist. Those who attempt to make a religion of humanism, which recognizes nothing greater than man, do not satisfy my emotions. And yet I am unable to believe that, in the world as known, there is anything that I can value outside human beings, and, to a much lesser extent, animals. Not the starry heavens, but their effects on human percipients, have excellence; to admire the universe for its size is slavish and absurd; impersonal non-human truth appears to be a delusion. And so my intellect goes with the humanists, though my emotions violently rebel. In this respect, the 'consolations of philosophy' are not for me.

In more purely intellectual ways, on the contrary, I have found as much satisfaction in philosophy as any one could reasonably have expected. Many matters which, when I was young, baffled me by the vagueness of all that had been said about them, are now amenable to an exact technique, which makes possible the kind of progress that is customary in science. Where definite knowledge is unattainable, it is sometimes possible to prove that it is unattainable, and it is usually possible to formulate a variety of exact hypotheses, all compatible with the existing evidence. Those philosophers who have adopted the methods derived from logical analysis can argue with each other, not in the old aimless way, but cooperatively, so that both sides can concur as to the outcome. All this is new during my lifetime; the pioneer was Frege, but he remained solitary until his old age. This extension of the sphere of reason to new provinces is something that I value very highly. Philosophic rationality may be choked in the shocks of war and the welter of new persecuting superstitions, but one may hope that it will not be lost utterly or for more than a few centuries. In this respect, my philosophic life has been a happy one.

From 'Reply to Criticisms'

Mr Brightman's essay on my philosophy of religion is a model of truly Christian forbearance; I do not believe that I should have been as kind to some one who had attacked my beliefs in the manner in which I have attacked beliefs which he holds. I will try to follow his example, and to deal with the questions involved as inoffensively as I am able. And first I will re-state in outline my general attitude towards religion, which is somewhat complex.

Religion has three main aspects. In the first place, there are a man's serious personal beliefs, in so far as they have to do with the nature of the world and the conduct of life. In the second place, there is theology. In the third place there is institutionalized religion, i.e. the Churches. The first of these aspects is somewhat vague, but the word 'religion' is coming more and more to be used in this sense. Theology is the part of religion with which the philosopher as such is most concerned. The historian and sociologist are chiefly occupied with religion as embodied in institutions. What makes my attitude towards religion complex is that, although I consider some form of personal religion highly desirable, and feel many people unsatisfactory through the lack of it, I cannot accept the theology of any well-known religion, and I incline to think that most Churches at most times have done more harm than good.

As regards my own personal religion, Mr Brightman has done full justice to it, and I need say no more about it, except that the expression of it which seems to me least unsatisfactory is the one in *Social Reconstruction* (Chapter VII).

As regards theology, Mr Brightman maintains that, in some sense, I believe in God; he says also that I ought to use my religious experiences as clues to the nature of the real. 'The appreciation of the religious sense of mystery and of the life of the Spirit, and the need for something more than human, are experiences of the divine.' I cannot agree. The fact that I feel a *need* for something more than human is no evidence that the need can be satisfied, any more than hunger is evidence that I shall get food. I do not see how any emotion of mine can be evidence of something outside me. If it is said that certain parts of human minds are divine, that may be allowed as a *façon de parler*, but it does not mean that there is a God in the sense in which Christians hitherto have believed in Him. In arguments to God from religious experience there seems to be an unexpressed premiss to the effect that what seem to us our deepest experiences cannot be deceptive, but must have all the significance they appear to have. For such a premiss there seems to me to be no good ground, if 'significance' means 'proving the existence of this or that'. In the realm of value, I admit the significance of religious experience.

The scholastic proofs of the existence of God are now out of fashion among Protestants. Mr Brightman mentions my discussion of Leibniz's proofs, but does not, perhaps, quite sufficiently recognize that I was discussing Leibniz, and had no occasion to notice any arguments which he does not use. For my part, although I think the old proofs fallacious, I prefer them to the modern ones, because they fail only through definite errors, whereas the modern ones, so far as they are known to me, do not even profess to be proofs in any strict sense. I do not know of any conclusive argument *against* the existence of God, not even the existence of evil. I think Leibniz, in his *Théodicée*, proved that the evil in the world *may* have been necessary in order to produce a greater good. He did not notice that the same argument proves that the good *may* have been necessary in order to produce a greater evil. If a world which is partly bad may have been created by a wholly benevolent God, a world which is partly good may have been created by a wholly malevolent Devil. Neither seems to me likely, but the one is as likely as the other. The fact that the unpleasant possibility is never noticed shows the optimistic bias which seems to me to infect most writing on the philosophy of religion.

As for the Churches, they belong to history, not to philosophy, and I shall therefore say nothing about them.

2

THE FREE MAN'S WORSHIP

To Dr Faustus in his study Mephistophilis told the history of the Creation, saying:

The endless praises of the choirs of angels had begun to grow wearisome; for, after all, did he not deserve their praise? Had he not given them endless joy? Would it not be more amusing to obtain undeserved praise, to be worshipped by beings whom he tortured? He smiled inwardly, and resolved that the great drama should be performed.

For countless ages the hot nebula whirled aimlessly through space. At length it began to take shape, the central mass threw off planets, the planets cooled, boiling seas and burning mountains heaved and tossed, from black masses of cloud hot sheets of rain deluged the barely solid crust. And now the first germ of life grew in the depths of the ocean, and developed rapidly, in the fructifying warmth, into vast forest trees, huge ferns springing from the damp mould, sea-monsters breeding, fighting, devouring, and passing away. And from the monsters, as the play unfolded itself, Man was born, with the power of thought, the knowledge of good and evil, and the cruel thirst for worship. And Man saw that all is passing in this mad monstrous world, that all is struggling to snatch, at any cost, a few brief moments of life before Death's inexorable decree. And Man said: 'There is a hidden purpose, could we but fathom it, and the purpose is good; for we must reverence something, and in the visible world there is nothing worthy of reverence.' And Man stood aside from the struggle, resolving that God intended harmony to come out of chaos by human efforts. And when he followed the instincts which God had transmitted to him from his ancestry of beasts of prey, he called it Sin, and asked God to forgive him. But he doubted whether he could be justly forgiven, until he invented a divine Plan by which God's wrath was to have been appeased. And seeing the present was bad, he made it yet worse, that thereby the future might be better. And he gave God thanks for the strength that enabled him to forego even the joys that were possible. And God smiled; and when he saw that Man had become perfect in renunciation and worship, he sent another sun through the sky, which crashed into Man's sun; and all returned again to nebula.

'Yes,' he murmured, 'it was a good play; I will have it performed again.'

Such, in outline, but even more purposeless, more void of meaning, is the world which Science presents for our belief. Amid such a world, if anywhere, our ideals henceforward must find a home. That Man is the product of causes which had no provision of the end they were achieving; that his origin, his growth, his hopes and fears, his loves and his beliefs, are but the outcome of accidental collocations of atoms; that no fire, no heroism, no intensity of thought and feeling, can preserve an individual life beyond the grave; that all the labours of the ages, all the devotion, all the inspiration, all the noonday brightness of human genius, are destined to extinction in the vast death of the solar system, and that the whole temple of Man's achievement must inevitably be buried beneath the debris of a universe in ruins — all these things, if not quite beyond dispute, are yet so nearly certain that no philosophy which rejects them can hope to stand. Only within the scaffolding of these truths, only on the firm foundation of unyielding despair, can the soul's habitation henceforth be safely built.

How, in such an alien and inhuman world, can so powerless a creature as Man preserve his aspirations untarnished? A strange mystery it is that Nature, omnipotent but blind, in the revolutions of her secular hurryings through the abysses of space, has brought forth at last a child subject still to her power, but gifted with sight, with knowledge of good and evil, with the capacity of judging all the works of his unthinking Mother. In spite of Death, the mark and seal of the parental control, Man is yet free, during his brief years, to examine, to criticize, to know, and in imagination to create. To him alone, in the world with which he is acquainted, this freedom belongs; and in this lies his superiority to the resistless forces that control his outward life.

The savage, like ourselves, feels the oppression of his impotence before the powers of Nature; but having in himself nothing that he respects more than Power, he is willing to prostrate himself before his gods, without inquiring whether they are worthy of his worship. Pathetic and very terrible is the long history of cruelty and torture, of degradation and human sacrifice, endured in the hope of placating the jealous gods: surely, the trembling believer thinks, when what is most precious has been freely given, their lust for blood must be appeased, and more will not be required. The religion of Moloch – as such creeds may be generically called – is in essence the cringing submission of the slave, who dare not, even in his heart, allow the thought that his master deserves no adulation. Since the independence of ideals is not yet acknowledged, Power may be freely worshipped, and receive an unlimited respect despite its wanton infliction of pain.

But gradually, as morality grows bolder, the claim of the ideal world begins to be felt, and worship, if it is not to cease, must be given to gods of another kind than those created by the savage. Some, though they feel the demands of the ideal, will still consciously reject them, still urging that naked Power is worthy of worship. Such is the attitude inculcated in God's answer to Job out of the whirlwind: the divine power and knowledge are paraded, but of the divine goodness there is no hint. Such, also, is the attitude of those who, in our own day, base their morality upon the struggle for survival, maintaining that the survivors are necessarily the fittest. But others, not content with an answer so repugnant to the moral sense, will adopt the position which we have become accustomed to regard as specially religious, maintaining that, in some hidden manner, the world of fact is really harmonious with the world of ideals. Thus Man creates God, all-powerful and all-good, the mystic unity of what is and what should be.

But the world of fact, after all, is not good, and in submitting our judgment to it there is an element of slavishness from which our thoughts must be purged. For in all things it is well to exalt the dignity of Man, by freeing him, as far as possible, from the tyranny of non-human Power. When we have realized that Power is largely bad, that Man, with his knowledge of good and evil, is but a helpless atom in a world which has no such knowledge, the choice is again presented to us: Shall we worship Force, or shall we worship

Goodness? Shall our God exist and be evil, or shall he be recognized as the creation of our own conscience?

The answer to this question is very momentous, and affects profoundly our whole morality. The worship of Force, to which Carlyle and Nietzsche and the creed of Militarism have accustomed us, is the result of failure to maintain our own ideals against a hostile universe: it is itself a prostrate submission to evil, a sacrifice of our best to Moloch. If strength indeed is to be respected, let us respect rather the strength of those who refuse that false 'recognition of facts' which fails to recognize that facts are often bad. Let us admit that, in the world we know, there are many things that would be better otherwise, and that the ideals to which we do and must adhere are not realized in the realm of matter. Let us preserve our respect for truth, for beauty, for the ideal of perfection which life does not permit us to attain, though none of these things meet with the approval of the unconscious universe. If Power is bad, as it seems to be, let us reject it from our hearts. In this lies Man's true freedom: in determination to worship only the God created by our own love of the good, to respect only the heaven which inspires the insight of our best moments. In action, in desire, we must submit perpetually to the tyranny of outside forces; but in thought, in aspiration, we are free, free from our fellow-men, free from the petty planet on which our bodies impotently crawl, free even, while we live, from the tyranny of death. Let us learn, then, that energy of faith which enables us to live constantly in the vision of the good; and let us descend, in action, into the world of fact, with that vision always before us.

When first the opposition of fact and ideal grows fully visible, a spirit of fiery revolt, of fierce hatred of the gods, seems necessary to the assertion of freedom. To defy with Promethean constancy a hostile universe, to keep its evil always in view, always actively hated, to refuse no pain that the malice of Power can invent, appears to be the duty of all who will not bow before the inevitable. But indignation is still a bondage, for it compels our thoughts to be occupied with an evil world; and in the fierceness of desire from which rebellion springs, there is a kind of self-assertion which it is necessary for the wise to overcome. Indignation is a submission of our thoughts, but not of our desires; the Stoic freedom in which wisdom consists is found in the submission of our desires, but not of our thoughts. From the submission of our desires springs the virtue of resignation; from the freedom of our thoughts springs the whole world of art and philosophy, and the vision of beauty by which, at last, we half reconquer the reluctant world. But the vision of beauty is possible only to unfettered contemplation, to thoughts not weighted by the load of eager wishes; and thus Freedom comes only to those who no longer ask of life that it shall yield them any of those personal goods that are subject to the mutations of Time.

Although the necessity of renunciation is evidence of the existence of evil, yet Christianity, in preaching it, has shown a wisdom exceeding that of the Promethean philosophy of rebellion. It must be admitted that, of the things we desire, some, though they prove impossible, are yet real goods; others, however, as ardently longed for, do not form part of a fully purified ideal. The belief that what must be renounced is bad, though sometimes false, is far less often false than untamed passion supposes; and the creed of religion, by providing a reason for proving that it is never false, has been the means of purifying our hopes by the discovery of many austere truths.

But there is in resignation a further good element: even real goods, when they are unattainable, ought not to be fretfully desired. To every man comes, sooner or later, the great renunciation. For the young, there is nothing unattainable; a good thing, desired with the whole force of a passionate will, and yet impossible, is to them not credible. Yet, by death, by illness, by poverty, or by the voice of duty, we must learn, each one of us, that the world was not made for us, and that, however beautiful may be the things we crave, Fate may nevertheless forbid them. It is the part of courage, when misfortune comes, to bear without repining the ruin of our hopes, to turn away our thoughts from vain regrets. This degree of submission to Power is not only just and right: it is the very gate of wisdom.

But passive renunciation is not the whole of wisdom, for not by renunciation alone can we build a temple for the worship of our own ideals. Haunting foreshadowings of the temple appear in the realm of imagination, in music, in architecture, in the untroubled kingdom of reason, and in the golden sunset magic of lyrics, where beauty shines and glows, remote from the touch of sorrow, remote from the fear of change, remote from the failures and disenchantments of the world of fact. In the contemplation of these things, the vision of heaven will shape itself in our hearts, giving at once a touchstone to judge the world about us, and an inspiration by which to fashion to our needs whatever is not incapable of serving as a stone in the sacred temple.

Except for those rare spirits that are born without sin, there is a cavern of darkness to be traversed before that temple can be entered.

The gate of the cavern is despair, and its floor is paved with the gravestones of abandoned hopes. There Self must die, there the eagerness, the greed of untamed desire must be slain, for only so can the soul be freed from the empire of Fate. But out of the cavern the Gate of Renunciation leads again to the daylight of wisdom, by whose radiance a new insight, a new joy, a new tenderness shine forth to gladden the pilgrim's heart.

When, without the bitterness of impotent rebellion, we have learnt both to resign ourselves to the outward rule of Fate and to recognize that the non-human world is unworthy of our worship, it becomes possible at last so to transform and refashion the unconscious universe, so to transmute it in the crucible of imagination, that a new image of shining gold replaces the old idol of clay. In all the multiform facts of the world – in the visual shapes of trees and mountains and clouds, in the events of the life of man, even in the very omnipotence of Death – the insight of creative idealism can find the reflection of a beauty which its own thoughts first made. In this way mind asserts its subtle mastery over the thoughtless forces of Nature. The more evil the material with which it deals, the more thwarting to untrained desire, the greater is its achievement in inducing the reluctant rock to yield up its hidden treasures, the prouder its victory in compelling the opposing forces to swell the pageant of its triumph. Of all the arts, Tragedy is the proudest, the most triumphant; for it builds its shining citadel in the very centre of the enemy's country, on the very summit of his highest mountain; from its impregnable watch-towers, his camps and arsenals, his columns and forts, are all revealed; within its walls the free life continues, while the legions of Death and Pain and Despair, and all the servile captains of tyrant Fate, afford the burghers of that dauntless city new spectacles of beauty. Happy those sacred ramparts, thrice happy the dwellers on that all-seeing eminence. Honour to those brave warriors who, through countless ages of warfare, have preserved for us the priceless heritage of liberty, and have kept undefiled by sacrilegious invaders the home of the unsubdued.

But the beauty of Tragedy does but make visible a quality which, in more or less obvious shapes, is present always and everywhere in life. In the spectacle of Death, in the endurance of intolerable pain, and in the irrevocableness of a vanished past, there is a sacredness, an overpowering awe, a feeling of the vastness, the depth, the inexhaustible mystery of existence, in which, as by some strange marriage of pain, the sufferer is bound to the world by bonds of sorrow. In these moments of insight, we lose all eagerness of temporary desire, all struggling and striving for petty ends, all care for the little trivial things that, to a superficial view, make up the common life of day by day; we see, surrounding the narrow raft illumined by the flickering light of human comradeship, the dark ocean on whose rolling waves we toss for a brief hour; from the great night without, a chill blast breaks in upon our refuge; all the loneliness of humanity amid hostile forces is concentrated upon the individual soul, which must struggle alone, with what of courage it can command, against the whole weight of a universe that cares nothing for its hopes and fears. Victory, in this struggle with the powers of darkness, is the true baptism into the glorious company of heroes, the true initiation into the overmastering beauty of human existence. From that awful encounter of the soul with the outer world, renunciation, wisdom, and charity are born; and with their birth a new life begins. To take into the inmost shrine of the soul the irresistible forces whose puppets we seem to be – Death and change, the irrevocableness of the past, and the powerlessness of man before the blind hurry of the universe from vanity to vanity – to feel these things and know them is to conquer them.

This is the reason why the Past has such magical power. The beauty of its motionless and silent pictures is like the enchanted purity of late autumn, when the leaves, though one breath would make them fall, still glow against the sky in golden glory. The Past does not change or strive; like Duncan, after life's fitful fever it sleeps well; what was eager and grasping, what was petty and transitory, has faded away, the things that were beautiful and eternal shine out of it like stars in the night. Its beauty, to a soul not worthy of it, is unendurable; but to a soul which has conquered Fate it is the key of religion.

The life of Man, viewed outwardly, is but a small thing in comparison with the forces of Nature. The slave is doomed to worship Time and Fate and Death, because they are greater than anything he finds in himself, and because all his thoughts are of things which they devour. But great as they are, to think of them greatly, to feel their passionless splendour, is greater still. And such thought makes us free men; we no longer bow before the inevitable in oriental subjection, but we absorb it, and make it a part of ourselves. To abandon the struggle for private happiness, to expel all eagerness of temporary desire, to burn with passion for eternal things – this is emancipation, and this is the free man's worship. And this liberation is effected by a contemplation of Fate; for Fate itself is subdued by the mind which leaves nothing to be purged by the purifying fire of Time.

United with his fellow-men by the strongest of all ties, the tie of a common doom, the free man finds that a new vision is with him always, shedding over every daily task the light of love. The life of Man is a long march through the night, surrounded by invisible foes, tortured by weariness and pain, towards a goal that few can hope to reach, and where none may tarry long. One by one, as they march, our comrades vanish from our sight, seized by the silent orders of omnipotent Death. Very brief is the time in which we can help them, in which their happiness or misery is decided. Be it ours to shed sunshine on their path, to lighten their sorrows by the balm of sympathy, to give them the pure joy of a never-tiring affection, to strengthen failing courage, to instil faith in hours of despair. Let us not weigh in grudging scales their merits and demerits, but let us think only of their need, of the sorrows, the difficulties, perhaps the blindnesses, that make the misery of their lives; let us remember that they are fellow-sufferers in the same darkness, actors in the same tragedy with ourselves. And so, when their day is over, when their good and their evil have become eternal by the immortality of the past, be it ours to feel that where they suffered, where they failed, no deed of ours was the cause; but wherever a spark of the divine fire kindled in their hearts, we were ready with encouragement, with sympathy, with brave words in which high courage glowed.

Brief and powerless is Man's life; on him and all his race the slow sure doom falls pitiless and dark. Blind to good and evil, reckless of destruction, omnipotent matter rolls on its relentless way; for Man, condemned today to lose his dearest, tomorrow himself to pass through the gate of darkness, it remains only to cherish, ere yet the blow falls, the lofty thoughts that ennoble his little day; disdaining the coward terrors of the slave of Fate, to worship at the shrine that his own hands have built; undismayed by the empire of chance, to preserve a mind free from the wanton tyranny that rules his outward life; proudly defiant of the irresistible forces that tolerate, for a moment, his knowledge and his condemnation, to sustain alone, a weary but unyielding Atlas, the world that his own ideals have fashioned despite the trampling march of unconscious power.

3

AUTOBIOGRAPHY: MYSTIC ILLUMINATION

During the Lent Term of 1901, we joined with the Whiteheads in taking Professor Maitland's house in Downing College. Professor Maitland had had to go to Madeira for his health. His housekeeper informed us that he had 'dried hisself up eating dry toast', but I imagine this was not the medical diagnosis. Mrs Whitehead was at this time becoming more and more of an invalid, and used to have intense pain owing to heart trouble. Whitehead and Alys and I were all filled with anxiety about her. He was not only deeply devoted to her but also very dependent upon her, and it seemed doubtful whether he would ever achieve any more good work if she were to die. One day, Gilbert Murray came to Newnham to read part of his translation of *The Hippolytus*, then unpublished. Alys and I went to hear him, and I was profoundly stirred by the beauty of the poetry. When we came home, we found Mrs Whitehead undergoing an unusually severe bout of pain. She seemed cut off from everyone and everything by walls of agony, and the sense of the solitude of each human soul suddenly overwhelmed me. Ever since my marriage, my emotional life had been calm and superficial: I had forgotten all the deeper issues, and had been content with flippant cleverness. Suddenly the ground seemed to give way beneath me, and I found myself in quite another region. Within five minutes I went through some such reflections as the following: the loneliness of the human soul is unendurable; nothing can penetrate it except the highest intensity of the sort of love that religious teachers have preached; whatever does not spring from this motive is harmful, or at best useless; it follows that war is wrong, that a public school education is abominable, that the use of force is to be deprecated, and that in human relations one should penetrate to the core of loneliness in each person and speak to that. The Whiteheads' youngest boy, aged three, was in the room. I had previously taken no notice of him, nor he of me. He had to be prevented from troubling his mother in the middle of her paroxysms of pain. I took his hand and led him away. He came willingly, and felt at home with me. From that day to his death in the war in 1918, we were close friends.

At the end of those five minutes, I had become a completely different person. For a time, a sort of mystic illumination possessed me. I felt that I knew the inmost thoughts of everybody that I met in the street, and though this was, no doubt, a delusion, I did in actual fact find myself in far closer touch than previously with all my friends, and many of my acquaintances. Having been an Imperialist, I became during those five minutes a pro-Boer and a Pacifist. Having for years cared only for exactness and analysis, I found myself filled with semi-mystical feelings about beauty, with an intense interest in children, and with a desire almost as profound as that of the Buddha to find some philosophy which should make human life endurable. A strange excitement possessed me, containing intense pain but also some element of triumph through the fact that I could dominate pain, and make it, as I thought, a gateway to wisdom. The mystic insight which I then imagined myself to possess has largely faded, and the habit of analysis has reasserted itself. But something of what I thought I saw in that moment has remained always with me, causing my attitude during the first war, my interest in children, my indifference to minor misfortunes, and a certain emotional tone in all my human relations.

4

WHAT IS AN AGNOSTIC?

What is an agnostic?

An agnostic is a man who thinks that it is impossible to know the truth in the matters such as God and a future life with which the Christian religion and other religions are concerned. Or, if not for ever impossible, at any rate impossible at present.

Are agnostics atheists?

No. An atheist, like a Christian, holds that we *can* know whether or not there is a God. The Christian holds that we can know there is a God, the atheist that we can know there is not. The agnostic suspends judgment, saying that there are not sufficient grounds either for affirmation or for denial. At the same time, an agnostic may hold that the existence of God, though not impossible, is very improbable; he may even hold it so improbable that it is not worth considering in practice. In that case, he is not far removed from atheism. His attitude may be that which a careful philosopher would have towards the gods of ancient Greece. If I were asked to *prove* that Zeus and Poseidon and Hera and the rest of the Olympians do not exist, I should be at a loss to find conclusive arguments. An agnostic may think the Christian God as improbable as the Olympians; in that case, he is, for practical purposes, at one with the atheists.

Since you deny 'God's law', what authority do you accept as a guide to conduct?

An agnostic does not accept any 'authority' in the sense in which religious people do. He holds that a man should think out questions of conduct for himself. Of course he will seek to profit by the wisdom of others, but he will have to select for himself the people he is to consider wise, and he will not regard even what they say as unquestionable. He will observe that what passes as 'God's law' varies from time to time. The Bible says both that a woman must not marry her deceased husband's brother, and that in certain circumstances she must do so. If you have the misfortune to be a childless widow with an unmarried brother-in-law, it is logically impossible for you to avoid disobeying 'God's law'.

How do you know what is good and what is evil? What does an agnostic consider a sin? Does an agnostic do whatever he pleases?

The agnostic is not quite so certain as some Christians are as to what is good and what is evil. He does not hold, as most Christians in the past held, that people who disagree with the Government on abstruse points of theology ought to suffer a painful death. He is against persecution, and rather chary of moral condemnation.

As for 'sin', he thinks it not a useful notion. He admits, of course, that some kinds of conduct are desirable and some undesirable, but he holds that the punishment of undesirable kinds is only to be commended when it is deterrent or reformatory, not when it is inflicted because it is thought a good thing on its own account that the wicked should suffer. It was this belief in vindictive punishment that made men accept hell. This is part of the harm done by the notion of 'sin'.

Does an agnostic do whatever he pleases? In one sense, no; in another sense, everyone does whatever he pleases. Suppose, for example, you hate someone so much that you would like to murder him. Why do you not do so? You may reply: 'Because religion tells me that murder is a sin.' But as a statistical fact agnostics are not more prone to murder than other people, in fact rather less so. They have the same motives for abstaining from murder as other people have. Far and away the most powerful of these motives is the fear of punishment. In lawless conditions, such as a gold rush, all sorts of people will commit crimes, although in ordinary circumstances they would have been law-abiding. There is not only actual legal punishment; there is the discomfort of dreading discovery, and the loneliness of knowing that, to avoid being hated, you must wear a mask even with your closest intimates. And there is also what may be called 'conscience': if you ever contemplated a murder, you would dread the horrible memory of your victim's last moments or lifeless corpse. All this, it is true, depends upon your living in a law-abiding community, but there are abundant secular reasons for creating and preserving such a community.

I said that there is another sense in which every man does as he pleases. No one but a fool indulges every impulse, but what holds a desire in check is always some other desire. A man's anti-social wishes may be restrained by a wish to please God, but they may also be restrained by a wish to please his friends, or to win the respect of his community, or to be able to contemplate himself without disgust. But if he has no such wishes, the mere abstract precepts of morality will not keep him straight.

How does an agnostic regard the Bible?

An agnostic regards the Bible exactly as enlightened clerics regard it. He does not think that it is divinely inspired; he thinks its early history legendary, and no more exactly true than that in Homer; he thinks its moral teaching sometimes good, but sometimes very bad. For example: Samuel ordered Saul, in a war, to kill not only every man, woman, and child of the enemy, but also all the sheep and cattle. Saul, however, let the sheep and cattle live, and for this we are told to condemn him. I have never been able to admire Elisha for cursing the children who laughed at him, or to believe (what the Bible asserts) that a benevolent Deity would send two she-bears to kill the children.

How does an agnostic regard Jesus, the Virgin Birth, and the Holy Trinity?

Since an agnostic does not believe in God, he cannot think that Jesus was God. Most agnostics admire the life and moral teaching of Jesus as told in the gospels, but not necessarily more than those of some other men. Some would place on an equality with him Buddha, some Socrates, and some Abraham Lincoln. Nor do they think that what he said is not open to question, since they do not accept any authority as absolute.

43

They regard the Virgin Birth as a doctrine taken over from pagan mythology, where such births were not uncommon. (Zoroaster was said to have been born of a virgin; Ishtar, the Babylonian goddess, is called the Holy Virgin.) They cannot give any credence to it, or to the doctrine of the Trinity, since neither is possible without belief in God.

Can an agnostic be a Christian?

The word 'Christian' has had various different meanings at different times. Throughout most of the centuries since the time of Christ, it has meant a person who believed in God and immortality and held that Christ was God. But Unitarians call themselves Christians, although they do not believe in the divinity of Christ, and many people nowadays use the word 'God' in a much less precise sense than that which it used to bear. Many people who say they believe in God no longer mean a person, or a trinity of persons, but only a vague tendency or power or purpose immanent in evolution. Others, going still further, mean by 'Christianity' merely a system of ethics which, since they are ignorant of history, they imagine to be characteristic of Christians only. When, in a recent book, I said that what the world needs is 'love, Christian love, or compassion', many people thought that this showed some change in my views although, in fact, I might have said the same thing at any time. If you mean by a 'Christian' a man who loves his neighbour, who has wide sympathy with suffering and who ardently desires a world freed from the cruelties and abominations which at present disfigure it, then, certainly, you will be justified in calling me a Christian. And, in this sense, I think you will find more 'Christians' among agnostics than among the orthodox. But, for my part, I cannot accept such a definition. Apart from other objections to it, it seems rude to Jews, Buddhists, Mohammedans, and other non-Christians, who, so far as history shows, have been at least as apt as Christians to practise the virtues which some modern Christians arrogantly claim as distinctive of their own religion. I think also that all who called themselves Christians in an earlier time and a great majority of those who do so at the present day, would consider that belief in God and immortality is essential to a Christian. On these grounds I should not call myself a Christian, and I should say that an agnostic cannot be a Christian. But, if the word 'Christianity' comes to be generally used to mean merely a kind of morality, then it will certainly be possible for an agnostic to be a Christian.

Does an agnostic deny that man has a soul?

This question has no precise meaning unless we are given a definition of the word 'soul'. I suppose what is meant is, roughly, something non-material which persists throughout a person's life and even, for those who believe in immortality, throughout all future time. If this is what is meant, an agnostic is not likely to believe that man has a soul. But I must hasten to add that this does not mean that an agnostic must be a materialist. Many agnostics (including myself) are quite as doubtful of the body as they are of the soul, but this is a long story taking one into difficult metaphysics. Mind and matter alike, I should say, are only convenient symbols in discourse, not actually existing things.

Does an agnostic believe in a hereafter, in heaven or hell?

The question whether people survive death is one as to which evidence is possible. Psychical research and spiritualism are thought by many to supply such evidence. An agnostic, as such, does not take a view about survival unless he thinks that there is evidence one way or the other. For my part, I do not think there is any good reason to believe that we survive death, but I am open to conviction if adequate evidence should appear.

Heaven and hell are a different matter. Belief in hell is bound up with the belief that the vindictive punishment of sin is a good thing, quite independently of any reformative or deterrent effect that it may have. Hardly any agnostic believes this. As for heaven, there might conceivably some day be evidence of its existence through spiritualism, but most agnostics do not think that there is such evidence, and therefore do not believe in heaven.

Are you never afraid of God's judgment in denying Him?

Most certainly not. I also deny Zeus and Jupiter and Odin and Brahma, but this causes me no qualms. I observe that a very large portion of the human race does not believe in God and suffers no visible punishment in consequence. And if there were a God, I think it very unlikely that He would have such an uneasy vanity as to be offended by those who doubt His existence.

How do agnostics explain the beauty and harmony of nature?

I do not understand where this 'beauty' and 'harmony' are supposed to be found. Throughout the animal kingdom, animals ruthlessly prey upon each other. Most of them are either cruelly killed by other animals or slowly die of hunger. For my part, I am unable to see any very great beauty or harmony in the tapeworm. Let it not be said that this creature is sent as a punishment for our sins, for it is more prevalent among animals than among humans. I suppose the questioner is thinking of such things as the beauty of the starry heavens. But one should remember that stars every now and again explode and reduce everything in their neighbourhood to a vague mist. Beauty, in any case, is subjective and exists only in the eye of the beholder.

How do agnostics explain miracles and other revelations of God's omnipotence?

Agnostics do not think that there is any evidence of 'miracles' in the sense of happenings contrary to natural law. We know that faith-healing occurs and is in no sense miraculous. At Lourdes certain diseases can be cured and others cannot. Those that can be cured at Lourdes can probably be cured by any doctor in whom the patient has faith. As for the records of other miracles, such as Joshua commanding the sun to stand still, the agnostic dismisses them as legends and points to the fact that all religions are plentifully supplied with such legends. There is just as much miraculous evidence for the Greek Gods in Homer, as for the Christian God in the Bible.

There have been base and cruel passions, which religion opposes. If you abandon religious principles, could mankind exist?

The existence of base and cruel passions is undeniable, but I find no evidence in history that religion has opposed these passions. On the contrary, it has sanctified them, and enabled people to indulge them without remorse. Cruel persecutions have been commoner in Christendom than anywhere else. What appears to justify persecution is dogmatic belief. Kindliness and tolerance only prevail in proportion as dogmatic belief decays. In our day a new dogmatic religion, namely Communism, has arisen. To this, as to other systems of dogma, the agnostic is opposed. The persecuting character of present-day Communism is exactly like the persecuting character of Christianity in earlier centuries. In so far as Christianity has become less persecuting, this is mainly due to the work of freethinkers who have made dogmatists rather less dogmatic. If they were as dogmatic now as in former times, they would still think it right to burn heretics at the stake. The spirit of tolerance which some modern Christians regard as essentially Christian is, in fact, a product of the temper which allows doubt and is suspicious of absolute certainties. I think that anybody who surveys past history in an impartial manner will be driven to the conclusion that religion has caused more suffering than it has prevented.

What is the meaning of life to the agnostic?

I feel inclined to answer by another question: What is the meaning of 'the meaning of life'? I suppose what is intended is some general purpose. I do not think that life in general has any purpose. It just happened. But individual human beings have purposes, and there is nothing in agnosticism to cause them to abandon these purposes. They cannot, of course, be certain of achieving the results at which they aim; but you would think ill of a soldier who refused to fight unless victory was certain. The person who needs religion to bolster up his own purposes is a timorous person, and I cannot think as well of him as of the man who takes his chances, while admitting that defeat is not impossible.

Does not the denial of religion mean the denial of marriage, chastity and other aspects of Christian virtue?

Here again one must reply by another question: Does the man who asks this question believe that marriage and chastity contribute to earthly happiness here below, or does he think that, while they cause misery here below, they are to be advocated as means of getting to heaven? The man who takes the latter view will no doubt expect agnosticism to lead to a decay of what he calls virtue, but he will have to admit that what he calls virtue is not what ministers to the happiness of the human race while on earth. If, on the other hand, he takes the former view, namely that there are terrestrial arguments in favour of marriage and chastity, he must also hold that these arguments are such as should appeal to an agnostic.

Agnostics, as such, have no distinctive views about sexual morality. Some of them think one thing, and some another. But most of them would admit that there are valid arguments against the unbridled indulgence of sexual desires. They would derive these arguments, however, from terrestrial sources and not from supposed divine commands.

Is not faith in reason alone a dangerous creed? Is not reason imperfect and inadequate without spiritual and moral laws?

No sensible man, however agnostic, has 'faith in reason alone'. Reason is concerned with matters of fact, some observed, some inferred. The question whether there is a future life and the question whether there is a God, concern matters of fact, and the agnostic will hold that they should be investigated in the same way as the question, 'Will there be an eclipse of the moon tomorrow?' But matters of fact alone are not sufficient to determine action, since they do not tell us what ends we ought to pursue. In the realm of ends we need something other than reason. The agnostic will find his ends in his own heart and not in an external command. Let us take an illustration: suppose you wish to travel by train from New York to Chicago, you will use reason to discover when the trains run, and a person who thought that there was some faculty of insight or intuition enabling him to dispense with the timetable would be thought rather silly. But no timetable will tell him that it is wise to travel to Chicago. No doubt, in deciding that it is wise, he will have to take account of further matters of fact; but behind all the matters of fact there will be the ends that he thinks fitting to pursue, and these, for an agnostic as for other men, belong to a realm which is not that of reason, though it should be in no degree contrary to it. The realm I mean is that of emotion and feeling and desire.

Do you regard all religions as forms of superstition or dogma? Which of the existing religions do you most respect, and why?

All the great organized religions that have dominated large populations have involved a greater or less amount of dogma, but 'religion' is a word of which the meaning is not very definite. Confucianism, for instance, might be called a religion, although it involves no dogma. And in some forms of liberal Christianity the element of dogma is reduced to a minimum. Of the great religions of history, I prefer Buddhism, especially in its earliest forms, because it has had the smallest element of persecution.

Communism like agnosticism opposes religion. Are agnostics Communists?

Communism does not oppose religion. It merely opposes the Christian religion, just as Mohammedanism does. Communism, at least in the form advocated by the Soviet Government and the Communist Party, is a new system of dogma of a peculiarly virulent and persecuting sort. Every genuine agnostic must therefore be opposed to it.

Do agnostics think that science and religion are impossible to reconcile?

The answer turns upon what is meant by 'religion'. If it means merely a system of ethics, it can be reconciled with science. If it means a system of dogma, regarded as unquestionably true, it is incompatible with the scientific spirit, which refuses to accept matters of fact without evidence, and also holds that complete certainty is hardly ever attainable.

What kind of evidence *could* convince you that God exists?

I think that if I heard a voice from the sky predicting all that was going to happen to me during the next twenty-four hours, including events that would have seemed highly improbable, and if all these events then proceeded to happen, I might perhaps be convinced at least of the existence of some superhuman intelligence. I can imagine other evidence of the same sort which might convince me, but so far as I know no such evidence exists.

Part II

RELIGION AND PHILOSOPHY

Parts II and III are devoted to Russell's views on the truth of religion in the light of philosophy and science. Russell proposed many definitions of 'religion', 'philosophy', and 'science', and his ideas as to how they were related to each other depended on the context.[1] In his introduction to *History of Western Philosophy* he states:

> Philosophy, as I shall understand the word, is something intermediate between theology and science. Like theology, it consists of speculations on matters as to which definite knowledge has, so far, been unascertainable; but like science, it appeals to human reason rather than to authority, whether that of tradition or that of revelation. All *definite* knowledge – so I should contend – belongs to science; all *dogma* as to what surpasses definite knowledge belongs to theology. But between theology and science there is a No Man's Land, exposed to attack from both sides; this No Man's Land is philosophy.
>
> (*Russell* 1993, p. 13)

But the relationship between religion, philosophy and science in the thinking of Russell is more complicated than the quotation above might indicate. Originally he had high expectations of finding certainty in mathematics and logic, but under the influence of Wittgenstein he reluctantly gave up these hopes and came to the conclusion that knowledge in all fields might turn out to be unreliable. In his *History of Western Philosophy* he writes that: 'To teach how to live without certainty, and yet without being paralysed by hesitation, is perhaps the chief thing that philosophy, in our age, can still do for those who study it' (Ibid., p. 14).

'The Essence of Religion' was first published in October 1912, in *The Hibbert Journal*, a liberal review of religion, theology and philosophy. It elaborates Russell's thinking about religion in the drafts of 'Prisons' (see *CPBR*, vol. 12, 1995), a projected book dealing with spiritual imprisonment from which there is release only through a union with the universe. Russell worked on 'Prisons' in 1911 at the same time as he was finishing *Principia Mathematica* and *The Problems of Philosophy*.

His interest in religion, which had been more or less dormant during the time he worked on *Principia* together with Whitehead, was inspired by his love affair with Lady Ottoline Morrell, who had deep religious feelings and beliefs. For her sake, Russell tried to formulate his own personal religion in order to offer some consolation to those who could no longer accept the Christian dogmas but still felt some sort of religious need.

'Prisons' was a testimony to his second 'conversion' in the summer of 1911. He used some parts of it in 'The Essence of Religion' and some paragraphs went into the last chapter, 'The Value of Philosophy', of *The Problems of Philosophy*.

The essay 'The Essence of Religion' received mixed reactions. Lady Ottoline thought it was very beautiful, even though it hardly contained enough religion to satisfy her. Rabindranath Tagore was appreciative, as were others who were sympathetic to mysticism. It was the subject of a paper written by J.H. Burn, who read it to the Heretics, a group at Cambridge devoted to open discussions on religion, literature, art and other relevant topics on 20 October 1912, when Russell was in Switzerland. When he came back, he led the Heretics in a discussion of his essay. Burn's paper has not survived nor have any reports of the discussion, but Russell gave his impression of the event in a letter to Lady Ottoline in which he said that it had been rather an effort, but he was pleased with the outcome.

Wittgenstein was not pleased with the essay;[2] he thought that one's private views on religion were too intimate for print.

At this time Russell was very sensitive to Wittgenstein's criticism and partly agreed. He never had the essay reprinted because he soon came to think it was 'too religious'. It was, however, reprinted in 1961 in *The Basic Writings of Bertrand Russell*, edited by Robert E. Egner and Lester E. Dennon.

'The Essence and Effect of Religion' was first published in February 1921 in *Young China*. In the autumn of 1920 Russell went to China accompanied by Dora Black, who became his second wife.

He had been invited to spend a year at the National University of Peking to give lectures on philosophy and mathematical logic, and a course on 'The Analysis of Mind'. However, he soon realized that his fame in China owed more to his writings on social philosophy than to his work in mathematical logic. People in China had been impressed by his *Principles of Social Reconstruction* (1916) and *Roads to Freedom* (1918) and wanted to hear him develop his ideas.

In his lecture 'The Essence and Effect of Religion' he addressed two questions: what is the essence of religions? and, is it necessary to preserve the essence of religions? Russell was very impressed by China and the Chinese people's relaxed attitude to religion. For example, he was impressed by the fact that the reigning Confucianism was concerned with ethics rather than dogma. This tolerant attitude was quite different from the dominating one in the West, which, in stressing dogma and correct belief, had caused much unnecessary suffering.

'Why I Am Not a Christian' is a lecture that Russell delivered at the Battersea Town Hall on Sunday 6 March 1927, under the auspices of the South London Branch of the National Secular Society. It was first published, as a pamphlet, by Watts and Company for the Rationalist Press Association Ltd of London in April 1927, which kept it in print until the 1950s. It was published in Australia and the United States in the same year. In 1957 it was reprinted in *Why I am Not a Christian and Other Essays on Religion and Related Topics*, edited by Paul Edwards, a professor of philosophy in New York University, and supplied with a preface by Russell. It has been reprinted numerous times in different anthologies and translated into more than twenty languages.

'Why I Am Not a Christian' is Russell's most incendiary anti-religious writing. It provoked a strong reaction among the pious. Those who were familiar with Russell's views on religion following the end of the First World War could not have been surprised, but those who had read only 'The Essence of Religion', or the sections on religion in *Principles of Social Reconstruction*, might have been struck by his change of tone.

'Why I Am Not a Christian' appeared at a time of religious revival, when many intellectuals were turning towards Catholicism, hence much of the response was hostile. T.S. Eliot ridiculed it and said in his review that all the arguments that Russell put forward were known to him at the age of five. He suggested pointedly that Russell stick to mathematics.

Eliot's reaction showed that Russell had hit a sensitive nerve among defenders of religion. Two devotees were so provoked that they felt obliged to respond by writing books refuting Russell's attack on their religious beliefs. H.G. Wood, who was an eminent member of the Society of Friends, at the time a lecturer on the New Testament at the Selly Oak Colleges and for the last six years of his life Professor of Theology in the University of Birmingham, wrote a book entitled *Why Bertrand Russell Is Not a Christian, an Essay in Controversy*, which was published the following year by the London Christian Movement. Russell responded in a review entitled 'Why Mr Wood Is Not a Freethinker'.

Kenneth Ingram also felt compelled to respond and wrote *The Unreasonableness of Anti-Christianity: a Reply to 'Why I Am Not a Christian,' by Mr Bertrand Russell* (1928), published on behalf of the Catholic Literature Association of the Anglo-Catholic Congress Committee by the Society of SS Peter and Paul Ltd in London. Ingram was, however, not a Catholic and his criticism of Russell is more balanced than Wood's. He took Russell to task for saying that the Privy Council had decided that 'hell was no longer necessary to a Christian'.

When Russell's essay was reprinted by Paul Edwards in 1957, two more Christians wrote books against it. C. H. Douglas Clark, a senior lecturer in inorganic and structural chemistry at the University of Leeds, wrote *Christianity and Bertrand Russell* (1958) and George S. Montgomery Jr launched a vehement attack in *Why Bertrand Russell Is Not a Christian, An American Reply* (New York, 1959).

Russell's standing with believers was not enhanced when his views were treated respectfully in the Soviet Union. But while many Christian theologians have denounced Russell's arguments against Christianity as the religion of love, the book remains a source of inspiration to many young honest doubters all over the world.

In the preface to the 1957 edition Russell responded to a rumour that he had become more religious. He reaffirmed agnosticism with regard to all dogmatic beliefs, religious or not. He wrote: 'The world needs open hearts and open minds, and it is not through rigid systems, whether old or new, that these can be derived' (*CPBR*, vol. 11, 1997).

'The Existence and Nature of God' is a lecture Russell delivered to an audience in the University of Michigan at Ann Arbor, on 18 February 1939. It was the first in a series of three sponsored by the Student Religious Association of the University of Michigan. It was followed by a lecture by the Rt Rev. Msgr Fulton J. Sheen of the Catholic University of America, who became a minor celebrity in the early days of television. The third lecturer was the famous Protestant theologian Professor Reinhold Niebuhr of Union Theological Seminar in New York. Russell's lecture attracted an audience of over two thousand people.

The Student Religious Association had been established by the Regents of the University of Michigan to stimulate and encourage interest in religion. Its first director was Kenneth Morgan, who taught in comparative religion. It was he who invited Russell and the others to speak. He interpreted 'religious' in a broader sense than was usual for his time, which probably did much to stimulate discussion of religious topics.

The lecture plus the discussion that followed was published for the first time as Paper 35 in Volume 10 of *The Collected Papers of Bertrand Russell*.

5

THE ESSENCE OF RELIGION

The decay of traditional religious beliefs, bitterly bewailed by upholders of the Churches, welcomed with joy by those who regard the old creeds as mere superstition, is an undeniable fact. Yet when the dogmas have been rejected, the question of the place of religion in life is by no means decided. The dogmas have been valued, not so much on their own account, as because they were believed to facilitate a certain attitude towards the world, an habitual direction of our thoughts, a life in the whole, free from the finiteness of self and providing an escape from the tyranny of desire and daily cares. Such a life in the whole is possible without dogma, and ought not to perish through the indifference of those to whom the beliefs of former ages are no longer credible. Acts inspired by religion have some quality of infinity in them: they seem done in obedience to a command, and though they may achieve great ends, yet it is no clear knowledge of these ends that makes them seem imperative. The beliefs which underlie such acts are often so deep and so instinctive as to remain unknown to those whose lives are built upon them. Indeed, it may be not belief but feeling that makes religion: a feeling which, when brought into the sphere of belief, may involve the conviction that this or that is good, but may, if it remains untouched by intellect, be only a feeling and yet be dominant in action. It is the quality of infinity that makes religion, the selfless, untrammelled life in the whole which frees men from the prison-house of eager wishes and little thoughts. This liberation from the prison is given by religion, but only by a religion without fettering dogmas; and dogmas become fettering as soon as assent to them becomes unnatural.

The soul of man is a strange mixture of God and brute, a battle-ground of two natures, the one particular, finite, self-centred, the other universal, infinite, and impartial. The finite life, which man shares with the brutes, is tied to the body, and views the world from the standpoint of the *here* and *now*. All those loves and hatreds which are based upon some service to the self belong to the finite life. The love of man and woman, and the love of parents and children, when they do not go beyond the promptings of instinct, are still part of the animal nature: they do not pass into the infinite life until they overcome instinct and cease to be subservient only to the purposes of the finite self. The hatred of enemies and the love of allies in battle are part of what man shares with other gregarious animals: they view the universe as grouped about one point, the single struggling self. Thus the finite part of our life contains all that makes the individual man essentially separate from other men and from the rest of the universe, all those thoughts and desires that cannot, in their nature, be shared by the inhabitant of a different body, all the distortions that make error, and all the insistent claims that lead to strife.

The infinite part of our life does not see the world from one point of view: it shines impartially, like the diffused light on a cloudy sea. Distant ages and remote regions of space are as real to it as what is present and near. In thought, it rises above the life of the senses, seeking always what is general and open to all men. In desire and will, it aims simply at the good, without regarding the good as mine or yours. In feeling, it gives love to all, not only to those who further the purposes of self. Unlike the finite life, it is impartial: its impartiality leads to truth in thought, justice in action, and universal love in feeling. Unlike the nature which man shares with the brutes, it has a life without barriers, embracing in its survey the whole universe of existence and essence; nothing in it is essentially private, but its thoughts and desires are such as all may share, since none depend upon the exclusiveness of *here* and *now* and *me*. Thus the infinite nature is the principle of union in the world, as the finite nature is the principle of division. Between the infinite nature in one man and the infinite nature in another, there can be no essential conflict: if its embodiments are incomplete, they supplement each other; its division among different men is accidental to its character, and the infinite in all constitutes one universal nature. There is thus a union of all the infinite natures of different men in a sense in which there is no union of all the finite natures. In proportion as the infinite grows strong in us, we live more completely the life of that one universal nature which embraces what is infinite in each of us.

The finite self, impelled by the desire for self-preservation, builds prison-walls round the infinite part of our nature, and endeavours to restrain it from that free life in the whole which constitutes its being. The finite self aims at dominion: it sees the world in concentric circles round the *here* and *now*, and itself as the God of that wished-for heaven. The universal soul mocks at this vision, but the finite self hopes always to make it true, and thus to quiet its troublesome critic. In many men, the finite self remains always the gaoler of the universal soul; in others, there is a rare and momentary escape; in a few, the prison-walls are demolished wholly, and the universal soul remains free through life. It is the escape from prison that gives to some moments and some thoughts a quality of infinity, like light breaking through from some greater world beyond. Sudden beauty in the midst of strife, uncalculating love, or the night-wind in the trees, seem to suggest the possibility of a life free from the conflicts and pettinesses of our everyday world, a life where there is peace which no misfortune can disturb. The things which have this quality of infinity seem to give an insight deeper than the piecemeal knowledge of our daily life. A life dominated by this insight, we feel, would be a life free from struggle, a life in harmony with the whole, outside the prison-walls built by the instinctive desires of the finite self.

It is this experience of sudden wisdom which is the source of what is essential in religion. Mysticism interprets this experience as a contact with a deeper, truer, more unified world than that of our common beliefs. Behind a thin veil, it sees the glory of God, dimly as a rule, sometimes with dazzling brightness. All the evils of our daily world it regards as merely shadows on the veil, illusions, nothings, which vanish from the sight of those who see the splendour beyond. But in this interpretation mysticism diminishes the value of the experience upon which it is based. The quality of infinity, which we feel, is not to be accounted for by the perception of new objects, other than those that at most times seem finite; it is to be accounted for, rather, by a different way of regarding the same objects, a contemplation more impersonal, more vast, more filled with love, than the fragmentary, disquiet consideration we give to things when we view them as means to help or hinder our own purposes. It is not in some other world that that beauty and that peace are to be found; it is in this actual everyday world, in the midst of action and the business of life. But it is in the everyday world as viewed by the universal soul, and in the midst of action and business inspired by its vision. The evils and the smallnesses are not illusions, but the universal soul finds within itself a love to which imperfections are no barrier, and thus unifies the world by the unity of its own contemplation.

The transition from the life of the finite self to the infinite life in the whole requires a moment of absolute self-surrender, when all personal will seems to cease, and the soul feels itself in passive submission to the universe. After passionate struggle for some particular good, there comes some inward or outward necessity to abandon the pursuit of the object which has absorbed all our desire, and no other desire is ready to replace the one that has been relinquished. Hence arises a state of suspension of the will, when the soul no longer seeks to impose itself upon the world, but is open to every impression that comes to it from the world. It is at such a time that the contemplative vision first comes into being, bringing with it universal love and universal worship. From universal worship comes joy, from universal love comes a new desire, and thence the birth of that seeking after universal good which constitutes the will of our infinite nature. Thus from the moment of self-surrender, which to the finite self appears like death, a new life begins, with a larger vision, a new happiness, and wider hopes.

The self-surrender in which the infinite life is born may be made easier to some men by belief in an all-wise God to whom submission is a duty. But it is not in its essence dependent upon this belief or upon any other. The religions of the past, it is true, have all depended to a greater or less degree upon dogma, upon some theory as to the nature and the purpose of the universe. But the decay of traditional beliefs has made every religion that rests on dogma precarious, and even impossible, to many whose nature is strongly religious. Hence those who cannot accept the creeds of the past, and yet believe that a religious outlook requires dogma, lose what is infinite in life, and become limited in their thoughts to everyday matters; they lose consciousness of the life of the whole, they lose that inexplicable sense of union which gives rise to compassion and the unhesitating service of humanity. They do not see in beauty the adumbration of a glory which a richer vision would see in every common thing, or in love a gateway to that transfigured world in which our union with the universe is fulfilled. Thus their outlook is impoverished, and their life is rendered smaller even in its finite parts. For right action they are thrown back upon bare morality; and bare morality is very inadequate as a motive for those who hunger and thirst after the infinite. Thus it has become a matter of the first importance to preserve religion without any dependence upon dogmas to which an intellectually honest assent grows daily more difficult.

There are in Christianity three elements which it is desirable to preserve if possible: worship, acquiescence, and love. Worship is given by Christianity to God; acquiescence is given to the inevitable because it is the will of God; love is enjoined towards my neighbours, my enemies, and, in fact, towards all men. The love which Christianity enjoins, and indeed any love which is to be universal and yet strong, seems in some way dependent upon worship and acquiescence. Yet these, in the form in which they appear in Christianity, depend upon belief in God, and are therefore no longer possible to those who cannot entertain this belief. Something, in worship, must be lost when we lose belief in the existence of supreme goodness and power combined. But much can be preserved, and what can be preserved seems sufficient to constitute a very strong religious life. Acquiescence, also, is rendered more difficult by loss of belief in God, since it takes away the assurance that apparent evil in the constitution of the world is really good. But it is not rendered impossible; and in consequence of its greater difficulty it becomes, when achieved, nobler, deeper, more filled by self-surrender than any acquiescence which Christianity produces. In some ways, therefore, the religion which has no dogma is greater and more religious than one which rests upon the belief that in the end our ideals are fulfilled in the outer world.

Worship

Worship is not easily defined, because it grows and changes as the worshipper grows. In crude religions it may be inspired by fear alone, and given to whatever is powerful. This element lingers in the worship of God, which may consist largely of fear and be given largely from respect for power. But the element of fear tends more and more to be banished by love, and in all the best worship fear is wholly absent. As soon as the worship inspired by fear has been surpassed, worship brings joy in the contemplation of what is worshipped. But joy alone does not constitute worship: there must be also some reverence and sense of mystery not easy to define. These three things, contemplation with joy, reverence, and sense of mystery, seem essential to constitute any of the higher forms of worship.

Within worship in this very wide sense there are varieties which it is important to distinguish. There is a selective worship, which demands that its object shall be good, and admits an opposite attitude towards a bad object; and there is an impartial worship, which can be given to whatever exists, regardless of its goodness or badness. Besides this division, there is another, equally important. There is a worship which can only be given to an actually existing object, and another worship which can be given to what merely has its place in the world of ideals; these two kinds may be distinguished as worship of the actual and worship of the ideal. The two are combined in worship of God, since God is conceived as both actual and the complete embodiment of the ideal.

Worship of God is selective, since it depends upon God's goodness. So is all worship of great men or great deeds, and of everything of which the worship depends upon some pre-eminent quality which calls forth our admiration. Worship of this sort, though it can be given to much of what exists in the actual world, cannot be given unreservedly and so as to produce a religious attitude towards the universe as a whole, except by those who believe in an omnipotent Creator or in a pantheistic all-pervading spiritual unity. For those in whom there is no such belief, the selective worship finds its full object only in the ideal good which creative contemplation imagines. The ideal good forms an essential part of the religious life, since it supplies the motive to action by giving content to the desire for universal good which forms a part of universal love. Without the knowledge and worship of the ideal good, the love of man is blind, not knowing in what direction to seek the welfare of those whom it loves. Every embodiment of good in the actual world is imperfect, if only by its brevity. Only the ideal good can satisfy fully our hunger for perfection. Only the ideal good demands no surrender to power, no sacrifice of aspiration to possibility, and no slavery of thought to fact. Only the vision of the ideal good gives infinity to our pursuit, in action, of those fragments of good which the world permits us to create, but the worship of the ideal good, though it brings with it the joy that springs from the contemplation of what is perfect, brings with it also the pain that results from the imperfection of the actual world. When this worship stands alone, it produces a sense of exile in a world of shadows, of infinite solitude amid alien forces. Thus this worship, though necessary to all religious action, does not alone suffice, since it does not produce that sense of union with the actual world which compels us to descend from the world of contemplation and seek, with however little success, to realize what is possible of the good here on earth.

For this purpose we need the kind of worship which is only given to what exists. Such worship, where there is belief in God, can be selective, since God exists and is completely good. Where there is not belief in God, such worship may be selective in regard to great men and great deeds, but towards such objects selective worship is always hampered by their imperfection and their limitation of duration and extent. The worship which can be given to whatever exists must not be selective, it must not involve any judgment as to the goodness of what is worshipped, but must be a direct impartial emotion. Such a worship is given by the contemplative vision, which finds mystery and joy in all that exists, and brings with it love to all that has life. This impartial worship has been thought, wrongly, to require belief in God, since it has been thought to involve the judgment that whatever exists is good. In fact, however, it involves no judgment whatever; hence it cannot be intellectually mistaken, and cannot be in any way dependent upon dogma. Thus the combination of this worship with the ideal good gives a faith wholly independent of beliefs as to the nature of the actual world, and therefore not assailable by the arguments which have destroyed the tenets of traditional religion.

Religion, therefore, results from the combination of two different kinds of worship – the selective, which is given to the good on account of its goodness, and the impartial, which is given to everything that exists. The former is the source of the belief in theism, the latter of the belief in pantheism, but in neither case is such a belief necessary for the worship which gives rise to it. The object of the selective worship is the ideal good, which belongs to the world of universals. Owing to oblivion of the world of universals, men have supposed that the ideal good could not have being or be worshipped unless it formed part of the actual world; hence they have believed that without God this worship could not survive. But the study of the world of universals shows that this was an error: the object of this worship need not exist, though it will be an essential part of the worship to wish it to exist as fully as possible. The object of the impartial worship, on the other hand, is whatever exists; in this case, though the object is known to exist, it is not known to be good, but it is an essential part of the worship to wish that it may be as good as possible. Pantheism, from the contemplative joy of impartial worship, and from the unity of its outlook on the universe, infers, mistakenly, that such worship involves the belief that the universe is good and is one. This belief is no more necessary to the impartial worship than the belief in God is to the selective worship. The two worships subsist side by side, without any dogma: the one involving the goodness but not the existence of its object, the other involving the existence but not the goodness of its object. Religious action is a continual endeavour to bridge the gulf between the objects of these two worships, by making more good exist and more of existence good. Only in the complete union of the two could the soul find permanent rest.

Acquiescence

Although, in a world where much evil exists and much good does not exist, no religion which is true can give permanent rest or free the soul from the need for action, yet religion can give acquiescence in evil which it is not within our power to cure. Christianity effects this by the belief that, since the apparent evil is in accordance with the will of God, it cannot really be evil. This view, however, demands a falsification of our standard of good and evil, since much that exists is evil to any unbiased consideration. Moreover, if pursued to a conclusion, it destroys all motive to action, since the reason given for acquiescence, namely that whatever happens must be for the best, is a reason which renders our efforts after the best superfluous. If, to avoid this consequence, we limit either the omnipotence or the goodness of God, acquiescence can no longer be urged on the same ground, since what happens may be either not in accordance with the will of God, or not good in spite of being in accordance with His will. For these reasons, though Christianity is in fact often effective both in causing acquiescence and in providing a religious motive for action, yet this effectiveness is due to a confusion of thought, and tends to cease as men grow more clear-sighted.

The problem we have to deal with is more difficult than the Christian's problem. We have to learn to acquiesce in the inevitable without judging that the inevitable must be good, to keep the feeling which prompts Christians to say, 'Thy will be done', while yet admitting that what is done may be evil.

Acquiescence, whatever our religion may be, must always require a large element of moral discipline. But this discipline may be made easier, and more visibly worth the pain which it involves, by religious considerations. There are two different though closely related kinds of acquiescence, the one in our private griefs, the other in the fundamental evils of the world. Acquiescence in our private griefs comes in the moment of submission which brings about the birth of the impartial will. Our private life, when it absorbs our thoughts and wishes, becomes a prison, from which, in times of grief, there is no escape but by submission. By submission our thoughts are freed, and our will is led to new aims which, before, had been hidden by the personal goods which had been uselessly desired. A large contemplation, or the growth of universal love, will produce a certain shame of absorption in our own life; hence the will is led away from protest against the inevitable, towards the pursuit of more general goods which are not wholly unattainable. Thus acquiescence in private griefs is an essential element in the growth of universal love and the impartial will.

Acquiescence does not consist in judging that things are not bad when in fact they are so. It consists in freedom from anger and indignation and preoccupied regret. Anger and indignation against those who cause our griefs will not be felt if universal love is strong; preoccupied regret will be avoided where the desire of contemplative freedom exists. The man to whom a large contemplation has become habitual will not readily allow himself to be long turned aside from the thoughts which give breadth to his life: in the absence of such thoughts he will feel something small and unworthy, a bondage of the infinite to the finite. In this way both contemplation and universal love will promote acquiescence so far as our own sorrows are concerned.

It is possible, however, to emerge from private protest, not into complete acquiescence, but into a Promethean indignation against the universe. Contemplation may only universalize our griefs; it may show us all life as a tragedy, so full of pain as to make us wish that consciousness could vanish wholly from the world. The belief that this would be desirable if it were possible is one which cannot be refuted, though it also cannot be shown to be true. But even this belief is not incompatible with acquiescence. What is incompatible is indignation, and a preoccupation with evils which makes goods invisible or only partially visible. Indignation seems scarcely possible in regard to evils for which no one is responsible; those who feel indignation in regard to the fundamental evils of the universe feel it against God or the Devil or an imaginatively personified Fate. When it is realized that the fundamental evils are due to the blind empire of matter, and are the wholly necessary effects of forces which have no consciousness and are therefore neither good nor bad in themselves, indignation becomes absurd, like Xerxes chastising the Hellespont. Thus the realization of necessity is the liberation from indignation. This alone, however, will not prevent an undue preoccupation with evil. It is obvious that some things that exist are good, some bad, and we have no means of knowing whether the good or the bad preponderate. In action, it is essential to have knowledge of good and evil; thus in all the matters subject to our will, the question what is good and what bad must be borne in mind. But in matters which lie outside our power, the question of good or bad, though knowledge about it, like all knowledge, is worth acquiring, has not that fundamental religious importance which has been assigned to it in discussions of theism and optimism. The dualism of good and bad, when it is too strongly present to our minds, prevents impartial contemplation and interferes with universal love and worship. There is, in fact, something finite and unduly human about the practice of emphasizing good and bad in regard to matters with which action is not concerned. Thus acquiescence in fundamental evils, like acquiescence in personal griefs, is furthered by the impartiality of contemplation and universal love and worship, and must already exist to some extent before these become possible. Acquiescence is at once a cause and an effect of faith, in much the same way when faith dispenses with dogma as when it rests upon a belief in God. In so far as acquiescence is a cause of faith, it rests upon moral discipline, a suppression of self and its demands, which is necessary to any life in harmony with the universe, and to any emergence from the finite into the infinite. This discipline is more severe in the absence of all optimistic dogma, but in proportion as it is more severe its outcome is greater, more unshakeable, more capable of so enlarging the bounds of self as to make it welcome with love whatever of good or evil may come before it.

Love

Love is of two kinds, the selective earthly love, which is given to what is delightful, beautiful, or good, and the impartial heavenly love, which is given to all indifferently. The earthly love is balanced by an opposing hatred: to friends are opposed foes; to saints, sinners; to God, the Devil. Thus this love introduces disunion into the world, with hostile camps and a doubtful warfare. But the heavenly love does not demand that its object shall be delightful, beautiful, or good; it can be given to everything that has life, to the best and the worst, to the greatest and to the least. It is not merely compassion, since it does not merely wish to relieve misfortune, but finds joy in what it loves, and is given to the fortunate as well as to the unfortunate. Though it includes benevolence, it is greater than benevolence: it is contemplative as well as active, and can be given where there is no possibility of benefiting the object. It is love, contemplative in origin, but becoming active wherever action is possible; and it is a kind of love to which there is no opposing hatred.

To the divine love, the division of the world into good and bad, though it remains true, seems lacking in depth; it seems finite and limited in comparison with the boundlessness of love. The division into two hostile camps seems unreal; what is felt to be real is the oneness of the world in love.

It is in the birth of divine love that the life of feeling begins for the universal soul. What contemplation is to the intellect of the universal soul, divine love is to its emotions. More than anything else, divine love frees the soul from its prison and breaks down the walls of self that prevent its union with the world. Where it is strong, duties become easy, and all service is filled with joy. Sorrow, it is true, remains, perhaps deeper and wider than before, since the lives of most human beings are largely tragic. But the bitterness of personal defeat is avoided, and aims become so wide that no complete overthrow of all hopes is possible. The loves of the natural life survive, but harmonized with universal love, and no longer setting up walls of division between the loved and the unloved. And above all, through the bond of universal love the soul escapes from the separate loneliness in which it is born, and from which no permanent deliverance is possible while it remains within the walls of its prison.

Christianity enjoins love of God and love of man as the two great commandments. Love of God differs, however, from love of man, since we cannot benefit God, while we cannot regard man as wholly good. Thus love of God is more contemplative and full of worship, while love of man is more active and full of service. In a religion which is not theistic, love of God is replaced by worship of the ideal good. As in Christianity, this worship is quite as necessary as love of man, since without it love of man is left without guidance in its wish to create the good in human lives. The worship of good is indeed the greater of the two commandments, since it leads us to know that love of man is good, and this knowledge helps us to feel the love of man. Moreover, it makes us conscious of what human life might be, and of the gulf between what it might be and what it is; hence springs an infinite compassion, which is a large part of love of man, and is apt to cause the whole. Acquiescence, also, greatly furthers love of man, since in its absence anger and indignation and strife come between the soul and the world, preventing the union in which love of man has its birth. The three elements of religion, namely worship, acquiescence, and love, are intimately interconnected; each helps to produce the others, and all three together form a unity in which it is impossible to say which comes first, which last. All three can exist without dogma, in a form which is capable of dominating life and of giving infinity to action and thought and feeling; and life in the infinite, which is the combination of the three, contains all that is essential to religion, in spite of its absence of dogmatic beliefs.

Religion derives its power from the sense of union with the universe which it is able to give. Formerly, union was achieved by assimilating the universe to our own conception of the good; union with God was easy since God was love. But the decay of traditional beliefs has made this way of union no longer one which can be relied upon: we must find a mode of union which asks nothing of the world and depends only upon ourselves. Such a mode of union is possible through impartial worship and universal love, which ignore the difference of good and bad and are given to all alike. In order to free religion from all dependence upon dogma, it is necessary to abstain from any demand that the world shall conform to our standards. Every such demand is an endeavour to impose self upon the world. From this endeavour the religion which can survive the decay of dogma must be freed. And in being freed from this endeavour, religion is freed from an element extraneous to its spirit and not compatible with its unhampered development. Religion seeks union with the universe by subordination of the demands of self; but this subordination is not complete if it depends upon a belief that the universe satisfies some at least of the demands of self. Hence for the sake of religion itself, as well as because such a belief appears unfounded, it is important to discover a form of union with the universe which is independent of all beliefs as to the nature of the universe. By life in the infinite, such a form of union is rendered possible; and to those who achieve it, it gives nearly all, and in some ways more than all, that has been given by the religions of the past.

The essence of religion, then, lies in subordination of the finite part of our life to the infinite part. Of the two natures in man, the particular or animal being lives in instinct, and seeks the welfare of the body and its descendants, while the universal or divine being seeks union with the universe, and desires freedom from all that impedes its seeking. The animal being is neither good nor bad in itself; it is good or bad solely as it helps or hinders the divine being in its search for union with the world. In union with the world the soul finds its freedom. There are three kinds of union: union in thought, union in feeling, union in will. Union in thought is knowledge, union in feeling is love, union in will is service. There are three kinds of disunion: error, hatred, and strife. What promotes disunion is insistent instinct, which is of the animal part of man; what promotes union is the combination of knowledge, love, and consequent service which is wisdom, the supreme good of man.

The life of instinct views the world as a means for the ends of instinct; thus it makes the world of less account than self. It confines knowledge to what is useful, love to allies in conflict of rival instincts, service to those with whom there is some instinctive tie. The world in which it finds a home is a narrow world, surrounded by alien and probably hostile forces; it is prisoned in a beleaguered fortress, knowing that ultimate surrender is inevitable.

The life of wisdom seeks an impartial end, in which there is no rivalry, no essential enmity. The union which it seeks has no boundaries: it wishes to know all, to love all, and to serve all. Thus it finds its home everywhere: no lines of circumvallation bar its progress. In knowledge it makes no division of useful and useless, in love it makes no division of friend and foe, in service it makes no division of deserving and undeserving.

The animal part of man, knowing that the individual life is brief and impotent, is appalled by the fact of death, and, unwilling to admit the hopelessness of the struggle, it postulates a prolongation in which its failures shall be turned into triumphs. The divine part of man, feeling the individual to be but of small account, thinks little of death, and finds its hopes independent of personal continuance.

The animal part of man, being filled with the importance of its own desires, finds it intolerable to suppose that the universe is less aware of this importance; a blank indifference to its hopes and fears is too painful to contemplate, and is therefore not regarded as admissible. The divine part of man does not demand that the world shall conform to a pattern: it accepts the world, and finds in wisdom a union which demands nothing of the world. Its energy is not checked by what seems hostile, but interpenetrates it and becomes one with it. It is not the strength of our ideals, but their weakness, that makes us dread the admission that they are ours, not the world's. We with our ideals must stand alone, and conquer, inwardly, the world's indifference. It is instinct, not wisdom, that finds this difficult and shivers at the solitude it seems to entail. Wisdom does not feel this solitude, because it can achieve union even with what seems most alien. The insistent demand that our ideals shall be already realized in the world is the last prison from which wisdom must be freed. Every demand is a prison, and wisdom is only free when it asks nothing.

6

THE ESSENCE AND EFFECT
OF RELIGION[1]

Religion is a large subject only one part of which I can talk about
today. The questions at issue are – first, what is the essence of
religion; and second, is it necessary to preserve this essence?

A definition of religion will be given after the following discussion. There are two sorts of religion – the institutional and the
personal. Those affecting society and public life are institutional
religions; those affecting inner beliefs and attitudes are personal
religions. Let us consider institutional religions first.

Different sorts of religions raise different questions. For institutional religions, the questions would be – does society need them? Are
these religions useful to society? As for personal religions, one might
ask, are these religions true? Should they be believed? Institutional
religions have emerged in two ways: there are those handed down from
earliest times whose origins are unknown, and there are those founded
by individuals and whose origins are traceable. At present most
religions belong to the second category. Those handed down from the
beginnings of recorded time are relatively few; existing examples are –
Chendu in Japan; such religious customs as the worship of heaven and
earth in pre-Confucian China; pre-Buddhist beliefs in India; and the
Judaism that antedated Christianity. These forms of worship may
have been a response to occurrences which might not be compre-
hended other than as miracles.

The 'native religions' handed down from the earliest times differ
from the 'historic religions' – the great religions of the world such as
Buddhism, Islam, Christianity and Marxism. (Marxian socialism has
been believed so widely and strongly that it will become a religion in
one or two thousand years.) For one thing, the various native
religions could not be compared because they were limited to one
culture and simply handed down from generation to generation. But
each of the great religions claims that only its own faith is true and

70

that all others are false. Each wants to spread itself over the entire world. It is scarcely possible for the Chinese to conceive that different religions sometimes cannot co-exist because, in China, Buddhism, Confucianism and other creeds can be believed in simultaneously and each is tolerant of the others. Westerners, by contrast, consider their religion to hold the absolute truth as soon as they believe in it. Alien religions are rejected, and, as a result of rival creeds failing to co-exist, there have been many religious wars. I think China is fortunate on two counts: (1) it is distant from Europe and has not been affected by religious wars, and (2) there are no poisonous and dangerous religions in Chinese history equivalent to those of the West. Someone who does not know the history of Western religion will not be able to comprehend that the word 'religion', as I have used it, has fearful connotations in the West. For example, the word 'persecution' has a horrific meaning,[1] because it is practised exclusively against those who do not conform to a specific religion.

Among the old religions only Judaism was intolerant of other religions. But its influence spread to Christianity and Islam, both of which have used the same methods. Even the intolerant side of Marxism might be attributed to the influence of Judaism. Thus an institutional religion not only has its own customs but also treats other religions as 'heresies', and wants the whole world to believe that it is the sole repository of truth while all others are false.

Now is this kind of religion useful? Usually when we ponder the usefulness of a social institution, we question whether it is valuable for national survival? Its so-called survival-value means that it can be used as a justification for killing others in order to preserve one's own life. That is why institutions useful for killing have been considered important and respectable. They are praised in poems and championed in education. Religions have been extremely effective in promoting wars in the past; indeed, they have played a lethal role throughout history!

There are many teachings in Christianity which condemn war. For example, is not killing incompatible with the lessons, 'love your neighbour as yourself' or 'turn the other cheek'? Nevertheless many wars have been caused by religions whose doctrines were held so tenaciously as t permit no toleration of rival creeds. When the end is preconceived the means to achieve it can be unscrupulous. Thus oppressive met ods have been employed with terrible results. In Christianity this kind of faith is called 'dogmatic', meaning that belief in a doctrine obliges one to put it into practice, not just to believe in it as a theory.

In the past, killing was believed useful, and religions were successful precisely because of their effectiveness in killing. In modern times science has been developed to a point where it can be more barbarous than religious fanaticism. For example, both the German and Russian Emperors were sincere believers, but both suffered crushing defeats in the War. As it is obvious that the effectiveness of religion in war has diminished, it is futile to continue to believe in religion.

It is said that religion has another use, that of promoting morality. Definitions of morality are vague, but for the time being I can say this – morality can increase human happiness. Does religion then help to increase human happiness? I think it undeniable that religion has made great contributions to history and might continue to contribute in the future. Thanks to religion there are sophisticated institutions which maintain social order. All religions, except those with revolutionary tendencies, are disposed to preserve the status quo by urging personal restraint and service to society. If a religion advocated destruction, and achieved catastrophic results, it would have been eliminated. All religions that still exist today support the status quo. Given that religion helps maintain social order, enabling people to enjoy a happier life, it cannot be denied that religion is useful. Unfortunately, the price of its usefulness is too high. First, many sacrifices are required to establish the strong institutions that guarantee social order. In Barbarian times we know that human beings were sacrificed to the Gods, and yet it is also true that today many aspects of happiness have been sacrificed for nothing. Second, since religion aims to preserve existing social institutions, it has promoted a conservative attitude which resists any institutional innovation or new ideas. It was believed that progress in thought would destroy faith and disturb the social order as individuals became unwilling to sacrifice themselves to the common good. Hence religious conservatism is incompatible with progress in thought. If the object of religion is to preserve social stability, then new ideas will be sacrificed and, thus, progress halted. How then do we increase happiness in the future?

Under a strict and conservative religious system individual development is stifled. Furthermore, oppressive religions make it particularly hard for those with unusual talents to develop freely and contribute intellectually and socially. Therefore, the civilization of a nation will definitely regress under the oppression of religion. Some nations may appear strong due to their religion but they are not able to progress.

Now let us deal with the second sort of religion, namely personal religion. How can a person be regarded as having a religious attitude? The so-called religious attitude must mean a faith which directs one's behaviour. Some have said recently that their religious beliefs are not unchangeable. But this retreat from dogmatism is incompatible with the religious attitude. All genuinely religious beliefs are absolute and will definitely influence one's behaviour.

In the native religions – the very native religions handed down from earliest times – beliefs were considered to be of practical use. For example, primitive people believed that an omnipotent heaven could help them in killing, so they were brave in fighting; farmers believed that, if they could win heaven's favour, then it would rain and their crops would grow. These beliefs were related to the harshness of existence. As to the religious attitude generally, it is not restricted to a single nation or state, but influences people the world over. It is said that God likes goodness and dislikes evil. Hence people are expected to do good, lest they make God angry. The doctrine of good and evil, therefore, is a tool for the propagation of religion. When talking about relations between Man and the universe, we have to ask about the destiny of Man and about good and evil. What is the universe? I dare not give a definite answer. It is even more difficult to explain what the universe expects of Man. In religion, if one believes that Man's desires are an insignificant part of the universe, this will definitely be regarded as 'irreligious'. In religion the desires of Man are significant, and, from this perspective, the universe is regarded as something that exists for Man. What makes us most comfortable in a religion is that it advances the egotistical notion that Man's desires are not trifling but are of great consequence in the universe.

There are many beliefs in science too. But belief in science is different from belief in religion. Scientific beliefs are not held dogmatically. The objects of belief, as well as the underlying attitudes, are quite different. We may have either a scientific attitude or a religious attitude towards the same object. For example, Marx's socialism may or may not be true scientifically. Yet when people believe in it dogmatically, it becomes a religious belief. In the pure domain of science, as in physics, for instance, the Law of Gravitation discovered by Newton has until recent years been presumed to be true. We can believe in it with either a religious fervour or with a scientific attitude. If we believe in it with a religious attitude, thinking that even the digits after the tenth decimal place cannot be changed, then Einstein ought to be killed because his new theory of gravitation is fundamentally different from Newton's. In fact, Newton himself was a scientist, and although he formulated an important theory that has not been challenged for three hundred years, he himself adopted a scientific attitude, believing that, no matter how accurate his theory, it might be corrected in the future. Many scientists take a scientific attitude. Einstein modified Newton's theory in a piecemeal way, by explaining something which was ignored by Newton, rather than by overthrowing his theory as a whole. It is obvious that the scientific and the religious attitudes are fundamentally different. If we treated science in a religious way, neither Einstein's theories Marx's, could have been born. Marx's theory of socialism was based on the science and philosophy of the 1860s when materialism was very popular. His observations were entirely based on materialism. Now, owing to progress in physics, the theory of relativity has been discovered and we know that matter and energy can be transformed into each other. If sixty-year-old assumptions are used to uphold Marx's theory as a body of unalterable doctrines, then Marxists are exhibiting a religious attitude, even though their theory is purportedly scientific.

Now let us tentatively define religion, although this remains difficult, for even if the friends of religion can arrive at a settled definition , the enemies of religion may not agree with it. I do not count as a friend of religion, so I do not accept the words of its adherents, nor is it necessary for them to accept mine. Let us agree for the moment that 'religions are beliefs with many dogmas which direct human behaviour and are neither based on – nor contradict – real evidence; and that the method employed by religions to direct people's minds are based on sentiment or power rather than reason.'

Now the question is, given that religion is like this, is there something essential to religion which can be preserved after the harmful dogmas are eliminated? I think not. Among present-day religions Buddhism is the best. The doctrines of Buddhism are profound, they are almost reasonable, and historically they have been the least harmful and the least cruel. But I cannot say that Buddhism is positively good, nor would I wish to have it spread all over the world and believed by everyone. This is because Buddhism only focuses on the question of what Man is, not on what the universe is like. Buddhism does not really pursue the truth; it appeals to sentiment and, ultimately, tries to persuade people to believe in doctrines which are based on subjective assumptions not objective evidence. Generally, subjective opinions produce false beliefs. I think that no matter what the religion, nor how ambiguously its faith is expressed, the same problem arises because of the substitution of subjective sentiment for objective evidence. Sentiment might be taken as the dominant force in our daily lives. But as for belief in facts, the farther we distance ourselves from sentiment the better. Never substitute sentiment for facts. It is absolutely harmful to do so.

Some people who profess to be open-minded believe that religions are useful because they occupy the same ground as morality. They claim that if there were no religions there would be no morality. But this is merely a problem of nomenclature. If religion and morality occupy the same ground, they are naturally inseparable. Nevertheless, if the term 'morality' exists, then there is certainly the idea of morality. The same holds for religion. Why should we confuse them? For example, it is a matter of religion, not morality, that in central Mexico children are killed as sacrifices to God. There are some people who are moral, yet they do not believe in religion, and even attack it. Can they be called immoral? It is apparent that the terms 'religion' and 'morality' can be easily distinguished and should not therefore be confused. It is said that those who love people of their own herd are good Christians. But in fact anyone may have a loving heart; not only Christians but also Buddhists may love others. It is fortunate to love other people, but it cannot be assumed that those who do are believers of this or that religion. I do not think that religion is beneficial to morality, first, because belief in religion is not completely based on fact, and is hence erroneous. Second, those who take a religious attitude either refuse to hold any beliefs other than those of their religion, or else they acquire the bad habits of insincerity and inconsistency by holding beliefs which they know to be false.

In fact, we can say, first, that the demerits of religion derive from its attitude of conservative opposition to new ideas and institutions. Religions reject anything opposed to the old customs, regardless of truth, so that any progress in ideas and institutions becomes impossible. Second, religions always make judgements exclusively in terms of human desires, substituting sentiment for objective evidence. As a result, they create a universe full of Gods; the more deeply people believe in a religion, the more Gods exist. It is always believed that the universe loves Man, that the Gods are representative of the universe, and, therefore, that the Gods may love and help Man. Man must not irritate the Gods since they can bring about disasters – all plagues have been the result of Man's wrongdoing.

I cannot claim that the universe is harmful to Man; nor can I say that the universe loves Man, since I do not have much evidence either way. I think that Nature is neutral to human beings and that it is better to believe that it may, to a certain degree, be controlled. We should study Nature rather than assume without evidence that the world is created by God. By doing so, our minds will become calm, and at last we will be able to perform our proper duty to Mankind.

7

WHY I AM NOT A
CHRISTIAN

As your Chairman has told you, the subject about which I am going to speak to you tonight is 'Why I am not a Christian'. Perhaps it would be as well, first of all, to try to make out what one means by the word 'Christian'. It is used in these days in a very loose sense by a great many people. Some people mean no more by it than a person who attempts to live a good life. In that sense I suppose there would be Christians in all sects and creeds; but I do not think that that is the proper sense of the word, if only because it would imply that all the people who are not Christians – all the Buddhists, Confucians, Mohammedans, and so on – are not trying to live a good life. I do not mean by a Christian any person who tries to live decently according to his lights. I think that you must have a certain amount of definite belief before you have a right to call yourself a Christian. The word does not have quite such a full-blooded meaning now as it had in the times of St Augustine and St Thomas Aquinas. In those days, if a man said that he was a Christian it was known what he meant. You accepted a whole collection of creeds which were set out with great precision, and every single syllable of those creeds you believed with the whole strength of your convictions.

What is a Christian?

Nowadays it is not quite that. We have to be a little more vague in our meaning of Christianity. I think, however, that there are two different items which are quite essential to anybody calling himself a Christian. The first is one of a dogmatic nature – namely that you must believe in God and in immortality. If you do not believe in those two things, I do not think that you can properly call yourself a Christian. Then, further than that, as the name implies, you must have some kind of belief about Christ. The Mohammedans, for

77

instance, also believe in God and in immortality, and yet they would not call themselves Christians. I think you must have at the very lowest the belief that Christ was, if not divine, at least the best and the wisest of men. If you are not going to believe that much about Christ, I do not think that you have any right to call yourself a Christian. Of course there is another sense which you find in *Whitaker's Almanack* and in geography books, where the population of the world is said to be divided into Christians, Mohammedans, Buddhists, fetish worshippers, and so on; and in that sense we are all Christians. The geography books count us all in, but that is a purely geographical sense, which I suppose we can ignore. Therefore I take it that when I tell you why I am not a Christian I have to tell you two different things: first, why I do not believe in God and in immortality; and, second, why I do not think that Christ was the best and the wisest of men, although I grant him a very high degree of moral goodness.

But for the successful efforts of unbelievers in the past, I could not take so elastic a definition of Christianity as that. As I said before, in olden days it had a much more full-blooded sense. For instance, it included the belief in hell. Belief in eternal hell fire was an essential item of Christian belief until pretty recent times. In this country, as you know, it ceased to be an essential item because of a decision of the Privy Council, and from that decision the Archbishop of Canterbury and the Archbishop of York dissented; but in this country our religion is settled by Act of Parliament, and therefore the Privy Council was able to override their Graces, and hell was no longer necessary to a Christian. Consequently I shall not insist that a Christian must believe in hell.

The existence of God

To come to this question of the existence of God, it is a large and serious question, and if I were to attempt to deal with it in any adequate manner I should have to keep you here until Kingdom Come, so that you will have to excuse me if I deal with it in a somewhat summary fashion. You know, of course, that the Catholic Church has laid it down as a dogma that the existence of God can be proved by the unaided reason. That is a somewhat curious dogma, but it is one of their dogmas. They had to introduce it because at one time the Freethinkers adopted the habit of saying that there were such and such arguments which mere reason might urge against the existence of God, but of course they knew as a matter of faith that God did exist. The arguments and the reasons were set out at great length, and the Catholic Church felt that they must stop it. Therefore they laid it down that the existence of God can be proved by the unaided reason, and they had to set up what they considered were arguments to prove it. There are, of course, a number of them, but I shall take only a few.

The First-Cause argument

Perhaps the simplest and easiest to understand is the argument of the First Cause. It is maintained that everything we see in this world has a cause, and as you go back in the chain of causes further and further you must come to a First Cause, and to that First Cause you give the name God. That argument, I suppose, does not carry very much weight nowadays, because, in the first place, cause is not quite what it used to be. The philosophers and the men of science have got going on cause, and it has not anything like the vitality that it used to have; but, apart from that, you can see that the argument that there must be a First Cause is one that cannot have any validity. I may say that when I was a young man, and was debating these questions very seriously in my mind, I for a long time accepted the argument of the First Cause, until one day, at the age of eighteen, I read John Stuart Mill's *Autobiography*, and I there found this sentence: 'My father taught me that the question, "Who made me?" cannot be answered, since it immediately suggests the further question, "Who made God?" ' That very simple sentence showed me, as I still think, the fallacy in the argument of the First Cause. If everything must have a cause, then God must have a cause. If there can be anything without a cause, it may just as well be the world as God, so that there cannot be any validity in that argument. It is exactly of the same nature as the Hindu's view, that the world rested upon an elephant and the elephant rested upon a tortoise; and when they said, 'How about the tortoise?' the Hindu said, 'Suppose we change the subject.' The argument is really no better than that. There is no reason why the world could not have come into being without a cause; nor, on the other hand, is there any reason why it should not have always existed. There is no reason to suppose that the world had a beginning at all. The idea that things must have a beginning is really due to the poverty of our imagination. Therefore, perhaps, I need not waste any more time upon the argument about the First Cause.

The natural law argument

Then there is a very common argument from natural law. That was a favourite argument all through the eighteenth century, especially under the influence of Sir Isaac Newton and his cosmogony. People observed the planets going round the sun according to the law of gravitation, and they thought that God had given a behest to these planets to move in that particular fashion, and that was why they did so. That was, of course, a convenient and simple explanation that saved them the trouble of looking any further for explanations of the law of gravitation. Nowadays we explain the law of gravitation in a somewhat complicated fashion that Einstein has introduced. I do not propose to give you a lecture on the law of gravitation, as interpreted by Einstein, because that again would take some time; at any rate, you no longer have the sort of natural law that you had in the Newtonian system, where, for some reason that nobody could understand, nature behaved in a uniform fashion. We now find that a great many things that we thought were natural laws are really human conventions. You know that even in the remotest depths of stellar space there are still three feet to a yard. That is, no doubt, a very remarkable fact, but you would hardly call it a law of nature. And a great many things that have been regarded as laws of nature are of that kind. On the other hand, where you can get down to any knowledge of what atoms actually do, you find that they are much less subject to law than people thought, and that the laws at which you arrive are statistical averages of just the sort that would emerge from chance. There is, as we all know, a law that if you throw dice you will get double sixes only about once in thirty-six times, and we do not regard that as evidence that the fall of the dice is regulated by design; on the contrary, if the double sixes came every time we should think that there was design. The laws of nature are of that sort as regards a great many of them. They are statistical averages such as would emerge from the laws of chance; and that makes this whole business of natural law much less impressive than it formerly was. Quite apart from that, which represents the momentary state of science that may change tomorrow, the whole idea that natural laws imply a law-giver is due to a confusion between natural and human laws. Human laws are behests commanding you to behave in a certain way, in which way you may choose to behave, or you may choose not to behave; but natural laws are a description of how things do in fact behave, and, being a mere description of what they in fact do, you cannot argue that there must be somebody who told them to do that, because even supposing that there were you are then faced with the question, Why did God issue just those natural laws and no others? If you say that He did it simply from his own good pleasure, and without any reason, you then find that there is something which is not subject to law, and so your train of natural law is interrupted. If you say, as more orthodox theologians do, that in all the laws which God issued He had a reason for giving those laws rather than others – the reason, of course, being to create the best universe, although you would never think it to look at it – if there was a reason for the laws which God gave, then God Himself was subject to law, and therefore you do not get any advantage by introducing God as an intermediary. You have really a law outside and anterior to the divine edicts, and God does not serve your purpose, because He is not the ultimate law-giver. In short, this whole argument about natural law no longer has anything like the strength that it used to have. I am travelling on in time in my review of the arguments. The arguments that are used for the existence of God change their character as time goes on. They were at first hard intellectual arguments embodying certain quite definite fallacies. As we come to modern times they become less respectable intellectually and more and more affected by a kind of moralizing vagueness.

The argument from design

The next step in this process brings us to the argument from design. You all know the argument from design: everything in the world is made just so that we can manage to live in the world, and if the world was ever so little different we could not manage to live in it. That is the argument from design. It sometimes takes rather a curious form; for instance, it is argued that rabbits have white tails in order to be easy to shoot. I do not know how rabbits would view that application. It is an easy argument to parody. You all know Voltaire's remark, that obviously the nose was designed to be such as to fit spectacles. That sort of parody has turned out to be not nearly so wide of the mark as it might have seemed in the eighteenth century, because since the time of Darwin we understand much better why living creatures are adapted to their environment. It is not that their environment was made to be suitable to them, but that they grew to be suitable to it, and that is the basis of adaptation. There is no evidence of design about it.

When you come to look into this argument from design, it is a most astonishing thing that people can believe that this world, with all the things that are in it, with all its defects, should be the best that omnipotence and omniscience has been able to produce in millions of years. I really cannot believe it. Do you think that, if you were granted omnipotence and omniscience and millions of years in which to perfect your world, you could produce nothing better than the Ku Klux Klan or the Fascisti? Really I am not much impressed with the people who say: 'Look at me: I am such a splendid product that there must have been design in the universe.' I am not very much impressed by the splendour of those people. Therefore I think that this argument of design is really a very poor argument indeed. Moreover, if you accept the ordinary laws of science, you have to suppose that human life and life in general on this planet will die out in due course: it is merely a flash in the pan; it is a stage in the decay of the solar system; at a certain stage of decay you get the sort of conditions of temperature and so forth which are suitable to protoplasm, and there is life for a short time in the life of the whole solar system. You see in the moon the sort of thing to which the earth is tending – something dead, cold, and lifeless.

I am told that that sort of view is depressing, and people will sometimes tell you that if they believed that they would not be able to go on living. Do not believe it; it is all nonsense. Nobody really worries much about what is going to happen millions of years hence. Even if they think they are worrying much about that, they are really deceiving themselves. They are worried about something much more mundane, or it may merely be a bad digestion; but nobody is really seriously rendered unhappy by the thought of something that is going to happen to this world millions and millions of years hence. Therefore, although it is of course a gloomy view to suppose that life will die out – at least I suppose we may say so, although sometimes when I contemplate the things that people do with their lives I think it is almost a consolation – it is not such as to render life miserable. It merely makes you turn your attention to other things.

The moral arguments for deity

Now we reach one stage further in what I shall call the intellectual descent that the Theists have made in their argumentations, and we come to what are called the moral arguments for the existence of God. You all know, of course, that there used to be in the old days three intellectual arguments for the existence of God, all of which were disposed of by Immanuel Kant in the *Critique of Pure Reason*; but no sooner had he disposed of those arguments than he invented a new one, a moral argument, and that quite convinced him. He was like many people: in intellectual matters he was sceptical, but in moral matters he believed implicitly in the maxims that he had imbibed at his mother's knee. That illustrates what the psycho-analysts so much emphasize – the immensely stronger hold upon us that our very early associations have than those of later times.

Kant, as I say, invented a new moral argument for the existence of God, and that in varying forms was extremely popular during the nineteenth century. It has all sorts of forms. One form is to say that there would be no right or wrong unless God existed. I am not for the moment concerned with whether there is a difference between right and wrong, or whether there is not: that is another question. The point I am concerned with is that, if you are quite sure there is a difference between right and wrong, you are then in this situation: Is that difference due to God's fiat or is it not? If it is due to God's fiat, then for God Himself there is no difference between right and wrong, and it is no longer a significant statement to say that God is good. If you are going to say, as theologians do, that God is good, you must then say that right and wrong have some meaning which is independent of God's fiat, because God's fiats are good and not bad independently of the mere fact that He made them. If you are going to say that, you will then have to say that it is not only through God that right and wrong come into being, but that they are in their essence logically anterior to God. You could, of course, if you liked, say that there was a superior deity who gave orders to the God who made this world, or you could take up the line that some of the gnostics took up – a line which I often thought was a very plausible one – that as a matter of fact this world that we know was made by the Devil at a moment when God was not looking. There is a good deal to be said for that, and I am not concerned to refute it.

The argument for the remedying of injustice

Then there is another very curious form of moral argument, which is this: they say that the existence of God is required in order to bring justice into the world. In the part of this universe that we know there is great injustice, and often the good suffer, and often the wicked prosper, and one hardly knows which of those is the more annoying; but if you are going to have justice in the universe as a whole you have to suppose a future life to redress the balance of life here on earth, and so they say that there must be a God, and there must be heaven and hell in order that in the long run there may be justice. That is a very curious argument. If you looked at the matter from a scientific point of view, you would say: 'After all, I know only this world. I do not know about the rest of the universe, but so far as one can argue at all on probabilities one would say that probably this world is a fair sample, and if there is injustice here the odds are that there is injustice elsewhere also.' Supposing you got a crate of oranges that you opened, and you found all the top layer of oranges bad, you would not argue: 'The underneath ones must be good, so as to redress the balance.' You would say: 'Probably the whole lot is a bad consignment'; and that is really what a scientific person would argue about the universe. He would say: 'Here we find in this world a great deal of injustice, and so far as that goes that is a reason for supposing that justice does not rule in the world; and therefore so far as it goes it affords a moral argument against a deity and not in favour of one.' Of course I know that the sort of intellectual arguments that I have been talking to you about are not what really moves people. What really moves people to believe in God is not any intellectual argument at all. Most people believe in God because they have been taught from early infancy to do it, and that is the main reason.

Then I think that the next most powerful reason is the wish for safety, a sort of feeling that there is a big brother who will look after you. That plays a very profound part in influencing people's desire for a belief in God.

The character of Christ

I now want to say a few words upon a topic which I often think is not quite sufficiently dealt with by Rationalists, and that is the question whether Christ was the best and the wisest of men. It is generally taken for granted that we should all agree that that was so. I do not myself. I think that there are a good many points upon which I agree with Christ a great deal more than the professing Christians do. I do not know that I could go with him all the way, but I could go with him much further than most professing Christians can. You will remember that he said: 'Resist not evil, but whosoever shall smite thee on thy right cheek, turn to him the other also.' That is not a new precept or a new principle. It was used by Lâo-Tse and Buddha some 500 or 600 years before Christ, but it is not a principle which as a matter of fact Christians accept. I have no doubt that the present Prime Minister[1], for instance, is a most sincere Christian, but I should not advise any of you to go and smite him on one cheek. I think that you might find that he thought this text was intended in a figurative sense.

Then there is another point which I consider is excellent. You will remember that Christ said: 'Judge not, lest ye be judged.' That principle I do not think you would find was popular in the law courts of Christian countries. I have known in my time quite a number of judges who were very earnest Christians, and they none of them felt that they were acting contrary to Christian principles in what they did. Then Christ says: 'Give to him that asketh of thee, and from him that would borrow of thee turn not thou away.' That is a very good principle. Your Chairman has reminded you that we are not here to talk politics, but I cannot help observing that the last General Election was fought on the question of how desirable it was to turn away from him that would borrow of thee, so that one must assume that the Liberals and Conservatives of this country are composed of people who do not agree with the teaching of Christ, because they certainly did very emphatically turn away on that occasion.

Then there is one other maxim of Christ which I think has a great deal in it, but I do not find that it is very popular among some of our Christian friends. He says: 'If thou wilt be perfect, go and sell that which thou hast, and give to the poor.' That is a very excellent maxim, but, as I say, it is not much practised. All these, I think, are good maxims, although they are a little difficult to live up to. I do not profess to live up to them myself; but then, after all, I am not by way of doing so, and it is not quite the same thing as for a Christian.

Defects in Christ's teaching

Having granted the excellence of these maxims, I come to certain points in which I do not believe that one can grant either the superlative wisdom or the superlative goodness of Christ as depicted in the Gospels; and here I may say that one is not concerned with the historical question. Historically it is quite doubtful whether Christ ever existed at all, and if he did we do not know anything about him, so that I am not concerned with the historical question, which is a very difficult one. I am concerned with Christ as he appears in the Gospels, taking the Gospel narrative as it stands, and there one does find some things that do not seem to be very wise. For one thing, he certainly thought that his second coming would occur in clouds of glory before the death of all the people who were living at that time. There are a great many texts that prove that. He says, for instance: 'Ye shall not have gone over the cities of Israel till the Son of Man be come.' Then he says: 'There are some standing here which shall not taste death till the Son of Man come into his kingdom'; and there are a lot of places where it is quite clear that he believed that his second coming would happen during the lifetime of many then living. That was the belief of his earlier followers, and it was the basis of a good deal of his moral teaching. When he said, 'Take no thought for the morrow', and things of that sort, it was very largely because he thought that the second coming was going to be very soon, and that all ordinary mundane affairs did not count. I have, as a matter of fact, known some Christians who did believe that the second coming was imminent. I knew a parson who frightened his congregation terribly by telling them that the second coming was very imminent indeed, but they were much consoled when they found that he was planting trees in his garden. The early Christians did really believe it, and they did abstain from such things as planting trees in their gardens, because they did accept from Christ the belief that the second coming was imminent. In that respect clearly he was not so wise as some other people have been, and he was certainly not superlatively wise.

The moral problem

Then you come to moral questions. There is one very serious defect to my mind in Christ's moral character, and that is that he believed in hell. I do not myself feel that any person who is really profoundly humane can believe in everlasting punishment. Christ certainly as depicted in the Gospels did believe in everlasting punishment, and one does find repeatedly a vindictive fury against those people who would not listen to his preaching – an attitude which is not uncommon with preachers, but which does somewhat detract from superlative excellence. You do not, for instance, find that attitude in Socrates. You find him quite bland and urbane towards the people who would not listen to him; and it is, to my mind, far more worthy of a sage to take that line than to take the line of indignation. You probably all remember the sort of things that Socrates was saying when he was dying, and the sort of things that he generally did say to people who did not agree with him.

You will find that in the Gospels Christ said: 'Ye serpents, ye generation of vipers, how can ye escape the damnation of hell.' That was said to people who did not like his preaching. It is not really to my mind quite the best tone, and there are a great many of these things about hell. There is, of course, the familiar text about the sin against the Holy Ghost: 'Whosoever speaketh against the Holy Ghost it shall not be forgiven him neither in this world nor in the world to come.' That text has caused an unspeakable amount of misery in the world, for all sorts of people have imagined that they have committed the sin against the Holy Ghost, and thought that it would not be forgiven them either in this world or in the world to come. I really do not think that a person with a proper degree of kindliness in his nature would have put fears and terrors of that sort into the world.

Then Christ says: 'The Son of Man shall send forth his angels, and they shall gather out of his kingdom all things that offend, and them which do iniquity, and shall cast them into a furnace of fire; there shall be wailing and gnashing of teeth'; and he goes on about the wailing and gnashing of teeth. It comes in one verse after another, and it is quite manifest to the reader that there is a certain pleasure in contemplating wailing and gnashing of teeth, or else it would not occur so often. Then you all, of course, remember about the sheep and the goats; how at the second coming he is going to divide the sheep from the goats, and he is going to say to the goats: 'Depart from me, ye cursed, into everlasting fire.' He continues: 'And these shall go away into everlasting fire.' Then he says again: 'If thy hand offend thee, cut it off; it is better for thee to enter into life maimed, than having two hands to go into hell, into the fire that never shall be quenched; where the worm dieth not and the fire is not quenched.' He repeats that again and again also. I must say that I think all this doctrine, that hell fire is a punishment for sin, is a doctrine of cruelty. It is a doctrine that put cruelty into the world and gave the world generations of cruel torture; and the Christ of the Gospels, if you could take him as his chroniclers represent him, would certainly have to be considered partly responsible for that.

There are other things of less importance. There is the instance of the Gadarene swine, where it certainly was not very kind to the pigs to put the devils into them and make them rush down the hill to the sea. You must remember that he was omnipotent, and he could have made the devils simply go away; but he chooses to send them into the pigs. Then there is the curious story of the fig-tree, which always rather puzzled me. You remember what happened about the fig-tree.

> He was hungry; and seeing a fig-tree afar off having leaves, he came if haply he might find anything thereon; and when he came to it he found nothing but leaves, for the time of figs was not yet. And Jesus answered and said unto it: 'No man eat fruit of thee hereafter for ever'...and Peter...saith unto him: 'Master, behold the fig-tree which thou cursedst is withered away.'

That is a very curious story, because it was not the right time of year for figs, and you really could not blame the tree. I cannot myself feel that either in the matter of wisdom or in the matter of virtue Christ stands quite as high as some other people known to history. I think I should put Buddha and Socrates above him in those respects.

The emotional factor

As I said before, I do not think that the real reason why people accept religion has anything to do with argumentation. They accept religion on emotional grounds. One is often told that it is a very wrong thing to attack religion, because religion makes men virtuous. So I am told; I have not noticed it. You know, of course, the parody of that argument in Samuel Butler's book, *Erewhon Revisited*. You will remember that in *Erewhon* there is a certain Higgs who arrives in a remote country, and after spending some time there he escapes from that country in a balloon. Twenty years later he comes back to that country and finds a new religion, in which he is worshipped under the name of the 'Sun Child'; and it is said that he ascended into heaven. He finds that the Feast of the Ascension is about to be celebrated, and he hears Professors Hanky and Panky say to each other that they never set eyes on the man Higgs, and they hope they never will; but they are the high priests of the religion of the Sun Child. He is very indignant, and he comes up to them, and he says: 'I am going to expose all this humbug and tell the people of Erewhon that it was only I, the man Higgs, and I went up in a balloon.' He was told: 'You must not do that, because all the morals of this country are bound round this myth, and if they once know that you did not ascend into heaven they will all become wicked'; and so he is persuaded of that, and he goes away quite quietly.

That is the idea – that we should all be wicked if we did not hold to the Christian religion. It seems to me that the people who have held to it have been for the most part extremely wicked. You find this curious fact, that the more intense has been the religion of any period and the more profound has been the dogmatic belief, the greater has been the cruelty and the worse has been the state of affairs. In the so-called ages of faith, when men really did believe the Christian religion in all its completeness, there was the Inquisition, with its tortures; there were millions of unfortunate women burnt as witches; and there was every kind of cruelty practised upon all sorts of people in the name of religion.

You find as you look round the world that every single bit of progress in humane feeling, every improvement in the criminal law, every step towards the diminution of war, every step towards better treatment of the coloured races, or every mitigation of slavery, every moral progress that there has been in the world, has been consistently opposed by the organized Churches of the world. I say quite deliberately that the Christian religion, as organized in its Churches, has been and still is the principal enemy of moral progress in the world.

How the Churches have retarded moral progress

You may think that I am going too far when I say that that is still so. I do not think that I am. Take one fact. You will bear with me if I mention it. It is not a pleasant fact, but the Churches compel one to mention facts that are not pleasant. Supposing that in this world that we live in today an inexperienced girl is married to a syphilitic man, in that case the Catholic Church says: 'This is an indissoluble sacrament. You must stay together for life', and no steps of any sort must be taken by that woman to prevent herself from giving birth to syphilitic children. That is what the Catholic Church says. I say that that is fiendish cruelty, and nobody whose natural sympathies have not been warped by dogma, or whose moral nature was not absolutely dead to all sense of suffering, could maintain that it is right and proper that that state of things should continue.

That is only an example. There are a great many ways in which at the present moment the Church, by its insistence upon what it chooses to call morality, inflicts upon all sorts of people undeserved and unnecessary suffering. And of course, as we know, it is in its major part an opponent still of progress and of improvement in all the ways that diminish suffering in the world, because it has chosen to label as morality a certain narrow set of rules of conduct which have nothing to do with human happiness; and when you say that this or that ought to be done because it would make for human happiness, they think that has nothing to do with the matter at all. 'What has human happiness to do with morals? The object of morals is not to make people happy. It is to fit them for heaven.' It certainly seems to unfit them for this world.

Fear the foundation of religion

Religion is based, I think, primarily and mainly upon fear. It is partly the terror of the unknown, and partly, as I have said, the wish to feel that you have a kind of elder brother who will stand by you in all your troubles and disputes. Fear is the basis of the whole thing – fear of the mysterious, fear of defeat, fear of death. Fear is the parent of cruelty, and therefore it is no wonder if cruelty and religion have gone hand-in-hand. It is because fear is at the basis of those two things. In this world we can now begin a little to understand things, and a little to master them by the help of science, which has forced its way step by step against the Christian religion, against the Churches, and against the opposition of all the old precepts. Science can help us to get over this craven fear in which mankind has lived for so many generations. Science can teach us, and I think our own hearts can teach us, no longer to look round for imaginary supports, no longer to invent allies in the sky, but rather to look to our own efforts here below to make this world a fit place to live in, instead of the sort of place that the Churches in all these centuries have made it.

What we must do

We want to stand upon our own feet and look fair and square at the world – its good facts, its bad facts, its beauties, and its ugliness; see the world as it is, and be not afraid of it. Conquer the world by intelligence, and not merely by being slavishly subdued by the terror that comes from it. The whole conception of God is a conception derived from the ancient Oriental despotisms. It is a conception quite unworthy of free men. When you hear people in church debasing themselves and saying that they are miserable sinners, and all the rest of it, it seems contemptible and not worthy of self-respecting human beings. We ought to stand up and look the world frankly in the face. We ought to make the best we can of the world, and if it is not so good as we wish, after all it will still be better than what these others have made of it in all these ages. A good world needs knowledge, kindliness, and courage; it does not need a regretful hankering after the past, or a fettering of the free intelligence by the words uttered long ago by ignorant men. It needs a fearless outlook and a free intelligence. It needs hope for the future, not looking back all the time towards a past that is dead, which we trust will be far surpassed by the future that our intelligence can create.

8

THE EXISTENCE AND
NATURE OF GOD

I am very much impressed by the liberalism of those who have
organized this series in inviting me to speak on the subject upon
which I am to address you tonight. I think it really is a very good
proof of a desire to have all views of the case presented that they
should have asked me to speak. I observe, of course, that the
trepidation which is caused by the thought of what I am to say is
somewhat mitigated by the fact that whatever poison is brought by
my speech is to be followed by its appropriate antidote on
subsequent occasions.

The existence and nature of God is a subject of which I can
discuss only half. If one arrives at a negative conclusion concerning
the first part of the question, the second part of the question does
not arise; and my position, as you may have gathered, is a negative
one on this matter.

I have been asking myself since it was arranged that I should
lecture, what are the reasons which are most potent in leading
people of our time to believe in God? They are not quite the same
reasons as in the Middle Ages or in early modern times. Modern
men believe for somewhat different reasons than the old ones.
Therefore, I don't propose to spend much time on the sort of
arguments that might be furnished by a scholastic on the subject.

There is one point of view which I think is quite irrelevant, but
nevertheless does have considerable influence. A good many people
seem to hold that a belief in God is necessary to virtue or to a
decent life, or that it is necessary for happiness or for social
cohesion, or in some way or another it must be preserved on account
of its social advantages. That sort of consideration I think we ought
to dismiss from our minds as quite irrelevant. However true it
might be that certain ethical and social advantages are connected
with the belief in God, that would not prove that there is a God,

and would leave that question in exactly the same position it was before. We might greatly regret that there should not be sound arguments in favour of a position so advantageous. But we should never be able to adopt that position if the arguments would seem to show that that was not the case. For my own part, while my own position is agnostic, if I were in any degree orthodox – if I did believe in God – I should be ashamed to deduce His existence from our terrestrial needs on this planet, which seems too petty a point of view for so cosmic a conclusion. I think that when you are thinking of God you must not think of God as the God of this planet or the God of some chosen race on this planet. You must take the matter up, thinking of God as a Universal God and consider us as unimportant as we are.

There has been a very great deal in traditional religion which one might call pre-Copernican, which speaks on the assumption that the earth is the centre of the universe, that Man was very magnificent and very important, and that the whole universe revolves about Man. I think that since the time of Copernicus it is rather preposterous to take that point of view. The earth is one of the smaller planets of a not particularly important star, a very minor portion of the Milky Way which is one of a very large number of galaxies; and altogether the idea that we who crawl about on this little planet are really the centre of the universe is one which I don't think would occur to anybody except us. It is just a trifle conceited, if I may [say] so.

But I want to come back to this question of believing some proposition because it is advantageous for us to believe it. That, I think, is always not only fallacious in logic but morally disastrous, because of all of the virtues one of the most important is veracity. I don't mean only to think what is true, but to think truthfully – as truly as you are able to think; to form your opinion upon the evidence obtainable. You would abandon that virtue of veracity if, instead of asking yourself, 'What evidence is there for this belief?' you asked yourself, 'Will the belief have good social consequences?' You would lend yourself to the view that people should be compelled by all kinds of non-rational arguments to adopt the beliefs which you hold to be socially useful and to adopt beliefs which are convenient to the ones in power. You would be a prosecutor. If it is desirable that people should believe a certain proposition, certainly it must be justifiable to persecute those who argue against it. Truth is to be decided by the police. All those consequences follow if you allow us in debating such a question on the existence of God to ask ourselves not 'is there evidence of the truth?' but 'is this belief going to have certain good consequences?' So I dismiss from my mind this question of the social consequences, which, if I were occupied with the second argument, would be favourable. You could argue on the virtues which were associated with Christianity, virtues which I should like to see preserved! Not all of them, though. I think faith is a vice, because faith means believing a proposition when there is no good reason for believing it. That may be taken as a definition of faith. But the great majority of Christian virtues I most wholeheartedly accept, and wish to see perpetuated.

I shall have to point out that there are also Christian vices. The attitude of the Christian towards certain religions was associated with a great increase of persecution. Christianity has ceased to be associated with persecution as it has ceased to control the governments of the world. All that would have to be borne in mind. If both sides were brought out, the argument might come out about even. But I don't wish to go into that.

Let us come on to tackle the question itself. I notice that moderns, unless they are Catholic, conceive God somewhat differently from the way in which God has been conceived until quite recently. Until quite recently, God was not only completely benevolent but also omnipotent. This position is nowadays not often claimed. But let's begin with a God both omnipotent and completely benevolent. Can we really believe that the world was created by such a God? I think that most of those who would answer that question affirmatively have not really considered what is involved in omnipotence. When you consider all the physical suffering that there is in the world; when you consider the stupidity of a good number of people; when you consider the cataclysms of nature; when you consider that all of human life is only a transitory phase of the universe, I think it is difficult to suppose that omnipotence could not possibly have done better.

I think of the only other occasion on which I have publicly discussed this question. I debated it with a bishop. It was maintained against me that suffering was no argument against the benevolence of the Deity because suffering was punishment against sin. It so happened that on the very day I was making the debate, my elder son was undergoing an operation for mastoid. He was suffering the most appalling pain. I could not think that by the age of six he could have committed such sins. And yet that is implied on the ground that it is a punishment of sin. Perhaps there are still some people who would say that this [is] a case of the sins of the father being visited upon the child.

I don't think myself that it is logical to maintain that evil can have been created by a creator who was completely good. If you could imagine yourself in a position to create the world, having the power to create such a world as you would like, you would realize that to create this world you would have to be a fiend beyond imagination. You would not have inflicted a great many of the sufferings that are inflicted. They are intolerable if considered as deliberate acts.

Of course, there are other arguments I can furnish. Leibniz, an ingenious thinker, said that there are a great many possible worlds and that some of these possible worlds perhaps contained no evil. But if they contained no evil they also contained much less good. And in this actual world there is a great preponderance of good over evil and therefore a creator who wanted to create a world would create this world rather than any other. Now, there is a great deal to be said about that. In the first place, there is no evidence that it is the best of all possible worlds. The argument is based, as all of these arguments are, on the fact that free will is a great good, and that you can't have free will without sin. That sort of argument caused a great deal of bewilderment among geologists because it had been held that before the fall no animal ate any other animal and even mosquitoes did not bite. All these things happened only after the fall. The geologists discovered the existence of carnivorous animals before man. That caused a great deal of dissension and alarm to orthodox theologians.

This whole question of the balance of good and evil does not strike one as very realistic. Is it quite just? What if you have had the bad luck to be evil and somebody else the good luck to be good? If you are a good philosopher, you might think that some one else happens to be good because you are so evil. It doesn't seem quite just.

This old position of an omnipotent creator is one which is not logically debatable. It is connected with another orthodox argument, the argument of the first cause. I am not going to waste time on most of the old arguments. Possibly this one influences some people who think that everything has a cause and therefore there must have been a first cause. To which I should reply, in the first place, we don't know whether everything has a cause. Why should it have had a beginning? This argument goes back indefinitely in time. Nor should the first cause have been an extraordinary cause. It might have been an ordinary event, just a little start. All that is needed is a little practice in the theory of infinite series to make the whole argument seem preposterous.

When I was adolescent, I was very much influenced by the argument of the first cause and believed in the existence of God because of that argument, until I read John Stuart Mill's autobiography in which he remarked, 'my father told me that the question "who made me?" cannot be answered because it supposes the question "who made God?" '. That is a complete answer.

I think that most moderns are not concerned with a God who is quite so omnipotent. They are concerned with a God who finds certain materials to manipulate, who is limited by his material, who does the best with what he has to work upon, and who, like an architect trying to construct a cathedral out of a heap of stones, is limited by the heap of stones and by the laws of nature. I think most moderns have that conception. One can think of a cosmic purpose which does not know how to perceive the future as infallibly as God would in orthodox theology: a purpose subject to the same kinds of limitations, though not to the same degree, as human beings are; the sort of God you may find in some of the writings of H.G. Wells, or in various other modern writers. There are a good many modern theologians who believe it too. That sort of God is, I think, not one [that] can be actually disproved, as I think the omnipotent and benevolent creator can. I should not maintain that one can be sure there is no such God. All that I should be inclined to say is that there is no reason to suppose there is such a God; I shouldn't go further and say that there is not.

This kind of God is supported, as a rule, by arguments from evolution. We are told that evolution of life refers especially to men and especially to the best type of men, who generally closely resemble the people who use the argument. We are told that evolution is so extraordinary and produced such marvellous results that it cannot have been the result of accident. There must have been a purpose behind it. And there must have been a God guiding the whole plan in order to get such marvellous results. I find myself in difficulties in dealing with those arguments because I am so little impressed by the results. First of all consider it quantitatively. The universe is quite large. It is not supposed to be infinite. The modern astronomer will tell you how large it is. It is quite a size. In that universe the only place where we know that there is life is this planet. A good many astronomers believe that there is no life at all except on this planet, and that if in any case there is, it is a very rare phenomenon indeed. It appears that planets in such stages of development as this one, with the same temperatures, with the same chemical ingredients, are exceptional, so that life, even if it does exist elsewhere, exists in very few parts of the universe. I can't help thinking that a very wise being, given all time to do it in, and assuming that he really did want to produce something like us, could have done it better. When I consider what a small space is occupied by life and what an amount of universe there is where there is nothing living, it seems to me that it is not a very satisfactory result. I think a really competent chemist probably could have done better. And there has been plenty of time. Not only is the universe of considerable size and space but of considerable time. In all that length of time, with the opportunity of experimentation that there has been, it seems to me just a little odd that there hasn't been more done, if it is really the purpose of the earth to produce life, and especially what is called intelligent life.

Moreover, it is quite clear, I think, that life could have developed simply by the steady operation of natural laws. Living matter is a chemical product. It hasn't come together very often. If it comes into being at all it is likely to multiply and increase. Once you get living matter you can quite easily see how on entirely mechanical principles it can develop into people like ourselves. Certainly the origin of living matter doesn't seem quite beyond the happenings of purely mechanical causes. Another point is this, that while we are told that the production of such minds as our own is the purpose of the universe, and perhaps in time even better ones, strange as it may seem, while we are told that that is the purpose of the universe, the men of science at the same time tell us that sooner or later the earth will become uninhabitable and life cease to be. The whole history of life will be a flash-in-the-pan, as something that existed for a moment in the universe and then stopped. It doesn't look as though the cosmos has been concerned with the production of life.

Of course you may say, and if you are religious you will say, that while life on this planet will cease, the human spirit will go on. But that is not a scientific argument. If you are arguing from what you know, you must take account of the upward march of man and also the downward march when the world grows cold. From the scientific point of view they are on the same level.

And if man is the result of evolution, is it a thing to be so very proud of? We think and we talk as if it was something very fine to be a human being; and generally as if evolution tended to produce continually better and better things. That, of course, is not true.

Evolution produced degenerate animals like the tapeworm which are just as much products of evolution as the animals we admire. Evolution produced the sort of man whom we hate and despise as well as the sort of man we love and admire. I don't feel very well about the sort of things happening in the world. Yet that is human life at the present time. When I think that in my own country we devote more than a quarter of everybody's income to the business of killing other people, when I think that in every country the main object seems to be mass murder, I cannot feel that man is really very fine. I like the animals better. I think if evolution would have stopped with sheep and deer and cows, it would have done better. You may say, 'Oh, yes, but man is intelligent.' But what's the good of being intelligent if you use your intelligence to slaughter others? That is the main purpose now. It is confidently hoped that perfectly enormous slaughter may be secured [when] the next war breaks out. That doesn't seem to be a cosmic purpose. Again I say if I were this struggling Deity I should become very discouraged at this point. I think I should feel as at the time of the flood. I should do it, I think, more thoroughly than it was done then.

About this whole question we can't get an impartial view. If you want to try to judge man as a product of evolution, you should try to imagine yourself not a man. Suppose you came from Mars or Venus and you learned to know our ways, what would you think of man? Well, I don't know what the Martians would think, but I judge they would think very ill of us indeed. It seems to me their view would be at least as impartial as our own view. Suppose you talked with a sheep on the humanity of man? They would say man is a monster who eats us. Suppose you take the opinion of turkeys on the celebration of Christmas. You would find that they had a poor opinion of mankind. I don't say that their view is wrong and ours is right. You can't give an impartial view. The verdict is partly good and partly bad, and therefore, if you are going to judge of the Creator by the creation you would have to suppose that God also is partly good and partly bad, that He likes poetry, music, art, and He also likes war and slaughter. On the other hand you may take the view that the evil in the world He can't help and that the good He has produced. But that is not more probable than the opposite view, that the world was created by the Devil who is unable to find any good in it and is very pleased with the bad. There is nothing to discriminate between these two views except that one is pleasant and one unpleasant. So that if you are going to judge of the Creator by His creation, I think you must single out the good bits. On the other hand, I should say that there is everything in the world to show that it is a haphazard and accidental world. I can't imagine the being who could have produced this world. It is too higgedly-piggedly, partly good, partly bad. Some people like some part of it, and some another. It doesn't seem at all likely that any purpose produced it, but it seems more likely it just grew, and that's why it is such a mess.

There is another argument often used: the argument from the moral sense. People say men have a sense of good and of evil, a sense of right and wrong. This, they say, must have been developed not by him but by the Deity. Your conscience is supposed to be the voice of God. That view was accepted before anthropology came in. Now that the science has become established you find that conscience varies with different people in different instances. Some people would think it cruelty not to sell their old men and women to a neighbouring tribe to be eaten. I think it is an abominable practice. At my age, I think it quite monstrous. But to these savages it is the voice of conscience. It is the right thing to do. Take such a thing as human sacrifice. It has existed in pretty nearly all races. It is the normal phase of a certain stage in the development of the race. To those who practised it, it was an essential part of their religion. They would have felt themselves monsters of inequity if they would have omitted this sacrifice. People on this continent thought the sun would go out if they didn't have the proper number of sacrifices. They sacrificed their enemies. That was a virtuous and religious act. You will find that what your conscience tells you varies according to the age and place, and is, in effect, what your parents tell you. There is hardly anything in conscience except the unconscious uprising of the precepts that you learned in early childhood. They come up as if they had an external source and seem like the voice of God. I don't think there is anything in conscience beyond that.

Take even a much higher religion than that of human sacrifice, compare Confucius with the Romans. The Romans preached sacrificing their sons to the public whenever their sons were traitors. On the other hand, Confucius praised very highly the young man who refused to give up his father who was a traitor because he held that duty to the parents is much more important than to the state. Their consciences were diametrically different and accepted by their community. To the Romans, the first duty was to the state; to the Chinese the first duty was to the home. That view which was held by the people who established the positive morality came to be held by all those in the community. Moral law is entirely temporary, accidental, and dependent upon the circumstances in which you are brought up.

I don't mean to say that people never disagree with their parents about moral law. When they do, it rises either from the fact that they have been influenced from somewhere else or that what they were taught didn't hang together. In those ways, men become moral innovators. The whole of moral law does not come in the moral instructions that you have had in early youth. Some people think that it is impossible that there should be morality without religion. I think there are a great deal of examples to the contrary. There have been a great many freethinkers in history who were quite as virtuous as any of the Christians. More than that, if you go into the question as to who were the people who did most to enlarge social sympathy, who were the people most conscious of the sufferings and injustices to the poorer portions in the community, and were the most anxious to remedy those sufferings, who protested most against cruelty to savages, you will find, I think, that very frequently the innovators were the people who did not accept orthodox Christianity. Take a very notable instance. You all know that incredible misgovernment and cruelty was practised by Leopold, King of Belgium, in the Congo. His government was so bad that in the course of ten years, the population was cut in half. In Belgium, these atrocities gradually came to be known. The Catholic Church supported the King and the socialists, who were mostly freethinkers, attacked it. There the practical morality was almost entirely outside the Christian Church. You can find plenty of examples on both sides. It is not by any means true as a formal proposition that belief in Christianity tends to promote a larger social sympathy. I don't see any reason, in the moral sense, for belief in the supernatural.

You remember that Kant, who is conventionally considered the greatest of philosophers – but whom I have been guilty of calling in print a misfortune – said that the two most sublime things are the starry heavens and the moral sense. In the first case, I agree with him. The moral sense I don't myself think very sublime. It takes so many odd forms in so many people. I find that one of the forms the most commonly heard, that sinners ought to be punished, has the minor premiss that the sinners have done something to hurt me. It is called moral indignation. I suppose I am a person without a moral sense. I can't feel that when A has caused pain to B you can make it right by B causing A pain. Yet that is right according to a view that is common.

Of course, I am quite willing to admit and I suppose everybody is willing to admit that there is a morality which is good. What I think is good is good because I think it is good. What I mean when I criticize the moral sense is that it takes forms which any one of us would reject. You can easily find a person who has an opposite belief to yours. You can't put any stress upon the moral sense. I think it is ultimately derived from the desire for a certain sort of world. You may desire a world in which everybody is happy, you may desire a world in which everybody is unhappy, you may desire a world in which everyone is just, in which you and your friends have all the power and other people are slaves. According to the world you desire, you will develop a different kind of moral sense.

I should like to sum up the sort of argument I have presented. I am conscious of presenting an argument that is inconclusive. My contention is that the matter is inconclusive. It would be irrational to arrive at a conclusion: the data don't exist. I think that if there is a God, it is a pity He didn't provide conclusive evidence of his existence. You will remember Pascal's argument. It is: if you disbelieve, and it so happens that orthodox religion is true, you will be damned; whereas, if you disbelieve and orthodox religion is not true, you will not suffer any punishment. Therefore, man should believe. Suppose one were to say, 'Oh, yes, there is a God, but He has quite deliberately created a world in which there is no conclusive evidence. He is going to damn all those who don't believe in Him despite the evidence.' I don't think the argument is one that you can lay much stress upon.

I should say in conclusion that it is possible that there may be an omnipotent God. He would have had to create evil without any temptation for creating evil. He must be infinitely weak, an absolute fiend. That God is possible. I don't see what conscience there will come out of it. I don't say an omnipotent God can fail to have that bad character. There may be a non-omnipotent God who is slowly, hesitatingly, and rather uncertainly guiding the universe towards something a little better than what we have now; or perhaps to something worse. How can we know? We can only know His major purposes from what we see in the world. We have to say the bad things in the world are inevitable. Then the good things are put there on purpose. I don't know why we should say that. I can think the good things are inevitable, the bad things put there on purpose. I don't think either is very plausible. If you are going to suppose at all that the world is the result of purpose you will have to say it is partly good, partly bad. It may be that our conceptions are not right.

If you take the Nietzschean view, the only thing that would matter would be what was pleasant to the Master. Most of us don't accept the Nietzschean philosophy. Most of us think that it is possible to arrive at happiness without harm to others. I think that if you are going to infer God from the world you will have to say He is partly good, partly bad, like ordinary mortals. I can't see any reason myself at all in the nature of the world for supposing any purpose at all. I don't see any evidence of any sort or kind that there is any purpose in the world or that it is anything other than a perfectly blind outcome of natural forces. The arguments from evolution seem to be quite fallacious. I don't want it thought that if orthodox religion, if the Church of God decays that there will be a moral degeneration. I know it may be argued plausibly that the worst things that are going on are associated with opposition to Christianity. That, I think, is true. But they have one factor in common with traditional Christianity, and that is that they inculcate irrational beliefs for which there is no evidence. My own feeling is that one absolutely vital factor in common progress must be an increase in the habit of forming our judgments from evidence, and eliminating our dangerous habit of accepting judgments on authority or because they are pleasant. I think all the irrational causes of belief do harm, and that it is very, very necessary for progress that we should learn to form our beliefs rationally. That habit is one which is even less evident in those bad men who have rejected traditional Christianity. It is less in them that it is in Christians of our time. Therefore I think that what I want to urge upon you is the habit of trying to think rationally. Try to reach the basic conclusions on the evidence. What that conclusion is won't matter much. The important thing is not what you believe so long as you believe with honest veracity. Do not allow your desires or likes to interfere. That seems to be the vital thing. What conclusion you come to is comparatively unimportant. The main thing about this question of God is that it is one of the questions upon which it is possible to think rationally. Think as truthfully as you can and then it won't matter what it is that you finally think.

Discussion which followed address

QUESTION: How do you answer the argument that God is beyond the conception of the human mind?

ANSWER: My answer to that would be that so far as it is true, God becomes quite irrelevant to our thinking, and those who say that God is beyond comprehension of the human mind profess to know a great deal about God. They don't really mean that God is beyond comprehension, only partly beyond comprehension. And generally they mean that He is beyond the comprehension of your mind and not beyond the comprehension of theirs.

QUESTION: If A does harm to B what do you suggest as a remedy to stop A from harming B again?

ANSWER: It is a very large question. It would take at least another hour to answer it. It depends enormously upon the circumstances. If A, for example, is a homicidal lunatic, he will have to be shut up. But shut him up as kindly as possible. I shouldn't bring in the conception of sin. The homicidal lunatic is an extreme case but a great many cases approximate that. Suppose A is a child. You really ought to begin with a child. If A is a child and you deal with him by punishment you put rage into his heart. He perhaps desists for the time being but as soon as he is old enough and strong enough he finds somebody else to inflict punishment upon. So that I don't think you do any real good by punishment except in so far as you can in the case of a homicidal lunatic. You don't cure the culprit by inflicting pain in turn. You have to use other methods. Use more sympathy, more understanding, getting him into a frame of mind where he no longer wishes to inflict pain. I think the whole thing goes back to childhood.

QUESTION: Please explain why we cannot have faith in something which has a basis of truth?

ANSWER: The reason is that you don't need faith in that case. Nobody talks about the faith in the multiplication table. You always use faith in doubtful situations, like that of the people in England having faith in the power of the British Navy. You don't need faith where the thing is obviously true. That's why I call faith an evil, because it means attaching more meaning to the evidence than it deserves.

QUESTION: If we take away the simple belief in God what will the poor uninformed populace have as the basis for their spiritual life?

ANSWER: I am rather glad to have [this] question brought up because it illustrates, I should say, one of the gravest defects of religion. It illustrates the fact that religion can be used to keep the poor contented with their lot, which is very convenient for the rich. I certainly have no wish that people whose lives are unfortunate should be contented with that unfortunate life. It is not necessary with our technical progress that anybody should be poverty stricken. I see nothing but evil in the consolation about the hereafter to those people who put up with injustices.

QUESTION: Would you say a word, please, about mysticism and modern religion?

ANSWER: Again it is difficult to say a word. A volume would seem more appropriate. I should say this about mysticism, that it has two different aspects. On the one hand it is an emotion. On the other hand as a result of that emotion people come to certain beliefs. Now, the emotion I value. I think it is a very important emotion indeed. I think the people who have experienced it are likely to be able to reach a higher level in certain respects than people who never reach it. But the beliefs that are based on that emotion vary according to the time and place. Mohammedans came to the conclusion that the Koran is in existence for all time. Buddhists came to beliefs about the life of Buddha. Taoists came to strange beliefs about what happened to Lâo-Tse. Everybody comes to conclusions which have to a certain extent half-existed before. I attach no truth whatever to the beliefs which mystics say result from their mystic insight.

QUESTION: You admit the existence of natural forces guiding the world. Should we not consider these laws and forces constituting the God-force in the universe?

ANSWER: I don't admit that natural forces guide the world. I may have said something that sounded like it. It is difficult always to speak in the language I consider logically correct. But force has been eliminated from physics. It occurred in Newtonian physics, but not in modern physics. I should never speak of natural forces as guiding the world, as I don't think the natural forces are anything but a shorthand in describing what does happen. If you arrange the names in the telephone book alphabetically, you must not think there is a natural force to cause people to take an alphabetical order. You are apt to think that occurs in the universe.

QUESTION: In your essay 'A Free Man's Worship' in *Mysticism and Logic* you say that victory over Fate and Death and suffering is the baptism into the galaxy of courageous heroes. What is the use? How would you inspire a despondent person without encouraging faith? What would you offer him?

ANSWER: I would encourage a despondent person by pointing out something that he could achieve. With every one of us there is something that we can do, and we would be better for doing it. There is no need for bringing in faith. It is always so much too large for what you need to do. Supposing it is your own welfare. You eat your breakfast but you don't bother about faith. If you bother about other people you will need very little faith to provide them with breakfast. There is always something you can do for somebody, and I include yourself as somebody. You don't need faith to know this, you just need a rational realization of what is possible.

QUESTION: What do people who do not believe in God use as a standard for right and wrong?

ANSWER: I should personally regard cruelty as the main bad thing, much the worst thing; and I should regard affection, and the kindly feeling, as the best thing. Then in addition to those there are more intellectual virtues and vices. I spoke about veracity and things of that sort. All those things you can inculcate in youth without having to bring in God. In actual fact, when you do bring in God it isn't in consequence of God being brought in that you succeed in persuading him that this or that is wrong, it is because of the way you speak about it if you really believe it yourself. One of the reasons why I think the precepts of parents are ineffective is that they are precepts that the parents think good for the children. What you really genuinely believe you can convey just as easily without God as with God. I speak with experience in dealing with children.

QUESTION: Is there such a thing as moral progress?

ANSWER: Well, there certainly have been ages of progress and ages of degeneracy. We live in the latter. There have been ages of moral progress, times when sympathy became wider. The chief element in moral progress is a widening of sympathy. If you confine it to your family it is not enough; if you confine it to your nation it is narrow, and so on. You ought to include the animals. I think it is the widening of sympathy that is the essential [thing]. In our age, we have gone the other way, we have narrowed sympathy down more and more.

QUESTION: What do you think of such a definition of God as offered by John Dewey: 'God is the synthesis of man's highest precepts'?

ANSWER: I should say if Dewey likes to use the word God he has a right to use it, as any person has a right to use it.

QUESTION: Is it possible, by maintaining a relative freedom from local customs and morals, to find in history a common form of the moral sense which can be taken as a standard (such as Huxley's principle of non-attachment)?

ANSWER: I should have said it was quite impossible. I should have said that all those attempts to collect a common effect are just plain humbug. You always find every fresh anthropologist saying that his views, being that of a savage, must be right. That view seems to be fallacious. You know how they talk about the noble savage of the eighteenth century. Certain savages were always monogamists. Another writer wrote a book about savages to prove quite the opposite.

QUESTION: Do you believe that emotions play as large a part in human existence as reason?

ANSWER: Most certainly I do. I think they play a larger part. I think the person who asked that question probably didn't mean exactly what he said. Our emotions about a thing and our belief in a thing are quite different. If somebody gives me two dollars and then another two dollars I might passionately desire it would be five dollars. To introduce emotion would get me into trouble. While I fully admit and should be prepared to urge that emotion is at least as important as reason, it is not the thing by which you ought to decide which of two propositions is true, or who has committed a murder. You can't decide that by emotion. You ought to go into the evidence. Emotion ought not to come in.

Part III

RELIGION AND
SCIENCE

In *Religion and Science* (1935) Russell wrote, 'Whatever knowledge is attainable, must be attained by scientific methods; and what science cannot discover, mankind cannot know' (p. 243). He allowed, however, that 'A purely personal religion, so long as it is content to avoid assertions which science can disprove, may survive undisturbed in the most scientific age' (p. 9) and in the following articles Russell considers proposals for a scientific basis for religion.

'Mysticism and Logic' was original published in *Hibbert Journal*, 12 (July 1914), whose editor, L.P. Jacks, deemed it of sufficient merit to be included without cuts in spite of its great length. It was composed as a lecture to be delivered in the US in conjunction with Russell's Lowell lectures, later published as *Our Knowledge of the External World*. The stimulus of the article was a prolonged and intense discussion with Lady Ottoline Morrell on the nature of religious belief. Russell, though sympathetic to a view of religion which emphasized 'feeling' inspired by mystical contemplation of nature, was not prepared to accept Ottoline's readiness to accept such feeling as sufficient ground for belief. Russell wrestled with this issue in the unpublished writings 'Prisons', 'The Pilgrimage of Life' and his published essay 'The Essence of Religion'. The essay 'Science and Religion' is another set of reflections on the subject. The unflattering references to Churchill indicate that this (probably unpublished) essay was written during the 1930s, after Hitler came into power.

In his review of Eddington's 'The Nature of the Physical World', published in *The Nation* (New York, 128, 20 February 1919), Russell announced the themes of his critique of the theology of the new physicists. This theology was presented by Sir Arthur Eddington, England's most eminent physicist and a gifted popularizer of scientific thought, in his Gifford lectures, January to

March 1927 (subsequently published as the volume under review). Eddington's book 'treats of the philosophical outcome of the great changes of scientific thought which have recently come about'. His aim was to revive the religion of reason, that is a theology which was supported by the results of science. The original eighteenth-century version of the religion of reason had fallen into decay because scientists and scientifically minded philosophers had come to agree with Laplace's announcement that a thoroughgoing determinism did not need God as a hypothesis. Eddington announced that 1927 was a turning point in the relation between science and religion, because the startling discoveries of the new physics which had undermined the old determinism, permitted us to reclaim the traditional theological accounts of freedom of the will and the spiritual life. Russell's review of Jeans's 'The Mysterious Universe' was published in the *Jewish Daily Forward*, 28 December 1930. Jeans was a mathematician and philosopher, and like Eddington a gifted writer. His theological speculation included the view that matter is created continuously throughout the universe. Russell's response is respectful, the review brief, but Russell took the problems with utmost seriousness. He devoted an entire book, *The Scientific Outlook*, to this subject.

The article 'Do Science and Religion Conflict?' appeared in *The Journal of the British Astronomic Association*, 64 (Jan 1954), pp. 94–96 and is a review of the seventh Eddington Memorial Lecture, delivered by H. H. Price and published as *Some Aspects of the Conflict between Science and Religion*. It is in the tradition of Russell's critiques – respectful but firm – of Eddington and other scientists who offer scientific evidence for belief in the supernatural.

9

MYSTICISM AND LOGIC

Metaphysics, or the attempt to conceive the world as a whole by means of thought, has been developed, from the first, by the union and conflict of two very different human impulses, the one urging men towards mysticism, the other urging them towards science. Some men have achieved greatness through one of these impulses alone, others through the other alone: in Hume, for example, the scientific impulse reigns quite unchecked, while in Blake a strong hostility to science coexists with profound mystic insight. But the greatest men who have been philosophers have felt the need both of science and of mysticism: the attempt to harmonize the two was what made their life, and what always must, for all its arduous uncertainty, make philosophy, to some minds, a greater thing than either science or religion.

Before attempting an explicit characterization of the scientific and the mystical impulses, I will illustrate them by examples from two philosophers whose greatness lies in the very intimate blending which they achieved. The two philosophers I mean are Heraclitus and Plato.

Heraclitus, as everyone knows, was a believer in universal flux: time builds and destroys all things. From the few fragments that remain, it is not easy to discover how he arrived at his opinions, but there are some sayings that strongly suggest scientific observation as the source.

'The things that can be seen, heard, and learned,' he says, 'are what I prize the most.' This is the language of the empiricist, to whom observation is the sole guarantee of truth. 'The sun is new every day' is another fragment; and this opinion, in spite of its paradoxical character, is obviously inspired by scientific reflection, and no doubt seemed to him to obviate the difficulty of understanding how the sun can work its way underground from west to east during the night. Actual observation must also have suggested to him his central doctrine, that Fire is the one permanent substance, of which all visible things are passing phases. In combustion we see things change utterly, while their flame and heat rise up into the air and vanish.

'This world, which is the same for all,' he says, 'no one of gods or men has made; but it was ever, is now, and ever shall be, an ever-living Fire, with measures kindling, and measures going out.'

'The transformations of Fire are, first of all, sea; and half of the sea is earth, half whirlwind.'

This theory, though no longer one which science can accept, is nevertheless scientific in spirit. Science, too, might have inspired the famous saying to which Plato alludes: 'You cannot step twice into the same rivers; for fresh waters are ever flowing in upon you.' But we find also another statement among the extant fragments: 'We step and do not step into the same rivers; we are and are not.'

The comparison of this statement, which is mystical, with the one quoted by Plato, which is scientific, shows how intimately the two tendencies are blended in the system of Heraclitus. Mysticism is, in essence, little more than a certain intensity and depth of feeling in regard to what is believed about the universe; and this kind of feeling leads Heraclitus, on the basis of his science, to strangely poignant sayings concerning life and the world, such as: 'Time is a child playing draughts, the kingly power is a child's.'

It is poetic imagination, not science, which presents time as despotic lord of the world, with all the irresponsible frivolity of a child. It is mysticism, too, which leads Heraclitus to assert the identity of opposites: 'Good and ill are one,' he says; and again: 'To God all things are fair and good and right, but men hold some things wrong and some right.'

Much of mysticism underlies the ethics of Heraclitus. It is true that a scientific determinism alone might have inspired the statement: 'Man's character is his fate'; but only a mystic would have said: 'Every beast is driven to the pasture with blows'; and again: 'It is hard to fight with one's heart's desire. Whatever it wishes to get, it purchases at the cost of soul'; and again: 'Wisdom is one thing. It is to know the thought by which all things are steered through all things.'[1]

Examples might be multiplied, but those that have been given are enough to show the character of the man: the facts of science, as they appeared to him, fed the flame in his soul, and in its light he saw into the depths of the world by the reflection of his own

110

dancing, swiftly penetrating fire. In such a nature we see the true union of the mystic and the man of science – the highest eminence, as I think, that it is possible to achieve in the world of thought.

In Plato, the same twofold impulse exists, though the mystic impulse is distinctly the stronger of the two, and secures ultimate victory whenever the conflict is sharp. His description of the cave is the classical statement of belief in a knowledge and reality truer and more real than that of the senses:

> Imagine a number of men living in an underground cavernous chamber, with an entrance open to the light, extending along the entire length of the cavern, in which they have been confined, from their childhood, with their legs and necks so shackled that they are obliged to sit still and look straight forwards, because their chains render it impossible for them to turn their heads round: and imagine a bright fire burning some way off, above and behind them, and an elevated roadway passing between the fire and the prisoners, with a low wall built along it, like the screens which conjurors put up in front of their audience, and above which they exhibit their wonders.
>
> I have it, he replied.
>
> Also figure to yourself a number of persons walking behind this wall, and carrying with them statues of men, and images of other animals, wrought in wood and stone and all kinds of materials, together with various other articles, which overtop the wall; and, as you might expect, let some of the passers-by be talking, and others silent.
>
> You are describing a strange scene, and strange prisoners.
>
> They resemble us, I replied.
>
> Now consider what would happen if the course of nature brought them a release from their fetters, and a remedy for their foolishness, in the following manner. Let us suppose that one of them has been released, and compelled suddenly to stand up, and turn his neck round and walk with open eyes towards the light; and let us suppose that he goes through all these actions with pain, and that the dazzling splendour renders him incapable of discerning those objects of which he used formerly to see the shadows. What answer should you expect him to make, if some one were to tell him that in those days he was watching foolish phantoms, but that now he is somewhat nearer to reality, and is turned

towards things more real, and sees more correctly; above all, if he were to point out to him the several objects that are passing by, and question him, and compel him to answer what they are? Should you not expect him to be puzzled, and to regard his old visions as truer than the objects now forced upon his notice?

Yes, much truer...

Hence, I suppose, habit will be necessary to enable him to perceive objects in that upper world. At first he will be most successful in distinguishing shadows; then he will discern the reflections of men and other things in water, and afterwards the realities; and after this he will raise his eyes to encounter the light of the moon and stars, finding it less difficult to study the heavenly bodies and the heaven itself by night, than the sun and the sun's light by day.

Doubtless.

Last of all, I imagine, he will be able to observe and contemplate the nature of the sun, not as it *appears* in water or on alien ground, but as it *is* in itself in its own territory.

Of course.

His next step will be to draw the conclusion, that the sun is the author of the seasons and the years, and the guardian of all things in the visible world, and in a manner the cause of all those things which he and his companions used to see.

Obviously, this will be his next step...

Now this imaginary case, my dear Glaucon, you must apply in all its parts to our former statements, by comparing the region which the eye reveals, to the prison house, and the light of the fire therein to the power of the sun: and if, by the upward ascent and the contemplation of the upper world, you understand the mounting of the soul into the intellectual region, you will hit the tendency of my own surmises, since you desire to be told what they are; though, indeed, God only knows whether they are correct. But, be that as it may, the view which I take of the subject is to the following effect. In the world of knowledge, the essential Form of Good is the limit of our enquiries, and can barely be perceived; but, when perceived, we cannot help concluding that it is in every case the source of all that is bright and beautiful, – in the visible world giving birth to light and its master, and in the intellectual world dispensing, immediately and with full authority, truth and reason; – and that whosoever would act wisely, either in private or in public, must set this Form of Good before his eyes.[2]

But in this passage, as throughout most of Plato's teaching, there is an identification of the good with the truly real, which became embodied in the philosophical tradition, and is still largely operative in our own day. In thus allowing a legislative function to the good, Plato produced a divorce between philosophy and science, from which, in my opinion, both have suffered ever since and are still suffering. The man of science, whatever his hopes may be, must lay them aside while he studies nature; and the philosopher, if he is to achieve truth, must do the same. Ethical considerations can only legitimately appear when the truth has been ascertained: they can and should appear as determining our feeling towards the truth, and our manner of ordering our lives in view of the truth, but not as themselves dictating what the truth is to be.

There are passages in Plato – among those which illustrate the scientific side of his mind – where he seems clearly aware of this. The most noteworthy is the one in which Socrates, as a young man, is explaining the theory of ideas to Parmenides.

After Socrates has explained that there is an idea of the good, but not of such things as hair and mud and dirt, Parmenides advises him 'not to despise even the meanest things', and this advice shows the genuine scientific temper. It is with this impartial temper that the mystic's apparent insight into a higher reality and a hidden good has to be combined if philosophy is to realize its greatest possibilities. And it is failure in this respect that has made so much of idealistic philosophy thin, lifeless, and insubstantial. It is only in marriage with the world that our ideals can bear fruit: divorced from it, they remain barren. But marriage with the world is not to be achieved by an ideal which shrinks from fact, or demands in advance that the world shall conform to its desires.

Parmenides himself is the source of a peculiarly interesting strain of mysticism which pervades Plato's thought – the mysticism which may be called 'logical' because it is embodied in theories on logic. This form of mysticism, which appears, so far as the West is concerned, to have originated with Parmenides, dominates the reasonings of all the great mystical metaphysicians from his day to that of Hegel and his modern disciples. Reality, he says, is uncreated, indestructible, unchanging, indivisible; it is 'immovable in the bonds of mighty chains, without beginning and without end; since coming into being and passing away have been driven afar, and true belief has cast them away'. The fundamental principle of his inquiry is stated in a sentence which would not be out of place in Hegel: 'Thou canst not know what is not – that is impossible – nor utter it; for it is the same thing that can be thought and that can be.' And again: 'It needs must be that what can be thought and spoken of is; for it is possible for it to be, and it is not possible for what is nothing to be.' The impossibility of change follows from this principle; for what is past can be spoken of, and therefore, by the principle, still is.

Mystical philosophy, in all ages and in all parts of the world, is characterized by certain beliefs which are illustrated by the doctrines we have been considering.

There is, first, the belief in insight as against discursive analytic knowledge: the belief in a way of wisdom, sudden, penetrating, coercive, which is contrasted with the slow and fallible study of outward appearance by a science relying wholly upon the senses. All who are capable of absorption in an inward passion must have experienced at times the strange feeling of unreality in common objects, the loss of contact with daily things, in which the solidity of the outer world is lost, and the soul seems, in utter loneliness, to bring forth, out of its own depths, the mad dance of fantastic phantoms which have hitherto appeared as independently real and living. This is the negative side of the mystic's initiation: the doubt concerning common knowledge, preparing the way for the reception of what seems a higher wisdom. Many men to whom this negative experience is familiar do not pass beyond it, but for the mystic it is merely the gateway to an ampler world.

The mystic insight begins with the sense of a mystery unveiled, of a hidden wisdom now suddenly become certain beyond the possibility of a doubt. The sense of certainty and revelation comes earlier than any definite belief. The definite beliefs at which mystics arrive are the result of reflection upon the inarticulate experience gained in the moment of insight. Often, beliefs which have no real connection with this moment become subsequently attracted into the central nucleus; thus in addition to the convictions which all mystics share, we find, in many of them, other convictions of a more local and temporary character, which no doubt become amalgamated with what was essentially mystical in virtue of their subjective certainty. We may ignore such inessential accretions, and confine ourselves to the beliefs which all mystics share.

The first and most direct outcome of the moment of illumination is belief in the possibility of a way of knowledge which may be called revelation or insight or intuition, as contrasted with sense, reason, and analysis, which are regarded as blind guides leading to the morass of illusion. Closely connected with this belief is the conception of a Reality behind the world of appearance and utterly different from it. This Reality is regarded with an admiration often amounting to worship; it is felt to be always and everywhere close at hand, thinly veiled by the shows of sense, ready, for the receptive mind, to shine in its glory even through the apparent folly and wickedness of Man. The poet, the artist, and the lover are seekers after that glory: the haunting beauty that they pursue is the faint reflection of its sun. But the mystic lives in the full light of the vision: what others dimly seek he knows, with a knowledge beside which all other knowledge is ignorance.

The second characteristic of mysticism is its belief in unity, and its refusal to admit opposition or division anywhere. We found Heraclitus saying 'good and ill are one'; and again he says, 'the way up and the way down is one and the same'. The same attitude appears in the simultaneous assertion of contradictory propositions, such as: 'We step and do not step into the same rivers; we are and are not.' The assertion of Parmenides, that reality is one and indivisible, comes from the same impulse towards unity. In Plato, this impulse is less prominent, being held in check by his theory of ideas; but it reappears, so far as his logic permits, in the doctrine of the primacy of the Good.

A third mark of almost all mystical metaphysics is the denial of the reality of Time. This is an outcome of the denial of division; if all is one, the distinction of past and future must be illusory. We have seen this doctrine prominent in Parmenides; and among moderns it is fundamental in the systems of Spinoza and Hegel.

The last of the doctrines of mysticism which we have to consider is its belief that all evil is mere appearance, an illusion produced by the divisions and oppositions of the analytic intellect. Mysticism does not maintain that such things as cruelty, for example, are good, but it denies that they are real: they belong to that lower world of phantoms from which we are to be liberated by the insight of the vision. Sometimes – for example in Hegel, and at least verbally in Spinoza – not only evil, but good also, is regarded as illusory, though nevertheless the emotional attitude towards what is held to be Reality is such as would naturally be associated with the belief that Reality is good. What is, in all cases, ethically characteristic of mysticism is absence of indignation or protest, acceptance with joy, disbelief in the ultimate truth of the division into two hostile camps, the good and the bad. This attitude is a direct outcome of the nature of the mystical experience: with its sense of unity is associated a feeling of infinite peace. Indeed it may be suspected that the feeling of peace produces, as feelings do in dreams, the whole system of associated beliefs which make up the body of mystic doctrine. But this is a difficult question, and one on which it cannot be hoped that mankind will reach agreement.

Four questions thus arise in considering the truth or falsehood of mysticism, namely:

1   Are there two ways of knowing, which may be called respectively reason and intuition? And if so, is either to be preferred to the other?
2   Is all plurality and division illusory?
3   Is time unreal?
4   What kind of reality belongs to good and evil?

On all four of these questions, while fully developed mysticism seems to me mistaken, I yet believe that, by sufficient restraint, there is an element of wisdom to be learned from the mystical way of feeling, which does not seem to be attainable in any other manner. If this is the truth, mysticism is to be commended as an attitude towards life, not as a creed about the world. The metaphysical creed, I shall maintain, is a mistaken outcome of the emotion, although this emotion, as colouring and informing all other thoughts and feelings, is the inspirer of whatever is best in Man. Even the cautious and patient investigation of truth by science, which seems the very antithesis of the mystic's swift certainty, may be fostered and nourished by that very spirit of reverence in which mysticism lives and moves.

Reason and intuition[3]

Of the reality or unreality of the mystic's world I know nothing. I have no wish to deny it, nor even to declare that the insight which reveals it is not a genuine insight. What I do wish to maintain – and it is here that the scientific attitude becomes imperative – is that insight, untested and unsupported, is an insufficient guarantee of truth, in spite of the fact that much of the most important truth is first suggested by its means. It is common to speak of an opposition between instinct and reason; in the eighteenth century, the opposition was drawn in favour of reason, but under the influence of Rousseau and the romantic movement instinct was given the preference, first by those who rebelled against artificial forms of government and thought, and then, as the purely rationalistic defence of traditional theology became increasingly difficult, by all who felt in science a menace to creeds which they associated with a spiritual outlook on life and the world. Bergson, under the name of 'intuition', has raised instinct to the position of sole arbiter of metaphysical truth. But in fact the opposition of instinct and reason is mainly illusory. Instinct, intuition, or insight is what first leads to the beliefs which subsequent reason confirms or confutes; but the confirmation, where it is possible, consists, in the last analysis, of agreement with other beliefs no less instinctive. Reason is a harmonizing, controlling force rather than a creative one. Even in the most purely logical realm, it is insight that first arrives at what is new.

Where instinct and reason do sometimes conflict is in regard to single beliefs, held instinctively, and held with such determination that no degree of inconsistency with other beliefs leads to their abandonment. Instinct, like all human faculties, is liable to error. Those in whom reason is weak are often unwilling to admit this as regards themselves, though all admit it in regard to others. Where instinct is least liable to error is in practical matters as to which right judgment is a help to survival: friendship and hostility in others, for instance, are often felt with extraordinary discrimination through very careful disguises. But even in such matters a wrong impression may be given by reserve or flattery; and in matters less directly practical, such as philosophy deals with, very strong instinctive beliefs are sometimes wholly mistaken, as we may come to know through their perceived inconsistency with other equally strong beliefs. It is such considerations that necessitate the harmonizing mediation of reason, which tests our beliefs by their mutual compatibility, and examines, in doubtful cases, the possible sources of error on the one side and on the other. In this there is no opposition to instinct as a whole, but only to blind reliance upon some one interesting aspect of instinct to the exclusion of other more commonplace but not less trustworthy aspects. It is such one-sidedness, not instinct itself, that reason aims at correcting.

These more or less trite maxims may be illustrated by application to Bergson's advocacy of 'intuition' as against 'intellect'. There are, he says, two profoundly different ways of knowing a thing. The first implies that we move round the object: the second that we enter into it. The first depends on the point of view at which we are placed and on the symbols by which we express ourselves. The second neither depends on a point of view nor relies on any symbol. The first kind of knowledge may be said to stop at the *relative*; the second, in those cases where it is possible, to attain the *absolute*.[4]

The second of these, which is intuition, is, he says, 'the kind of *intellectual sympathy* by which one places oneself within an object in order to coincide with what is unique in it and therefore inexpressible' (p. 6). In illustration, he mentions self-knowledge: 'there is one reality, at least, which we all seize from within, by intuition and not by simple analysis. It is our own personality in its flowing through time – our self which endures' (p. 8). The rest of Bergson's philosophy consists in reporting, through the imperfect medium of words, the knowledge gained by intuition, and the consequent complete condemnation of all the pretended knowledge derived from science and common sense.

This procedure, since it takes sides in a conflict of instinctive beliefs, stands in need of justification by proving the greater trustworthiness of the beliefs on one side than of those on the other. Bergson attempts this justification in two ways, first by explaining that intellect is a purely practical faculty to secure biological success, second by mentioning remarkable feats of instinct in animals and by pointing out characteristics of the world which, though intuition can apprehend them, are baffling to intellect as he interprets it.

Of Bergson's theory that intellect is a purely practical faculty, developed in the struggle for survival, and not a source of true beliefs, we may say, first, that it is only through intellect that we know of the struggle for survival and of the biological ancestry of man: if the intellect is misleading, the whole of this merely inferred history is presumably untrue. If, on the other hand, we agree with him in thinking that evolution took place as Darwin believed, then it is not only intellect but all our faculties that have been developed under the stress of practical utility. Intuition is seen at its best where it is directly useful, for example in regard to other people's characters and dispositions. Bergson apparently holds that capacity for this kind of knowledge is less explicable by the struggle for existence than, for example, capacity for pure mathematics. Yet the savage deceived by false friendship is likely to pay for his mistake with his life; whereas even in the most civilized societies men are not put to death for mathematical incompetence. All the most striking of his instances of intuition in animals have a very direct survival value. The fact is, of course, that both intuition and intellect have been developed because they are useful, and that, speaking broadly, they are useful when they give truth and become harmful when they give falsehood. Intellect, in civilized man, like artistic capacity, has occasionally been developed beyond the point where it is useful to the individual; intuition, on the other hand, seems on the whole to diminish as civilization increases. It is greater, as a rule, in children than in adults, in the uneducated than in the educated. Probably in dogs it exceeds anything to be found in human beings. But those who see in these facts a recommendation of intuition ought to return to running wild in the woods, dyeing themselves with woad and living on hips and haws.

Let us next examine whether intuition possesses any such infallibility as Bergson claims for it. The best instance of it, according to him, is our acquaintance with ourselves; yet self-knowledge is proverbially rare and difficult. Most men, for example, have in their nature meannesses, vanities, and envies of which they are quite unconscious, though even their best friends can perceive them without any difficulty. It is true that intuition has a convincingness which is lacking to intellect: while it is present, it is almost impossible to doubt its truth. But if it should appear, on examination, to be at least as fallible as intellect, its greater subjective certainty becomes a demerit, making it only the more irresistibly deceptive. Apart from self-knowledge, one of the most notable examples of intuition is the knowledge people believe themselves to possess of those with whom they are in love: the wall between different personalities seems to become transparent, and people think they see into another soul as into their own. Yet deception in such cases is constantly practised with success; and even where there is no intentional deception, experience gradually proves, as a rule, that the supposed insight was illusory, and that the slower, more groping methods of the intellect are in the long run more reliable.

Bergson maintains that intellect can only deal with things in so far as they resemble what has been experienced in the past, while intuition has the power of apprehending the uniqueness and novelty that always belong to each fresh moment. That there is something unique and new at every moment, is certainly true; it is also true that this cannot be fully expressed by means of intellectual concepts. Only direct acquaintance can give knowledge of what is unique and new. But direct acquaintance of this kind is given fully in sensation, and does not require, so far as I can see, any special faculty of intuition for its apprehension. It is neither intellect nor intuition, but sensation, that supplies new data; but when the data are new in any remarkable manner, intellect is much more capable of dealing with them than intuition would be. The hen with a brood of ducklings no doubt has intuition which seems to place her inside them, and not merely to know them analytically; but when the ducklings take to the water, the whole apparent intuition is seen to be illusory, and the hen is left helpless on the shore. Intuition, in fact, is an aspect and development of instinct, and, like all instinct, is admirable in those customary surroundings which have moulded the habits of the animal in question, but totally incompetent as soon as the surroundings are changed in a way which demands some non-habitual mode of action.

The theoretical understanding of the world, which is the aim of philosophy, is not a matter of great practical importance to animals, or to savages, or even to most civilized men. It is hardly to be supposed, therefore, that the rapid, rough-and-ready methods of instinct or intuition will find in this field a favourable ground for their application. It is the older kinds of activity, which bring out our kinship with remote generations of animal and semi-human ancestors, that show intuition at its best. In such matters as self-preservation and love, intuition will act sometimes (though not always) with a swiftness and precision which are astonishing to the critical intellect. But philosophy is not one of the pursuits which illustrate our affinity with the past: it is a highly refined, highly civilized pursuit, demanding, for its success, a certain liberation from the life of instinct, and even, at times, a certain aloofness from all mundane hopes and fears. It is not in philosophy, therefore, that we can hope to see intuition at its best. On the contrary, since the true objects of philosophy, and the habits of thought demanded for their apprehension, are strange, unusual, and remote, it is here, more almost than anywhere else, that intellect proves superior to intuition, and that quick unanalysed convictions are least deserving of uncritical acceptance.

In advocating the scientific restraint and balance, as against the self-assertion of a confident reliance upon intuition, we are only urging, in the sphere of knowledge, that largeness of contemplation, that impersonal disinterestedness, and that freedom from practical preoccupations which have been inculcated by all the great religions of the world. Thus our conclusion, however it may conflict with the explicit beliefs of many mystics, is, in essence, not contrary to the spirit which inspires those beliefs, but rather the outcome of this very spirit as applied in the realm of thought.

Unity and plurality

One of the most convincing aspects of the mystic illumination is the apparent revelation of the oneness of all things, giving rise to pantheism in religion and to monism in philosophy. An elaborate logic, beginning with Parmenides, and culminating in Hegel and his followers, has been gradually developed, to prove that the universe is one indivisible Whole, and that what seem to be its parts, if considered as substantial and self-existing, are mere illusion. The conception of a reality quite other than the world of appearance, a reality one, indivisible, and unchanging, was introduced into Western philosophy by Parmenides, not, nominally at least, for mystical or religious reasons, but on the basis of a logical argument as to the impossibility of not-being, and most subsequent meta-physical systems are the outcome of this fundamental idea.

The logic used in defence of mysticism seems to me faulty as logic, and open to technical criticisms, which I have explained elsewhere. I shall not here repeat these criticisms, since they are lengthy and difficult, but shall instead attempt an analysis of the state of mind from which mystical logic has arisen.

Belief in a reality quite different from what appears to the senses arises with irresistible force in certain moods, which are the source of most mysticism, and of most metaphysics. While such a mood is dominant, the need of logic is not felt, and accordingly the more thoroughgoing mystics do not employ logic, but appeal directly to the immediate deliverance of their insight. But such fully developed mysticism is rare in the West. When the intensity of emotional conviction subsides, a man who is in the habit of reasoning will search for logical grounds in favour of the belief which he finds in himself. But since the belief already exists, he will be very hospitable to any ground that suggests itself. The paradoxes apparently proved by his logic are really the paradoxes of mysticism, and are the goal which he feels his logic must reach if it is to be in accordance with insight. The resulting logic has rendered most philosophers incapable of giving any account of the world of science and daily life. If they had been anxious to give such an account, they would probably have discovered the errors of their logic; but most of them were less anxious to understand the world of science and daily life than to convict it of unreality in the interests of a super-sensible 'real' world.

It is in this way that logic has been pursued by those of the great philosophers who were mystics. But since they usually took for granted the supposed insight of the mystic emotion, their logical doctrines were presented with a certain dryness, and were believed by their disciples to be quite independent of the sudden illumination from which they sprang. Nevertheless their origin clung to them, and they remained – to borrow a useful word from Mr Santayana – 'malicious' in regard to the world of science and common sense. It is only so that we can account for the complacency with which philosophers have accepted the inconsistency of their doctrines with all the common and scientific facts which seem best established and most worthy of belief.

The logic of mysticism shows, as is natural, the defects which are inherent in anything malicious. The impulse to logic, not felt while the mystic mood is dominant, reasserts itself as the mood fades, but with a desire to retain the vanishing insight, or at least to prove that it *was* insight, and that what seems to contradict it is illusion. The logic which thus arises is not quite disinterested or candid, and is inspired by a certain hatred of the daily world to which it is to be applied. Such an attitude naturally does not tend to the best results. Everyone knows that to read an author simply in order to refute him is not the way to understand him; and to read the book of Nature with a conviction that it is all illusion is just as unlikely to lead to understanding. If our logic is to find the common world intelligible, it must not be hostile, but must be inspired by a genuine acceptance such as is not usually to be found among metaphysicians.

Time

The unreality of time is a cardinal doctrine of many metaphysical systems, often nominally based, as already by Parmenides, upon logical arguments, but originally derived, at any rate in the founders of new systems, from the certainty which is born in the moment of mystic insight. As a Persian Sufi poet says:

> Past and future are what veil God from our sight.
> Burn up Both of them with fire! How long
> Wilt thou be partitioned by these segments as a reed?[4]

The belief that what is ultimately real must be immutable is a very common one: it gave rise to the metaphysical notion of substance, and finds, even now, a wholly illegitimate satisfaction in such scientific doctrines as the conservation of energy and mass.

It is difficult to disentangle the truth and the error in this view. The arguments for the contention that time is unreal and that the world of sense is illusory must, I think, be regarded as fallacious. Nevertheless there is some sense – easier to feel than to state – in which time is an unimportant and superficial characteristic of reality. Past and future must be acknowledged to be as real as the present, and a certain emancipation from slavery to time is essential to philosophic thought. The importance of time is rather practical than theoretical, rather in relation to our desires than in relation to truth. A truer image of the world, I think, is obtained by picturing things as entering into the stream of time from an eternal world outside, than from a view which regards time as the devouring tyrant of all that is. Both in thought and in feeling, even though time be real, to realize the unimportance of time is the gate of wisdom.

That this is the case may be seen at once by asking ourselves why our feelings towards the past are so different from our feelings towards the future. The reason for this difference is wholly practical: our wishes can affect the future but not the past – the future is to some extent subject to our power, while the past is unalterably fixed. But every future will some day be past; if we see the past truly now, it must, when it was still future, have been just what we now see it to be, and what is now future must be just what we shall see it to be when it has become past. The felt difference of quality between past and future, therefore, is not an intrinsic difference, but only a difference in relation to us: to impartial contemplation, it ceases to exist. And impartiality of contemplation is, in the intellectual sphere, that very same virtue of disinterestedness which, in the sphere of action, appears as justice and unselfishness. Whoever wishes to see the world truly, to rise in thought above the tyranny of practical desires, must learn to overcome the difference of attitude towards past and future, and to survey the whole stream of time in one comprehensive vision.

The kind of way in which, as it seems to me, time ought not to enter into our theoretic philosophical thought, may be illustrated by the philosophy which has become associated with the idea of evolution, and which is exemplified by Nietzsche, pragmatism, and Bergson. This philosophy, on the basis of the development which has led from the lowest forms of life up to man, sees in *progress* the fundamental law of the universe, and thus admits the difference between *earlier* and *later* into the very citadel of its contemplative outlook. With its past and future history of the world, conjectural as it is, I do not wish to quarrel. But I think that, in the intoxication of a quick success, much that is required for a true understanding of the universe has been forgotten. Something of Hellenism, some-thing, too, of Oriental resignation, must be combined with its hurrying Western self-assertion before it can emerge from the ardour of youth into the mature wisdom of manhood. In spite of its appeals to science, the true scientific philosophy, I think, is something more arduous and more aloof, appealing to less mundane hopes, and requiring a severer discipline for its successful practice.

Darwin's *Origin of Species* persuaded the world that the difference between different species of animals and plants is not the fixed immutable difference that it appears to be. The doctrine of natural kinds, which had rendered classification easy and definite, which was enshrined in the Aristotelian tradition, and protected by its supposed necessity for orthodox dogma, was suddenly swept away for ever out of the biological world. The difference between man and the lower animals, which to our human conceit appears enormous, was shown to be a gradual achievement, involving intermediate beings who could not with certainty be placed either within or without the human family. The sun and the planets had already been shown by Laplace to be very probably derived from a primitive more or less undifferentiated nebula. Thus the old fixed landmarks became wavering and indistinct, and all sharp outlines were blurred. Things and species lost their boundaries, and none could say where they began or where they ended.

But if human conceit was staggered for a moment by its kinship with the ape, it soon found a way to reassert itself, and that way is the 'philosophy' of evolution. A process which led from the amoeba to Man appeared to the philosophers to be obviously a progress – though whether the amoeba would agree with this opinion is not known. Hence the cycle of changes which science had shown to be the probable history of the past was welcomed as revealing a law of development towards good in the universe – an evolution or unfolding of an ideal slowly embodying itself in the actual. But such a view, though it might satisfy Spencer and those whom we may call Hegelian evolutionists, could not be accepted as adequate by the more whole-hearted votaries of change. An ideal to which the world continuously approaches is, to these minds, too dead and static to be inspiring. Not only the aspiration, but the ideal too, must change and develop with the course of evolution: there must be no fixed goal, but a continual fashioning of fresh needs by the impulse which is life and which alone gives unity to the process.

Life, in this philosophy, is a continuous stream, in which all divisions are artificial and unreal. Separate things, beginnings and endings, are mere convenient fictions: there is only smooth unbroken transition. The beliefs of today may count as true today, if they carry us along the stream; but tomorrow they will be false, and must be replaced by new beliefs to meet the new situation. All our thinking consists of convenient fictions, imaginary congealings of the stream: reality flows on in spite of all our fictions, and though it can be lived, it cannot be conceived in thought. Somehow, without explicit statement, the assurance is slipped in that the future, though we cannot foresee it, will be better than the past or the present: the reader is like the child which expects a sweet because it has been told to open its mouth and shut its eyes. Logic, mathematics, physics disappear in this philosophy, because they are too 'static'; what is real is an impulse and movement towards a goal which, like the rainbow, recedes as we advance, and makes every place different when we reach it from what it appeared to be at a distance.

I do not propose to enter upon a technical examination of this philosophy. I wish only to maintain that the motives and interests which inspire it are so exclusively practical, and the problems with which it deals are so special, that it can hardly be regarded as touching any of the questions that, to my mind, constitute genuine philosophy.

The predominant interest of evolutionism is in the question of human destiny, or at least of the destiny of Life. It is more interested in morality and happiness than in knowledge for its own sake. It must be admitted that the same may be said of many other philosophies, and that a desire for the kind of knowledge which philosophy can give is very rare. But if philosophy is to attain truth, it is necessary first and foremost that philosophers should acquire the disinterested intellectual curiosity which characterizes the genuine man of science. Knowledge concerning the future – which is the kind of knowledge that must be sought if we are to know about human destiny – is possible within certain narrow limits. It is impossible to say how much the limits may be enlarged with the progress of science. But what is evident is that any proposition about the future belongs by its subject-matter to some particular science, and is to be ascertained, if at all, by the methods of that science. Philosophy is not a short cut to the same kind of results as those of the other sciences: if it is to be a genuine study, it must have a province of its own, and aim at results which the other sciences can neither prove nor disprove.

Evolutionism, in basing itself upon the notion of *progress*, which is change from the worse to the better, allows the notion of time, as it seems to me, to become its tyrant rather than its servant, and thereby loses that impartiality of contemplation which is the source of all that is best in philosophic thought and feeling. Metaphysicians, as we saw, have frequently denied altogether the reality of time. I do not wish to do this; I wish only to preserve the mental outlook which inspired the denial, the attitude which, in thought, regards the past as having the same reality as the present and the same importance as the future. 'In so far,' says Spinoza,[6] 'as the mind conceives a thing according to the dictate of reason, it will be equally affected whether the idea is that of a future, past, or present thing.' It is this 'conceiving according to the dictate of reason' that I find lacking in the philosophy which is based on evolution.

Good and evil

Mysticism maintains that all evil is illusory, and sometimes maintains the same view as regards good, but more often holds that all reality is good. Both views are to be found in Heraclitus: 'Good and ill are one', he says, but again, 'To God all things are fair and good and right, but men hold some things wrong and some right.' A similar twofold position is to be found in Spinoza, but he uses the word 'perfection' when he means to speak of the good that is not merely human. 'By reality and perfection I mean the same thing,' he says[5] but elsewhere we find the definition: 'By *good* I shall mean that which we certainly know to be useful to us.'[6] Thus perfection belongs to reality in its own nature, but goodness is relative to ourselves and our needs, and disappears in an impartial survey. Some such distinction, I think, is necessary in order to understand the ethical outlook of mysticism: there is a lower mundane kind of good and evil, which divides the world of appearance into what seem to be conflicting parts; but there is also a higher, mystical kind of good, which belongs to reality and is not opposed by any correlative kind of evil.

It is difficult to give a logically tenable account of this position without recognizing that good and evil are subjective, that what is good is merely that towards which we have one kind of feeling, and what is evil is merely that towards which we have another kind of feeling. In our active life, where we have to exercise choice, and to prefer this to that of two possible acts, it is necessary to have a distinction of good and evil, or at least of better and worse. But this distinction, like everything pertaining to action, belongs to what mysticism regards as the world of illusion, if only because it is essentially concerned with time. In our contemplative life, where action is not called for, it is possible to be impartial, and to overcome the ethical dualism which action requires. So long as we remain *merely* impartial, we may be content to say that both the good and the evil of action are illusions. But if, as we must do if we have the mystic vision, we find the whole world worthy of love and worship, if we see

The earth, and every common sight...
Apparell'd in celestial light

we shall say that there is a higher good than that of action, and that this higher good belongs to the whole world as it is in reality. In this way the twofold attitude and the apparent vacillation of mysticism are explained and justified.

The possibility of this universal love and joy in all that exists is of supreme importance for the conduct and happiness of life, and gives inestimable value to the mystic emotion, apart from any creeds which may be built upon it. But if we are not to be led into false beliefs, it is necessary to realize exactly *what* the mystic emotion reveals. It reveals a possibility of human nature – a possibility of a nobler, happier, freer life than any that can be otherwise achieved. But it does not reveal anything about the non-human, or about the nature of the universe in general. Good and bad, and even the higher good that mysticism finds everywhere, are the reflections of our own emotions on other things, not part of the substance of things as they are in themselves. And therefore an impartial contemplation, freed from all preoccupation with Self, will not judge things good or bad, although it is very easily combined with that feeling of universal love which leads the mystic to say that the whole world is good.

The philosophy of evolution, through the notion of progress, is bound up with the ethical dualism of the worse and the better, and is thus shut out, not only from the kind of survey which discards good and evil altogether from its view, but also from the mystical belief in the goodness of everything. In this way the distinction of good and evil, like time, becomes a tyrant in this philosophy, and introduces into thought the restless selectiveness of action. Good and evil, like time, are, it would seem, not general or fundamental in the world of thought, but late and highly specialized members of the intellectual hierarchy.

Although, as we saw, mysticism can be interpreted so as to agree with the view that good and evil are not intellectually fundamental, it must be admitted that here we are no longer in verbal agreement with most of the great philosophers and religious teachers of the past. I believe, however, that the elimination of ethical considerations from philosophy is both scientifically necessary and – though this may seem a paradox – an ethical advance. Both these contentions must be briefly defended.

The hope of satisfaction to our more human desires – the hope of demonstrating that the world has this or that desirable ethical characteristic – is not one which, so far as I can see, a scientific philosophy can do anything whatever to satisfy. The difference between a good world and a bad one is a difference in the particular characteristics of the particular things that exist in these worlds: it is not a sufficiently abstract difference to come within the province of philosophy. Love and hate, for example, are ethical opposites, but to philosophy they are closely analogous attitudes towards objects. The general form and structure of those attitudes towards objects which constitute mental phenomena is a problem for philosophy, but the difference between love and hate is not a difference of form or structure, and therefore belongs rather to the special science of psychology than to philosophy. Thus the ethical interests which have often inspired philosophers must remain in the background: some kind of ethical interest may inspire the whole study, but none must obtrude in the detail or be expected in the special results which are sought.

If this view seems at first sight disappointing, we may remind ourselves that a similar change has been found necessary in all the other sciences. The physicist or chemist is not now required to prove the ethical importance of his ions or atoms; the biologist is not expected to prove the utility of the plants or animals which he dissects. In pre-scientific ages this was not the case. Astronomy, for example, was studied because men believed in astrology: it was thought that the movements of the planets had the most direct and important bearing upon the lives of human beings. Presumably, when this belief decayed and the disinterested study of astronomy began, many who had found astrology absorbingly interesting decided that astronomy had too little human interest to be worthy of study. Physics, as it appears in Plato's *Timaeus* for example, is full of ethical notions: it is an essential part of its purpose to show that the earth is worthy of admiration. The modern physicist, on the contrary, though he has no wish to deny that the earth is admirable, is not concerned, as physicist, with its ethical attributes: he is merely concerned to find out facts, not to consider whether they are good or bad. In psychology, the scientific attitude is even more recent and more difficult than in the physical sciences: it is natural to consider that human nature is either good or bad, and to suppose that the difference between good and bad, so all-important in practice, must be important in theory also. It is only during the last century that an ethically neutral psychology has grown up; and here too, ethical neutrality has been essential to scientific success.

In philosophy, hitherto, ethical neutrality has been seldom sought and hardly ever achieved. Men have remembered their wishes, and have judged philosophies in relation to their wishes. Driven from the particular sciences, the belief that the notions of good and evil must afford a key to the understanding of the world has sought a refuge in philosophy. But even from this last refuge, if philosophy is not to remain a set of pleasing dreams, this belief must be driven forth. It is a commonplace that happiness is not best achieved by those who seek it directly; and it would seem that the same is true of the good. In thought, at any rate, those who forget good and evil and seek only to know the facts are more likely to achieve good than those who view the world through the distorting medium of their own desires.

We are thus brought back to our seeming paradox, that a philosophy which does not seek to impose upon the world its own conceptions of good and evil is not only more likely to achieve truth, but is also the outcome of a higher ethical standpoint than one which, like evolutionism and most traditional systems, is perpetually appraising the universe and seeking to find in it an embodiment of present ideals. In religion, and in every deeply serious view of the world and of human destiny, there is an element of submission, a realization of the limits of human power, which is somewhat lacking in the modern world, with its quick material successes and its insolent belief in the boundless possibilities of progress. 'He that loveth his life shall lose it'; and there is danger lest, through a too confident love of life, life itself should lose much of what gives it its highest worth. The submission which religion inculcates in action is essentially the same in spirit as that which science teaches in thought; and the ethical neutrality by which its victories have been achieved is the outcome of that submission.

The good which it concerns us to remember is the good which it lies in our power to create – the good in our own lives and in our attitude towards the world. Insistence on belief in an external realization of the good is a form of self-assertion, which, while it cannot secure the external good which it desires, can seriously impair the inward good which lies within our power, and destroy that reverence towards fact which constitutes both what is valuable in humility and what is fruitful in the scientific temper.

Human beings cannot, of course, wholly transcend human nature; something subjective, if only the interest that determines the direction of our attention, must remain in all our thought. But scientific philosophy comes nearer to objectivity than any other human pursuit, and gives us, therefore, the closest contact and the most intimate relation with the outer world that it is possible to achieve. To the primitive mind, everything is either friendly or hostile; but experience has shown that friendliness and hostility are not the conceptions by which the world is to be understood. Scientific philosophy thus represents, though as yet only in a nascent condition, a higher form of thought than any pre-scientific belief or imagination, and, like every approach to self-transcendence, it brings with it a rich reward in increase of scope and breadth and comprehension. Evolutionism, in spite of its appeals to particular scientific facts, fails to be a truly scientific philosophy because of its slavery to time, its ethical preoccupations, and its predominant interest in our mundane concerns and destiny. A truly scientific philosophy will be more humble, more piecemeal, more arduous, offering less glitter of outward mirage to flatter fallacious hopes, but more indifferent to fate, and more capable of accepting the world without the tyrannous imposition of our human and temporary demands.

10

SCIENCE AND RELIGION

The conflict between science and religion, which began to be acute in the sixteenth century has, in varying forms, continued down to our own day. As compared with other wars, it has had some rather peculiar features. In every battle without exception, science has been victorious; but when, in consequence, religion evacuated territory formerly claimed as its own, its champions blandly explained that the claim had been unfounded, and that the true realm of religion remained inviolate. The result has been a profound change in the character of religion, which has become progressively more inward and spiritual, more moral and less dogmatic. As for science, each new department of inductive knowledge has had to fight for its existence, but after achieving its own freedom has tended to join with religion in attacking the newer upstart sciences which had not yet become respectable by victory. This process, both in religion and science, is still going on at the present day.

The attack of science upon the dogmas which were universally accepted in the Christian world at the beginning of the sixteenth century has proceeded, broadly speaking, from without inward, beginning with the heavens, going on to the geological history of the earth, coming next to the origin of forms of life, thence to the human body, and last to the human mind. I shall begin with a brief survey of this history, and then try to disentangle the essentials of the conflict as it exists in the present day.

Let us first consider what Christians believed before science had begun its onslaughts. They held that the earth was the centre of the universe, being surrounded by the spheres of the various heavenly bodies, outside all of which was the empyrean and the abode of God and His angels. Everything in the heavens, from the moon upwards, was indestructible; the things that pass away were thought to be all below the moon – a belief which gave rise to the word 'sublunary'.

The whole visible universe was created about six thousand years ago. Bishop Usher fixed the date at 4004 BC, and Dr Lightfoot, Vice-Chancellor of the University of Cambridge, was able to add further precision by determining that Man was created on October 23 at 9 a.m. God created Man in His own image, and gave him free will, although He foresaw that free will would lead men to sin, and that justice would demand the punishment of sinners. He told Adam and Eve not to eat of the fruit of a certain tree, but they nevertheless did so; for this crime, they and all their descendants deserve to burn eternally in hell fire. But after waiting 4004 years, during which He destroyed all human beings except eight in a universal deluge, God in His infinite mercy decided that some people should not go to hell, but that the punishment which they deserved should be inflicted upon God the Son. Some of those who believed that this had been done went to heaven instead of to hell. The truth on all matters of religious importance was stated in the Bible, or could be inferred from things there stated, for the Bible was God's word, dictated by Him to its human authors.

Very little of this is believed by most modern Christians. The doctrine of invincible ignorance has enabled even Roman Catholics to hold that salvation is possible outside the Church. The Copernican astronomy is universally accepted. The date 4004 BC is abandoned at the bidding of geologists. Most educated Christians no longer accept the literal truth of everything in the Bible. It is true that no man can become a clergyman of the Church of England without giving an affirmative answer to the question: 'Do you unfeignedly believe the whole of the Scriptures of the Old and New Testaments?' but it is recognized that those who give this answer need not be deemed to be speaking the truth. Modern Christians are indignant if one supposes that they still believe the ancient formulas, but they do not sufficiently recognize that only the pressure of science has driven them into their present comparatively rational position. It is essential to religion as understood in the West to hold that the universe has a purpose which is concerned with Man. The most severe blow to this belief was the first, the Copernican astronomy. If the universe was made with reference to Man, it was natural that the earth which he inhabits should be at the centre. So far from this being the case, it was found that the sun is the centre of that part of the cosmos which is in our immediate neighbourhood, that the sun is vastly larger than the earth, and that the sun itself is merely one among the countless multitude of stars. Certain Greeks (Aristarchus), who were disciples of Pythagoras, had taught that the earth rotates daily and goes round the sun annually. But this view never won wide acceptance in antiquity, and had been forgotten when Copernicus revived it. He, prudently, refrained from publishing his book until he was dying; the first copy reached him on his deathbed in 1543.

As Copernicus – at least according to his editor's preface – had not asserted his theory, but only advanced it as an interesting hypothesis, he escaped formal condemnation until Kepler and Galileo had given proofs that the hypothesis must be accepted. From the first, however, religious leaders were bitterly opposed to the new astronomy. Does not the first verse of the ninety-third Psalm tell us that 'The world also is stablished, that it cannot be moved'? Luther said:

> People give ear to an upstart astrologer who strives to show that the earth revolves, not the heavens or the firmament, the sun or the moon. Whoever wishes to appear clever must devise some new system, which of all systems is of course the very best. This fool wishes to reverse the entire science of astronomy; but sacred Scripture tells us that Joshua commanded the sun to stand still, and not the earth.

And Calvin said: 'Who will venture to place the authority of Copernicus above that of the Holy Spirit?' But on the whole Copernicus attracted little attention. He had given no good grounds for his theory, and it was therefore possible to ignore him.

It was Galileo's work which caused the Catholic Church to pronounce the Copernican theory heretical, first in 1616, and again in 1633. The bitterness of the attack was very great. The Jesuit Inchofer, one of its leaders, said in 1631:

> The opinion of the earth's motion is of all heresies the most abominable, the most pernicious, the most scandalous; the immovability of the earth is thrice sacred; argument against the immortality of the soul, the existence of God, and the incarnation, should be tolerated sooner than an argument to prove that the earth moves.

I think this worthy ecclesiastic was right, from his point of view. Nothing has done so much as astronomy to make it incredible that Man is the purpose of Creation, which is the central belief of Christianity. Nevertheless, Newton succeeded in combining piety with Copernicanism, since he held that the planets were originally hurled by the hand of God. Laplace, who 'had no need of the hypothesis' of God, took the next step with the nebular hypothesis, according to which planets grew. Perhaps God made the nebula, but it seemed a round-about method for omnipotence to arrive at Man.

After astronomy came geology. Fossils, and evidences that mountains were once under water, were taken to prove the deluge; but gradually it was found that the earth must be immeasurably older than had been thought. Sir Charles Lyell's *Principles of Geology*, published in 1830, set forth the evolutionary view of geology, and persuaded almost all men of science that millions of years had been required to form the rocks on the earth's surface, and that extinct flora and fauna could not have all perished so recently as the supposed date of the deluge. Theologians denounced Lyell, and for a while he was regarded as a wicked man, but the time was past when legal persecution could be inflicted.

The next step – a very important one – was the application of the doctrine of evolution to the origin of species. Aristotle and Genesis combined in asserting that different species had been separately created, and this view, though not unquestioned, was accepted by most biologists until the appearance of Darwin's book in 1859. Darwin's doctrine reached theologians and the uneducated public in the form of the theory that men were descended from monkeys. This would never do. Men have immortal souls, monkeys have not; Christ died to save men, not monkeys; men have a divinely implanted sense of right and wrong, whereas monkeys are guided solely by instinct. If men developed by imperceptible steps out of monkeys, at what moment did they suddenly acquire these theologically important characteristics? Bishop Wilberforce thundered against Darwinism at the British Association in 1860[1], but in vain: men were no longer afraid of the Church's displeasure, and the evolution of animal and vegetable species was soon the accepted doctrine among biologists.

The gulf set by theology between Man and the lower animals is illustrated by the attitude of the Pope Pius IX to the SPCA.[2] Lord Odo Russell asked him to support it, but he replied that 'such an association could not be sanctioned by the Holy See, being founded on a theological error, to wit, that Christians owed a duty to animals'. It was difficult for an evolutionist to maintain such a view, since no sharp line could be drawn between Man and animals.

The substitution of science for superstition in the treatment of the human body has been a very gradual process. In the Middle

Ages, plagues were regarded as evidences of the divine displeasure; until very recent times, insanity of certain kinds was attributed to demoniacal possession, as it is in the Gospels. Much was thought to be due to witchcraft, and until late in the seventeenth century countless harmless women were burnt as witches. Sir Thomas Browne in 1664 helped, as magistrate, to get two witches hanged, and nearly a century later Wesley maintained that 'to give up witchcraft is to give up the Bible'. I think it must be admitted that Wesley was right, for the Bible says 'Thou shalt not suffer a witch to live.'³ Modern liberal Christians, who still hold that the Bible is ethically valuable, are apt to forget such texts and the millions of innocent victims who have died in agony because, at one time, men genuinely accepted the Bible as a guide to conduct.

The use of anaesthetics was at first denounced as impious, particularly in childbirth, since the Bible declared that the pains of labour are a punishment for the sin of Eve. In 1591, a Scotch lady named Eufame Macalyane was burnt alive for seeking relief from the pains of childbirth; and in the nineteenth century Simpson's use of chloroform was denounced by innumerable parsons. He succeeded in proving that it was all right to give anaesthetics to *men*, because God put Adam into a deep sleep when He extracted his rib to make Eve; but male ecclesiastics remained unconvinced as regards the sufferings of *women*. In regard to insanity, the belief in demoniacal possession made it seem rational to torture the victim so as to make the demon uncomfortable. Prevention of sleep was a common treatment. And even George III, when he was mad, was beaten with a view to restoring his sanity. It is only in our own day that a rational treatment of mental disorders has become common.

The sciences which deal with the mental life of Man have been the latest to develop, and their attack upon religious beliefs is still only beginning. Early history has shown, not only that Genesis is unhistorical, but also that it is largely borrowed from Babylonian myths. The higher criticism has disintegrated the Bible itself. Anthropology has made it plain that much of what was formerly Christian orthodoxy is a survival of very primitive modes of thought. But none of these studies are so deadly to the outlook of modern Christians as scientific psychology, since this seems to prove that the traditional conception of sin is wholly untenable. Virtue and sin are notions that depend upon free will; as we come to understand the causes of character, these notions melt away. It is common nowadays even among liberal Christians to urge a charitable view of crime (i.e. of socially undesirable conduct) on the ground that it is a product of social conditions. But those who use this argument do not, as a rule, perceive its scope. Socially desirable conduct also, where it exists, is a product of antecedent causes. A man's character is determined by his heredity, his diet, his glands, his education, and so on; these are, at any rate in the important years of childhood, outside his control. If he becomes a man who does harm, he is not to blame; if he becomes a man who does good, this is equally traceable to causes outside himself. I do not mean to say that his efforts are not essential links in the causal chain determining his actions; I mean merely that his efforts are themselves due to antecedent circumstances which have made him the sort of person he is. If God planned the world, Calvin was right in saying that some people were foredoomed to what is called virtue and others to what is called wickedness; it would seem hardly fair, therefore, to reward the former and punish the latter. Nor does our criminal law, which, historically, is an attempt to imitate divine justice, seem warranted by the notion of a man's 'deserts'. Clearly we should wish men not to commit murders, just as we wish them not to spread cholera. A man infected with cholera is not allowed to mix freely with the population, but we do not think him wicked. We may similarly be obliged to interfere with the liberty of a murderer, but we should not have a feeling of moral reprobation in the one case any more than in the other.

The theory that our acts have antecedent causes is one which seems, at first sight, to have more consequences than it in fact has. It does not show that there is no use in making efforts, since our efforts are among the causes of our acts, though they in turn have other causes. It does not have any bearing on the question of what is desirable. It does not show that people should be left free to commit socially undesirable actions. It shows only that, in arranging law and social custom, we should aim at causing socially desirable actions, and that the infliction of pains upon those who act in ways that are unpleasant to others is to be justified by its effects in preventing such acts, not on the ground that the wicked deserve to suffer. In orthodox theology, hell does not reform sinners, but is justified simply on the ground that punishment is their due. Such a view as this is unscientific.

In Protestant ethics, the notion of 'conscience' has played an important part. It has been supposed that God reveals to each human heart what is right and what is wrong, so that in order to avoid sin we only have to listen to the inner voice. Unfortunately conscience says different things to different people. It tells one man that he ought to defend his country in case of invasion, while it tells another that all participation in warfare is wicked. It told George III that his Coronation Oath forbade him to grant Catholic Emancipation, while it told George IV no such thing. It leads some to condemn spoliation of the rich by the poor, as advocated by Communists, and others to condemn exploitation of the poor by the rich, as practised by capitalists. As a guide to conduct, therefore, conscience is a failure. Scientifically, conscience is the stored up discomfort due to disapproval experienced or imagined in the past, particularly in early youth. So far from having a divine origin, it is a product of education, and can be trained to approve or disapprove as educators see fit.

In what I have been saying I have assumed determinism; I have assumed, that is to say, that there are scientific laws which make it possible, at least approximately, to infer later events from earlier ones. This assumption has been made both in science and in daily life, although metaphysically and theologically it has been questioned. For the first time since the seventeenth century, there is now a school of physicists which questions it. Eddington, who is the chief English exponent of this school, holds that the apparent regularity in the behaviour of large bodies is a matter of averages, and is not to be found in the behaviour of individual atoms. The possibility of this view depends upon quantum physics. According to quantum theory, atoms undergo certain changes which occur at undetermined times, and which may be any one of a number of possibilities. Among a large number of atoms, a certain discoverable proportion will, in any given time, undergo any one of the possible changes, just as a certain proportion of a large population will have measles, another proportion cancer, and so on. But nothing at present known enables us to be definite as to any particular atom, beyond enumerating the list of changes that are possible to it.

It is suggested, on these grounds, that atoms have something like free will, and that, in a brain, there may be a condition of unstable equilibrium which would cause a measurable difference in the result if a given atom chose one course instead of another. Thus Eddington avoids the belief that our bodily actions are controlled by the laws of physics.

As against this view, one might be content to appeal to authority; Einstein, for instance, still believes in strict causality. But I think we can say something rather more definite. The quantum laws of atomic behaviour began to be studied in 1913; most of our knowledge concerning them has been acquired since 1925. It is no wonder if we do not yet know them completely. One new law would make the behaviour of atoms again completely deterministic; who shall say that such a law will not be discovered during the next few years?

But, further, if the atom really enjoys a measure of caprice, will any pleasant consequences follow? I think not. It must be remembered that, if there are really no laws deciding which of several possible things an atom will do, we cannot suppose that on the whole it will do things having one result rather than things having another. We shall simply not know what it will do. Eddington seems to imagine – though of course not explicitly – that if atoms can do what they like they will do what he likes. But there is no evidence that their tastes are the same as his, and genuine caprice is not compatible with having any tastes at all. Caprice is a conception which is difficult to grasp, since all our acts have motives, and are therefore deterministic, not capricious. Those who derive pleasure from the belief that nature is more or less lawless have not, I think, quite grasped what their view involves.

There is a further argument against the practical application which Eddington wishes to make of atomic caprice, and that is the existence of causal laws in human and animal behaviour. For this no recondite researches are necessary. If any of you question what I say, I advise you to pull the nose of every stranger you meet. When you find one who, instead of getting angry, says, 'Thank you very much, please do it again', I shall begin to think that perhaps human behaviour is not subject to laws. In the meantime, inability to predict is quite sufficiently explained, where it exists, by the complexity of the phenomena.

There are some, especially among biologists, who still profess to see purpose in the course of nature. They say that the nebula, the formation of the planets, the millions of years during which the earth cooled, and the ages during which primitive forms of life evolved, were all only a prelude to the glorious blossoming which we are now witnessing. God's purpose throughout the ages is at last revealed, in Hitler and Mr Winston Churchill, in the men who invent poison gases and the politicians who engineer war scares. Or, if these are not yet the full revelation, we may hope hereafter for more statesmanlike statesmen and more dictatorial dictators. Even if this consummation be thought adequate to so long a prologue, what are we to say of the epilogue? The earth will grow cold, and life on it will become extinct. There may, for a time, be life somewhere else, but the universe is tending towards a uniform temperature, and ultimately, we are bound to suppose, there will be no life anywhere. There will then, at any rate, be nothing to regret and no one to regret it; but the result, one would think, could have been achieved more easily by not creating the world at all. As the leisurely effort of an omnipotent Being, I cannot say that I think it a success. But as the Bible tells us, God's ways are not our ways.

The universe, as science reveals it, is very old and very large. Our planet, long after it separated from the sun, was too hot to support life. After countless ages the chemical combination which we call living matter came into existence, and increased in amount and complexity of structure by means of ordinary chemical laws. At last, through elaboration of structure, living bodies acquired that peculiar relation of present to past behaviour which we call consciousness. These little conscious lumps on a tiny planet then imagined themselves to be the purpose of the whole. They were so pleased with themselves that they thought only Omnipotence could have created them, and only the creation of them could have satisfied Omnipotence. I do not know whether the world was or was not created by a Deity, but if it was, I cannot regard Man as a worthy culmination, and I sincerely hope that in some other corner there are beings more intelligent, more merciful, and less conceited.

11

REVIEW OF SIR ARTHUR EDDINGTON, *THE NATURE OF THE PHYSICAL WORLD*

Professor Eddington is unquestionably the most delightful of all the writers on physics at the present time, and his qualities are shown almost equally in his popular writings and in his technical mathematics. As a theoretical physicist he has a rare clarity and systematic comprehensiveness which is probably the basis of his extraordinary skill as a popularizer. He is a past master of the art of humorous illustration; take as an example what he says in his chapter on the definition of reality. 'Reality', he says, is generally used with the intention of evoking sentiment and is a grand word for a peroration; of such a peroration he proceeds to give an imaginary example: 'The right honourable speaker went on to declare that the concord and amity for which he had unceasingly striven had now become a reality [loud cheers].' He goes on to remark: 'The conception which it is so troublesome to apprehend is not "reality" but "reality [loud cheers]".' I do not know how an important point could have been put more convincingly or more amusingly. Three-quarters of his course of Gifford lectures is occupied with a popular exposition of the leading ideas of modern physics, while the last quarter is concerned with adapting these ideas to theology. The first three-quarters is wholly admirable, but as to the last quarter opinions will be divided according to the prejudices which the reader brings to bear.

The last few chapters, which are those of most interest to the general reader, are devoted to the exposition of an idealist philosophy and the advocacy of free will. These two points are not necessarily connected; let us take first the idealist philosophy. Professor Eddington is very well aware how little physics tells us about the physical world, but being no psychologist he somewhat exaggerates what psychology can tell us about the mental world. He believes that we have direct self-knowledge, a view which has been

140

widely held, but which cannot, I think, survive a scrutiny of what is meant by 'knowledge'. I am prepared to admit that we are nearer to knowing about our own minds than about anything else, because the causal chain from an event to my knowledge of it is shorter when it is in my own brain than when it is anywhere else; but there is still a causal chain, and the knowledge is still a separate event only causally connected with what is known. Professor Eddington disagrees with neutral monism, and holds instead to the doctrine of 'mind-stuff', although he is careful to explain that this need not be either mind or stuff. I disagree with this doctrine, because I hold that mentality is a form of organization, not a property of individual events, just as, say, democracy is a property of a community and not of an individual citizen. Lack of space, however, forbids me to develop this theme.

We come now to the question of free will. So far as physics is concerned, it seems that the acts of individual atoms can no longer be regarded as rigidly determined by physical laws, but what is so determined is the action of large aggregates. And here the matter is only one of probability, not a demonstrative certainty. I do not mean by this merely that our knowledge is only probable; I mean that it is knowledge *of* a probability, like the knowledge that continued shuffling will not bring the pack of cards back into its original order. Now, as Eddington rightly points out, indeterminateness in the doings of individual atoms is not enough to give any valuable kind of free will. When we speak, for example, a great many atoms are involved in the motions of throat, tongue, and lips. Therefore, if the doings of large aggregates of atoms are always subject to law, all that we say is determined in spite of the indeterminateness of minute phenomena.

Eddington holds, however, that mind can undo the statistical and merely probable laws which control large aggregates of atoms, and that, therefore, the visible movements of our bodies are not necessarily mechanically determined. I do not know of any reason either to believe or to disbelieve this, though I think it probable that reasons for belief or disbelief will be known before long. Eddington's idea seems to be that mind can exercise a selective action, which interferes with the laws of chance as, for example, in the case of a pack of cards which we deliberately rearrange. The fact that the laws of physics, in so far as they concern large aggregates, are only probable laws, has, of course, many great advantages from this point of view, for a probability can always be altered by the introduction of a new factor. But although this action of mind is a possibility, it cannot be said that there is any positive evidence in its favour; it is as yet merely an hypothesis to be considered.

I do not know whether Eddington thinks that mind can in any degree act contrary to the second law of thermodynamics, but I rather gather that he does not think so, for he says that this law makes the distinction between past and future, so that if mind could undo it, it would make time run backwards. He seems to accept with equanimity the view, which follows from this law, that the world is running down and must in the end cease to contain anything interesting. He has apparently a God, but his God seems to have made the world long ago and forgotten all about it. He is like a man who presents a city with an excellent free library and then allows everybody to take books out without any rule as to their return, or as to their being put in their right places if they are returned, so that before very long the library becomes unusable. It requires a certain robustness to be optimistic on the basis of such a philosophy; but I suspect that Eddington has secret beliefs in reserve which he has not set forth in these lectures. In this respect, however, we are, no doubt, all alike.

12

REVIEW OF JAMES JEANS,
THE MYSTERIOUS UNIVERSE

Sir James Jeans has long been known to the world of mathematicians and to mathematical physicists, but it is only recently that he became known to the general public through his admirable book, *The Universe Around Us*. His new book, *The Mysterious Universe*, is not quite so good as its predecessor: it is considerably shorter, and the last quarter of it is occupied with matters on which the author does not speak as an expert. The first three-quarters, however, have the same fascinating quality as one finds in *The Universe Around Us*, though perhaps the unscientific reader may not follow the exposition of relativity any better than those of previous popular writers.

The book begins with a biography of the sun, one might almost say an epitaph. It seems that not more than one star in about one hundred thousand has planets, but that some two thousand million years ago the sun had the good fortune to have a fruitful meeting with another star, which led to the existing planetary offspring. The stars that do not have planets cannot give rise to life, so that life must be a very rare phenomenon in the universe. 'It seems incredible,' says Sir James Jeans, 'that the universe can have been designed primarily to produce life like our own: had it been so, surely we might have expected to find a better proportion between the magnitude of the mechanism and the amount of the product.' And even in this rare corner of the universe the possibility of life exists only during an interlude between weather that is too hot and weather that is too cold. 'It is a tragedy of our race that it is probably destined to die of cold, while the greater part of the substance of the universe still remains too hot for life to obtain a footing.' Theologians who argue as if human life were the purpose of creation seem to be as faulty in their astronomy as they are excessive in their estimation of themselves and their fellow-creatures. I shall not attempt to summarize the admirable chapters on modern physics, matter and radiation, and relativity and the ether; they are already as brief as possible, and no summary can do them justice. I will, however, quote Professor Jeans's own summary in order to whet the reader's appetite.

> To sum up, a soap-bubble with irregularities and corrugations on its surface is perhaps the best representation, in terms of simple and familiar materials, of the new universe revealed to us by the theory of relativity. The universe is not the interior of the soap-bubble but its surface, and we must always remember that, while the surface of the soap-bubble has only two dimensions, the universe-bubble has four – three dimensions of space and one of time. And the substance out of which this bubble is blown, the soap-film, is empty space welded on to empty time.

The last chapter of the book is concerned to argue that this soap-bubble has been blown by a mathematical Deity because of His interest in its mathematical properties. This part has pleased the theologians. It is nowadays expected of all eminent men of science that they should join in the defence of property against the Bolsheviks by showing that God made the world and therefore the capitalist system. Theologians have grown grateful for small mercies, and they do not much care what sort of God the man of science gives them so long as he gives them one at all. Sir James Jeans's God, like Plato's, is one who has a passion for doing sums, but, being a pure mathematician, is quite indifferent as to what the sums are about. By prefacing his arguments by a lot of difficult and recent physics, the eminent author manages to give it an air of profundity which it would not otherwise possess. In essence the argument is as follows: since two apples and two apples together always make four apples, it follows that the Creator must have known that two and two are four. It might be objected that, since one man and one woman together sometimes make three, the Creator was not yet quite as well versed in sums as one could wish. To speak seriously: Sir James Jeans reverts explicitly to the theory of Bishop Berkeley, according to which the only things that exist are thoughts, and the quasi-permanence which we observe in the external world is due to the fact that God keeps on thinking about things for quite a long time. Material objects, for example, do not cease to exist when no human being is looking at them, because

God is looking at them all the time, or rather because they are thoughts in His mind at all times. The universe, he says, 'can best be pictured, although still very imperfectly and inadequately, as consisting of pure thought, the thought of what, for want of a wider word, we must describe as a mathematical thinker'. A little later we are told that the laws governing God's thoughts are those which govern the phenomena of our waking hours, but not apparently of our dreams.

The argument is, of course, not set out with the formal precision which Sir James would demand in a subject not involving his emotions. Apart from all detail, he has been guilty of a fundamental fallacy in confusing the realms of pure and applied mathematics. Pure mathematics at no point depends upon observation; it is concerned with symbols, and with proving that different collections of symbols have the same meaning. It is because of this symbolic character that it can be studied without the help of experiment. Physics, on the contrary, however mathematical it may become, depends throughout on observation and experiment, that is to say, ultimately upon sense perception. The mathematician provides all kinds of mathematics, but only some of what he provides is useful to the physicist. And what the physicist asserts when he uses mathematics is something totally different from what the pure mathematician asserts. The physicist asserts that the mathematical symbols which he is employing can be used for the interpretation, colligation, and prediction of sense impressions. However abstract his work may become, it never loses its relation to experience. It is found that mathematical formulae can express certain laws governing the world that we observe. Jeans argues that the world must have been created by a mathematician for the pleasure of seeing these laws in operation. If he had ever attempted to set out this argument formally, I cannot doubt that he would have seen how fallacious it is. To begin with, it seems probable that any world, no matter what, could be brought by a mathematician of sufficient skill within the scope of general laws. If this be so, the mathematical character of modern physics is not a fact about the world, but merely a tribute to the skill of the physicists. In the second place, if God were as pure a pure mathematician as His knightly champion supposes, He would have no wish to give a gross external existence to His thoughts. The desire to trace curves and make geometrical models belongs to the schoolboy stage, and would be considered *infra dig* by a professor. Nevertheless it is this desire that Sir James imputes to his Maker. The world, he tells us, consists of thoughts; of these there are, it would seem, three grades: the thoughts of God, the thoughts of men when they are awake, and the thoughts of men when they are asleep and have bad dreams. One does not quite see what the two latter kinds of thought add to the perfection of the universe, since clearly God's thoughts are the best, and one does not quite see what can have been gained by creating so much muddle-headedness. I once knew an extremely learned and orthodox theologian who told me that as the result of long study he had come to understand everything except why God created the world. I commend this puzzle to the attention of Sir James Jeans, and I hope that he will comfort the theologians and the defenders of private property by dealing with it at no distant date.

13

DO SCIENCE AND RELIGION CONFLICT?

Sir Arthur Eddington, the Memorial Lecture in whose honour was delivered this year by Professor H.H. Price, combined science and piety in equal proportions. I do not know, and I think none except his close intimates ever knew, by what considerations he would have defended his religious beliefs in discussion with a sceptic. The only thing about which all who knew him can feel no doubt is the profound sincerity of his convictions.

Professor Price, in this lecture, sets forth what he believes to be the present position in the centuries-old conflict between science and theology. I think he somewhat overstates the extent to which science has got the upper hand in the minds of educated men. Certainly, whatever may be the case in Western Europe, nominal Christianity is still, I should say, predominant in the United States. I think also that Professor Price's account of what he believes to be the prevailing scientific outlook is something of a caricature. He calls this outlook materialistic and assumes that its thoroughgoing advocates are Behaviourists who reject introspection as a method of ascertaining facts. I think those of whom this is true are, except east of the Iron Curtain, a dwindling minority. Consider, for example, the vogue of psycho-analysis, with its dependence upon dreams, for which the only possible evidence is introspection; and consider, to begin at the other end, what physicists are making of matter. In old days physicists thought of matter as made of nice little billiard balls behaving in a thoroughly intelligible manner. But the modern physicists have exploded matter as completely as if they had subjected it to a thermo-nuclear bomb. All that is left of it is a wave of statistical probability, the probability being that something – we know not what – may be somewhere – we know not where – in a space quite different from that of common sense.

One might say that modern physics is materialist except in one small point: namely, that it does not believe there is any such thing as matter.

Professor Price, I think quite rightly, rejects the view that religion can be divorced from dogma. There are those who consider that religion can be regarded merely as an ethic recommending a certain way of life and that this ethic can be maintained without such beliefs as the future life and the existence of God. Professor Price is ready to admit that this or that dogma is unnecessary. For example, Buddhism in its earlier forms was not theistic. But he maintains, and in this I am in agreement with him, that all the great religions of the world have advocated moral precepts for which the evidence was derived from theological beliefs. When I say that I agree with him in this, I am not saying that religious dogmas are necessary for what I consider virtue. I am only saying that they are necessary for some parts of what the adherents of various religions consider to be virtue. For example, I do not think it is possible to prove, without the help of religious dogma, that birth-control is wicked.

Professor Price, like most modern people, rejects the old philosophical proofs of the existence of God which were invented by the Scholastics, refurbished by Descartes, and, as most non-Catholic philosophers think, demolished by Kant. He holds that, if there is to be satisfactory evidence in favour of religious belief, it must be empirical evidence derived from facts unduly neglected by the outlook which he calls materialist. Such facts, he maintains, are to be found in the sphere of extra-sensory perception. From these facts, according to him, it emerges that we all in varying degrees possess means of knowledge which transcend the senses. He infers that, although as yet facts of extra-sensory perception do not suffice to prove the future life or the existence of God, they already suffice to weaken the arguments against these beliefs. Some people maintain that they have a consciousness of the Divine and that other people, who have not this consciousness, ought to accept it as we accept the testimony of those whose senses are more acute than our own. Everybody believes that bats can hear sounds which are inaudible to us. Why then refuse to believe that mystics can hear the voice of God?

The investigators of extra-sensory perception have amassed a number of testimonies to what, if true, are very curious facts. Some people can cause material objects to move without touching them; other people have visions of friends at the moment when these friends are dying; yet other people, when somebody is dealing cards, can guess whether the next card will be red or black in a slightly larger percentage of cases than the laws of probability would lead us to expect. This faculty, however, so far, is apparently confined to people living in North Carolina.

The conclusions which Professor Price draws from investigations of extra-sensory perception are cautious. 'My conclusion is,' he says, 'that psychical research, so far as it has gone at present, gives only indirect support to the "other-worldly" assertions which are an essential part of the religious outlook.' Professor Price thinks that psychical research proves the inadequacy of the conception of human personality which has become common among scientifically educated people. He says:

> We shall not be justified in jumping to the conclusion that the religious conception of human personality is certainly the right one. But we *shall* be justified in concluding that it is not certainly and obviously false, as the majority of Western educated people now assume that it is.

For my part I should hesitate to say that anything is 'certainly and obviously false'. But I should hesitate also to assign as much weight as Professor Price does to some parts of the evidence for extra-sensory perception. I think most of the investigators in this field have taken insufficient note of past evidence for marvels which no one now accepts. During the first weeks of the 1914–18 War practically everybody in England believed that Russian troops had passed through England on their way to France. The evidence was overwhelming – much more so, I should say, than a good deal of the evidence for extra-sensory perception – and yet it was very soon admitted that the whole of this evidence was untrue. I wish psychical researchers would examine the evidence that the Templars paid indecent bodily homage to Satan who was present with horns and hooves complete. I think they will find the evidence much more convincing than that of Paley's twelve honest men. Or again, take the miracles performed in the Diocese of Hippo while St Augustine was bishop, and personally vouched for by that revered sage. (An account of these will be found in Gibbon in Chapter XXVIII.)

In all such investigations, we have to be on our guard against two of the most powerful motives promoting human credulity: I mean, the love of the marvellous and the fear of death. I knew a man at one time who used to perform conjuring tricks before a small audience, and afterwards get them all to relate what had happened. Practically all related something more astonishing than the truth. As for survival after death, whatever metaphysical opinion we may hold about mind and body, the evidence for an intimate causal relationship between the two is overwhelming, and it is difficult to believe that, whatever a 'mind' may be, a human mind can exist apart from a physical organism.

I do not mean to deny that many things of great interest have emerged from the kind of investigation to which Professor Price appeals. There was a time when hypnotism seemed an almost incredible marvel. The evidence for telepathy is strong. But when it comes to pre-cognition I, for my part, feel the antecedent improbability so great that much more than the usual weight of evidence would be required to establish it. I shall certainly be more impressed when I find this evidence carrying conviction to men who are not already passionately desirous to be convinced.

In conclusion, I had better confess what will in any case be obvious to my readers, that my own bias is very strong, though in the opposite direction to that of the believers in extra-sensory perception. I do not like to think that after I am dead I shall be at the beck and call of silly mediums, and be obliged to utter whatever may appear to them to be words of wisdom. Every sceptic should take warning from Voltaire's rejection of marine fossils found on mountain tops. He refused to believe in them because they were thought to afford evidence for the flood. I do not wish to commit a similar folly, and so I try to keep an open mind. I hope that if ever the evidence is sufficient I shall be convinced, but as yet I think suspense of judgment is the only intellectually justifiable attitude.

Part IV

RELIGION AND MORALITY

'Religion and the Churches' was part of a series of eight lectures on the principles of social reconstruction that Russell wrote in 1915 and delivered in the beginning of 1916 at Caxton Hall in Westminster. Originally Russell collaborated with D.H. Lawrence, but they could not come to an agreement, so Russell wrote them himself. These lectures were an attempt to create a 'new religion'. During the collaboration D.H. Lawrence wrote to Lady Ottoline that, apart from the lectures, they also had the idea to 'establish a little society or body around a *religious belief, which leads to action*. We must centre in the knowledge of the Infinite, of God.' The new religion would differ in several ways from the old ones. In the last chapter, 'What We Can Do', Russell says:

> The world has need of a philosophy, or a religion, which will promote life. But in order to promote life it is necessary to value something other than mere life. Life devoted only to life is animal, without any real human value, incapable of preserving men permanently from weariness and the feeling that all is vanity. If life is to be fully human it must serve some end which seems, in some sense, outside human life, some end which is impersonal and above mankind, such as God or truth or beauty. Those who best promote life do not have life for their purpose. They aim rather at what seems like a gradual incarnation, a bringing into our human existence of something eternal, something that appears to imagination to live in a heaven remote from strife and failure and the devouring jaws of Time. Contact with this eternal world – even if it be only a world of our imagination – brings a strength and a fundamental peace which cannot be wholly destroyed by the struggles and ap-

parent failures of our temporal life. It is this happy contemplation of what is eternal that Spinoza calls the intellectual love of God. To those who have once known it, it is
the key of wisdom.

(Russell (1916) 1980, p. 168ff.)

The lectures, published in 1916 as *Principles of Social Reconstruction*, constitute one of Russell's most original contributions to social
and political thought. 'Religion and the Churches' was the seventh
of eight lectures and it was first published in *The Unpopular Review*
(April–June 1916) and then in the book with minor additions and
changes. In 1944 he cited this essay as the 'least unsatisfactory' of
his statements on religion.

'Inherent Tendencies of Industrialism' is a section of a chapter of
Prospects of Industrial Civilization and is included as a sample of
Russell's sociology of religion.

'Has Religion Made Useful Contributions to Civilization?' was
originally published in 1929 both as a pamphlet and as an article in
The Debunker and the American Parade. In Great Britain it first
appeared in *The Rationalist Annual* for the year 1930. In 1957 it was
reprinted in Paul Edwards' collection of Russell's writings on
religion. It can be seen as a sequel to Russell's essay 'Why I Am
Not a Christian'.

'The Sense of Sin' is taken from Chapter 7 of *The Conquest of
Happiness*, which was published in 1930. The book was written
during a time when Russell was very unhappy because his marriage
to Dora was falling apart. Like the Freudians he argues that the
sense of sinfulness has enhanced neither human happiness nor
human goodness. In the first part Russell again criticizes the view
that societies need religion to sustain public morality. The second
part is devoted to a criticism of Herbert Butterfield's book
Christianity and History (London, 1950). Russell argues that
religion, and Christianity in particular, has created more suffering
than it has abolished. He argues that only wisdom and intelligence
can create a happier world.

14

RELIGION AND THE CHURCHES

Almost all the changes which the world has undergone since the end of the Middle Ages are due to the discovery and diffusion of new knowledge. This was the primary cause of the Renaissance, the Reformation, and the industrial revolution. It was also, very directly, the cause of the decay of dogmatic religion. The study of classical texts and early church history, Copernican astronomy and physics, Darwinian biology and comparative anthropology, have each in turn battered down some part of the edifice of Catholic dogma, until, for almost all thinking and instructed people, the most that seems defensible is some inner spirit, some vague hope, and some not very definite feeling of moral obligation. This result might perhaps have remained limited to the educated minority, but for the fact that the Churches have almost everywhere opposed political progress with the same bitterness with which they have opposed progress in thought. Political conservatism has brought the Churches into conflict with whatever was vigorous in the working classes, and has spread free thought in wide circles which might otherwise have remained orthodox for centuries. The decay of dogmatic religion is, for good or evil, one of the most important facts in the modern world. Its effects have hardly yet begun to show themselves: what they will be it is impossible to say, but they will certainly be profound and far-reaching.

Religion is partly personal, partly social: to the Protestant primarily personal, to the Catholic primarily social. It is only when the two elements are intimately blended that religion becomes a powerful force in moulding society. The Catholic Church, as it existed from the time of Constantine to the time of the Reformation, represented a blending which would have seemed incredible if it had not been actually achieved, the blending of Christ and Caesar, of the morality of humble submission with the pride of Imperial

Rome. Those who loved the one could find it in the Thebaid; those who loved the other could admire it in the pomp of metropolitan archbishops. In St Francis and Innocent III the same two sides of the Church are still represented. But since the Reformation personal religion has been increasingly outside the Catholic Church, while the religion which has remained Catholic has been increasingly a matter of institutions and politics and historic continuity. This division has weakened the force of religion: religious bodies have not been strengthened by the enthusiasm and single-mindedness of the men in whom personal religion is strong, and these men have not found their teaching diffused and made permanent by the power of ecclesiastical institutions.

The Catholic Church achieved, during the Middle Ages, the most organic society and the most harmonious inner synthesis of instinct, mind, and spirit, that the Western world has ever known. St Francis, Thomas Aquinas, and Dante represent its summit as regards individual development. The cathedrals, the mendicant Orders, and the triumph of the Papacy over the Empire represent its supreme political success. But the perfection which had been achieved was a narrow perfection: instinct, mind, and spirit all suffered from curtailment in order to fit into the pattern; laymen found themselves subject to the Church in ways which they resented, and the Church used its power for rapacity and oppression. The perfect synthesis was an enemy to new growth, and after the time of Dante all that was living in the world had first to fight for its right to live against the representatives of the old order. This fight is even now not ended. Only when it is quite ended, both in the external world of politics and in the internal world of men's own thoughts, will it be possible for a new organic society and a new inner synthesis to take the place which the Church held for a thousand years.

The clerical profession suffers from two causes, one of which it shares with some other professions, while the other is peculiar to itself. The cause peculiar to it is the convention that clergymen are more virtuous than other men. Any average selection of mankind, set apart and told that it excels the rest in virtue, must tend to sink below the average. This is an ancient commonplace in regard to princes and those who used to be called 'the great'. But it is no less true as regards those of the clergy who are not genuinely and by nature as much better than the average as they are conventionally supposed to be. The other source of harm to the clerical profession is endowments. Property which is only available for those who will

154

support an established institution has a tendency to warp men's judgments as to the excellence of the institution. The tendency is aggravated when the property is associated with social consideration and opportunities for petty power. It is at its worst when the institution is tied by law to an ancient creed, almost impossible to change, and yet quite out of touch with the unfettered thought of the present day. All these causes combine to damage the moral force of the Church.

It is not so much that the creed of the Church is the wrong one. What is amiss is the mere existence of a creed. As soon as income, position, and power are dependent upon acceptance of no matter what creed, intellectual honesty is imperilled. Men will tell themselves that a formal assent is justified by the good which it will enable them to do. They fail to realize that, in those whose mental life has any vigour, loss of complete intellectual integrity puts an end to the power of doing good, by producing gradually in all directions an inability to see truth simply. The strictness of party discipline has introduced the same evil in politics; there, because the evil is comparatively new, it is visible to many who think it unimportant as regards the Church. But the evil is greater as regards the Church, because religion is of more importance than politics, and because it is more necessary that the exponents of religion should be wholly free from taint.

The evils we have been considering seem inseparable from the existence of a professional priesthood. If religion is not to be harmful in a world of rapid change, it must, like the Society of Friends, be carried on by men who have other occupations during the week, who do their religious work from enthusiasm, without receiving any payment. And such men, because they know the everyday world, are not likely to fall into a remote morality which no one regards as applicable to common life. Being free, they will not be bound to reach certain conclusions decided in advance, but will be able to consider moral and religious questions genuinely, without bias. Except in a quite stationary society, no religious life can be living or a real support to the spirit unless it is freed from the incubus of a professional priesthood.

It is largely for these reasons that so little of what is valuable in morals and religion comes nowadays from the men who are eminent in the religious world. It is true that among professed believers there are many who are wholly sincere, who feel still the inspiration which Christianity brought before it had been weakened by the progress of knowledge. These sincere believers are valuable to the world because they keep alive the conviction that the life of the spirit is what is of most importance to men and women. Some of them, in all the countries now at war, have had the courage to preach peace and love in the name of Christ, and have done what lay in their power to mitigate the bitterness of hatred. All praise is due to these men, and without them the world would be even worse than it is.

But it is not through even the most sincere and courageous believers in the traditional religion that a new spirit can come into the world. It is not through them that religion can be brought back to those who have lost it because their minds were active, not because their spirit was dead. Believers in the traditional religion necessarily look to the past for inspiration rather than to the future. They seek wisdom in the teaching of Christ, which, admirable as it is, remains quite inadequate for many of the social and spiritual issues of modern life. Art and intellect and all the problems of government are ignored in the Gospels. Those who, like Tolstoy, endeavour seriously to take the Gospels as a guide to life are compelled to regard the ignorant peasant as the best type of man, and to brush aside political questions by an extreme and impracticable anarchism.

If a religious view of life and the world is ever to reconquer the thoughts and feelings of free-minded men and women, much that we are accustomed to associate with religion will have to be discarded. The first and greatest change that is required is to establish a morality of initiative, not a morality of submission, a morality of hope rather than fear, of things to be done rather than of things to be left undone. It is not the whole duty of man to slip through the world so as to escape the wrath of God. The world is *our* world, and it rests with us to make a heaven or a hell. The power is ours, and the kingdom and the glory would be ours also if we had courage and insight to create them. The religious life that we must seek will not be one of occasional solemnity and superstitious prohibitions, it will not be sad or ascetic, it will concern itself little with rules of conduct. It will be inspired by a vision of what human life may be, and will be happy with the joy of creation, living in a large free world of initiative and hope. It will love mankind, not for what they are to the outward eye, but for what imagination shows that they have it in them to become. It will not readily condemn, but it will give praise to positive achievement rather than negative sinlessness, to the joy of life, the quick affection, the creative insight, by which the world may grow young and beautiful and filled with vigour.

'Religion' is a word which has many meanings and a long history. In origin, it was concerned with certain rites, inherited from a remote past, performed originally for some reason long since forgotten, and associated from time to time with various myths to account for their supposed importance. Much of this lingers still. A religious man is one who goes to church, a communicant, one who 'practises', as Catholics say. How he behaves otherwise, or how he feels concerning life and man's place in the world, does not bear upon the question whether he is 'religious' in this simple but historically correct sense. Many men and women are religious in this sense without having in their natures anything that deserves to be called religion in the sense in which I mean the word. The mere familiarity of the church service has made them impervious to it; they are unconscious of all the history and human experience by which the liturgy has been enriched, and unmoved by the glibly repeated words of the Gospel, which condemn almost all the activities of those who fancy themselves disciples of Christ. This fate must overtake any habitual rite: it is impossible that it should continue to produce much effect after it has been performed so often as to grow mechanical.

The activities of men may be roughly derived from three sources, not in actual fact sharply separate one from another, but sufficiently distinguishable to deserve different names. The three sources I mean are instinct, mind, and spirit, and of these three it is the life of the spirit that makes religion.

The life of instinct includes all that man shares with the lower animals, all that is concerned with self-preservation and reproduction and the desires and impulses derivative from these. It includes vanity and love of possession, love of family, and even much of what makes love of country. It includes all the impulses that are essentially concerned with the biological success of oneself or one's group – for among gregarious animals the life of instinct includes the group. The impulses which it includes may not in fact make for success, and may often in fact militate against it, but are nevertheless those of which success is the *raison d'être*, those which express the animal nature of man and his position among a world of competitors.

The life of the mind is the life of pursuit of knowledge, from mere childish curiosity up to the greatest efforts of thought. Curiosity exists in animals, and serves an obvious biological purpose; but it is only in men that it passes beyond the investigation of particular objects which may be edible or poisonous, friendly or hostile. Curiosity is the primary impulse out of which the whole edifice of scientific knowledge has grown. Knowledge has been found so useful that most actual acquisition of it is no longer prompted by curiosity; innumerable other motives now contribute to foster the intellectual life. Nevertheless, direct love of knowledge and dislike of error still play a very large part, especially with those who are most successful in learning. No man acquires much knowledge unless the acquisition is in itself delightful to him, apart from any consciousness of the use to which the knowledge may be put. The impulse to acquire knowledge and the activities which centre round it constitute what I mean by the life of the mind. The life of the mind consists of thought which is wholly or partially impersonal, in the sense that it concerns itself with objects on their own account, and not merely on account of their bearing upon our instinctive life.

The life of the spirit centres round impersonal feeling, as the life of the mind centres round impersonal thought. In this sense, all art belongs to the life of the spirit, though its greatness is derived from its being also intimately bound up with the life of instinct. Art starts from instinct and rises into the region of the spirit; religion starts from the spirit and endeavours to dominate and inform the life of instinct. It is possible to feel the same interest in the joys and sorrows of others as in our own, to love and hate independently of all relation to ourselves, to care about the destiny of man and the development of the universe without a thought that we are personally involved. Reverence and worship, the sense of an obligation to mankind, the feeling of imperativeness and acting under orders which traditional religion has interpreted as Divine inspiration, all belong to the life of the spirit. And deeper than all these lies the sense of a mystery half revealed, of a hidden wisdom and glory, of a transfiguring vision in which common things lose their solid importance and become a thin veil behind which the ultimate truth of the world is dimly seen. It is such feelings that are the source of religion, and if they were to die most of what is best would vanish out of life.

Instinct, mind, and spirit are all essential to a full life; each has its own excellence and its own corruption. Each can attain a spurious excellence at the expense of the others; each has a tendency to encroach upon the others; but in the life which is to be sought all three will be developed in co-ordination, and intimately blended in a single harmonious whole. Among uncivilized men instinct is supreme, and mind and spirit hardly exist. Among educated men at the present day mind is developed, as a rule, at the expense of both instinct and spirit, producing a curious inhumanity and lifelessness, a paucity of both personal and impersonal desires, which leads to cynicism and intellectual destructiveness. Among ascetics and most of those who would be called saints, the life of the spirit has been developed at the expense of instinct and mind, producing an outlook which is impossible to those who have a healthy animal life and to those who have a love of active thought. It is not in any of these one-sided developments that we can find wisdom or a philosophy which will bring new life to the civilized world.

Among civilized men and women at the present day it is rare to find instinct, mind, and spirit in harmony. Very few have achieved a practical philosophy which gives its due place to each; as a rule, instinct is at war with either mind or spirit, and mind and spirit are at war with each other. This strife compels men and women to direct much of their energy inwards, instead of being able to expend it all in objective activities. When a man achieves a precarious inward peace by the defeat of a part of his nature, his vital force is impaired, and his growth is no longer quite healthy. If men are to remain whole, it is very necessary that they should achieve a reconciliation of instinct, mind, and spirit.

Instinct is the source of vitality, the bond that unites the life of the individual with the life of the race, the basis of all profound sense of union with others, and the means by which the collective life nourishes the life of the separate units. But instinct by itself leaves us powerless to control the forces of Nature, either in ourselves or in our physical environment, and keeps us in bondage to the same unthinking impulse by which the trees grow. Mind can liberate us from this bondage, by the power of impersonal thought, which enables us to judge critically the purely biological purposes towards which instinct more or less blindly tends. But mind, in its dealings with instinct, is *merely* critical: so far as instinct is concerned, the unchecked activity of the mind is apt to be destructive and to generate cynicism. Spirit is an antidote to the cynicism of mind: it universalizes the emotions that spring from instinct, and by universalizing them makes them impervious to mental criticism. And when thought is informed by spirit it loses its cruel, destructive quality; it no longer promotes the death of instinct, but only its purification from insistence and ruthlessness and its emancipation from the prison walls of accidental circumstance. It is instinct that gives force, mind that gives the means of directing force to desired ends, and spirit that suggests impersonal uses for force of a kind that thought cannot discredit by criticism. This is an outline of the parts that instinct, mind, and spirit would play in a harmonious life.

Instinct, mind, and spirit are each a help to the others when their development is free and unvitiated; but when corruption comes into any one of the three, not only does that one fail, but the others also become poisoned. All three must grow together. And if they are to grow to their full stature in any one man or woman, that man or woman must not be isolated, but must be one of a society where growth is not thwarted and made crooked.

The life of instinct, when it is unchecked by mind or spirit, consists of instinctive cycles, which begin with impulses to more or less definite acts, and pass on to satisfaction of needs through the consequences of these impulsive acts. Impulse and desire are not directed towards the whole cycle, but only towards its initiation: the rest is left to natural causes. We desire to eat, but we do not desire to be nourished unless we are valetudinarians. Yet without the nourishment eating is a mere momentary pleasure, not part of the general impulse to life. Men desire sexual intercourse, but they do not as a rule desire children strongly or often. Yet without the hope of children and its occasional realization, sexual intercourse remains for most people an isolated and separate pleasure, not uniting their personal life with the life of mankind, not continuous with the central purposes by which they live, and not capable of bringing that profound sense of fulfilment which comes from completion by children. Most men, unless the impulse is atrophied through disuse, feel a desire to create something, great or small according to their capacities. Some few are able to satisfy this desire: some happy men can create an Empire, a science, a poem, or a picture. The men of science, who have less difficulty than any others in finding an outlet for creativeness, are the happiest of intelligent men in the modern world, since their creative activity affords full satisfaction to mind and spirit as well as to the instinct of creation.[1] In them a beginning is to be seen of the new way of life which is to be sought; in their happiness we may perhaps find the germ of a future happiness for all mankind. The rest, with few exceptions, are thwarted in their creative impulses. They cannot build their own house or make their own garden, or direct their own labour to producing what their free choice would lead them to produce. In this way the instinct of creation, which should lead on to the life of mind and spirit, is

160

checked and turned aside. Too often it is turned to destruction, as the only effective action which remains possible. Out of its defeat grows envy, and out of envy grows the impulse to destroy the creativeness of more fortunate men. This is one of the greatest sources of corruption in the life of instinct.

The life of instinct is important, not only on its own account, or because of the direct usefulness of the actions which it inspires, but also because, if it is unsatisfactory, the individual life becomes detached and separated from the general life of man. All really profound sense of unity with others depends upon instinct, upon co-operation or agreement in some instinctive purpose. This is most obvious in the relations of men and women and parents and children. But it is true also in wider relations. It is true of large assemblies swayed by a strong common emotion, and even of a whole nation in times of stress. It is part of what makes the value of religion as a social institution. Where this feeling is wholly absent, other human beings seem distant and aloof. Where it is actively thwarted, other human beings become objects of instinctive hostility. The aloofness or the instinctive hostility may be masked by religious love, which can be given to all men regardless of their relation to ourselves. But religious love does not bridge the gulf that parts man from man: it looks across the gulf, it views others with compassion or impersonal sympathy, but it does not live with the same life with which they live. Instinct alone can do this, but only when it is fruitful and sane and direct. To this end it is necessary that instinctive cycles should be fairly often completed, not interrupted in the middle of their course. At present they are constantly interrupted, partly by purposes which conflict with them for economic or other reasons, partly by the pursuit of pleasure, which picks out the most agreeable part of the cycle and avoids the rest. In this way instinct is robbed of its importance and seriousness; it becomes incapable of bringing any real fulfilment, its demands grow more and more excessive, and life becomes no longer a whole with a single movement, but a series of detached moments, some of them pleasurable, most of them full of weariness and discouragement.

The life of the mind, although supremely excellent in itself, cannot bring health into the life of instinct, except when it results in a not too difficult outlet for the instinct of creation. In other cases it is, as a rule, too widely separated from instinct, too detached, too destitute of inward growth, to afford either a vehicle for instinct or a means of subtilizing and refining it. Thought is in its essence impersonal and detached, instinct is in its essence personal and tied to particular circumstances: between the two, unless both reach a high level, there is a war which is not easily appeased. This is the fundamental reason for vitalism, futurism, pragmatism, and the various other philosophies which advertise themselves as vigorous and virile. All these represent the attempt to find a mode of thought which shall not be hostile to instinct. The attempt, in itself, is deserving of praise, but the solution offered is far too facile. What is proposed amounts to a subordination of thought to instinct, a refusal to allow thought to achieve its own ideal. Thought which does not rise above what is personal is not thought in any true sense: it is merely a more or less intelligent use of instinct. It is thought and spirit that raise man above the level of the brutes. By discarding them we may lose the proper excellence of men, but cannot acquire the excellence of animals. Thought must achieve its full growth before a reconciliation with instinct is attempted.

When refined thought and unrefined instinct coexist, as they do in many intellectual men, the result is a complete disbelief in any important good to be achieved by the help of instinct. According to their disposition, some such men will as far as possible discard instinct and become ascetic, while others will accept it as a necessity, leaving it degraded and separated from all that is really important in their lives. Either of these courses prevents instinct from remaining vital, or from being a bond with others; either produces a sense of physical solitude, a gulf across which the minds and spirits of others may speak, but not their instincts. To very many men, the instinct of patriotism, when the war broke out, was the first instinct that had bridged the gulf, the first that had made them feel a really profound unity with others. This instinct, just because, in its intense form, it was new and unfamiliar, had remained uninfected by thought, not paralysed or devitalized by doubt and cold detachment. The sense of unity which it brought is capable of being brought by the instinctive life of more normal times, if thought and spirit are not hostile to it. And so long as this sense of unity is absent, instinct and spirit cannot be in harmony, nor can the life of the community have vigour and the seeds of new growth.

The life of the mind, because of its detachment, tends to separate a man inwardly from other men, so long as it is not balanced by the life of the spirit. For this reason, mind without spirit can render instinct corrupt or atrophied, but cannot add any excellence to the life of instinct. On this ground, some men are hostile to thought. But no good purpose is served by trying to prevent the growth of thought, which has its own insistence, and if checked in the directions in which it tends naturally, will turn into other directions where it is more harmful. And thought is in itself God-like: if the composition between thought and instinct were irreconcilable, it would be thought that ought to conquer. But the opposition is not irreconcilable: all that is necessary is that both thought and instinct should be informed by the life of the spirit.

In order that human life should have vigour, it is necessary for the instinctive impulses to be strong and direct; but in order that human life should be good, these impulses must be dominated and controlled by desires less personal and ruthless, less liable to lead to conflict than those that are inspired by instinct alone. Something impersonal and universal is needed over and above what springs out of the principle of individual growth. It is this that is given by the life of the spirit.

Patriotism affords an example of the kind of control which is needed. Patriotism is compounded out of a number of instinctive feelings and impulses: love of home, love of those whose ways and outlook resemble our own, the impulse to co-operation in a group, the sense of pride in the achievements of one's group. All these impulses and desires, like everything belonging to the life of instinct, are personal, in the sense that the feelings and actions which they inspire towards others are determined by the relation of those others to ourselves, not by what those others are intrinsically. All these impulses and desires unite to produce a love of a man's own country which is more deeply implanted in the fibre of his being, and more closely united to his vital force, than any love not rooted in instinct. But if spirit does not enter in to generalize love of country, the exclusiveness of instinctive love makes it a source of hatred of other countries. What spirit can effect is to make us realize that other countries equally are worthy of love, that the vital warmth which makes us love our own country reveals to us that it deserves to be loved, and that only the poverty of our nature prevents us from loving all countries as we love our own. In this way instinctive love can be extended in imagination, and a sense of the value of all mankind can grow up, which is more living and intense than any that is possible to those whose instinctive love is weak. Mind can only show us that it is irrational to love our own country best; it can weaken patriotism, but cannot strengthen the love of all mankind. Spirit alone can do this, by extending and universalizing the love that is born of instinct. And in doing this it checks and purifies whatever is insistent or ruthless or oppressively personal in the life of instinct.

The same extension through spirit is necessary with other instinctive loves, if they are not to be enfeebled or corrupted by thought. The love of husband and wife is capable of being a very good thing, and when men and women are sufficiently primitive, nothing but instinct and good fortune is needed to make it reach a certain limited perfection. But as thought begins to assert its right to criticize instinct the old simplicity becomes impossible. The love of husband and wife, as unchecked instinct leaves it, is too narrow and personal to stand against the shafts of satire, until it is enriched by the life of the spirit. The romantic view of marriage, which our fathers and mothers professed to believe, will not survive an imaginative peregrination down a street of suburban villas, each containing its couple, each couple having congratulated themselves as they first crossed the threshold, that here they could love in peace, without interruption from others, without contact with the cold outside world. The separateness and stuffiness, the fine names for cowardices and timid vanities, that are shut within the four walls of thousands upon thousands of little villas, present themselves coldly and mercilessly to those in whom mind is dominant at the expense of spirit.

Nothing is good in the life of a human being except the very best that his nature can achieve. As men advance, things which have been good cease to be good, merely because something better is possible. So it is with the life of instinct: for those whose mental life is strong, much that was really good while mind remained less developed has now become bad merely through the greater degree of truth in their outlook on the world. The instinctive man in love feels that his emotion is unique, that the lady of his heart has perfections such as no other woman ever equalled. The man who has acquired the power of impersonal thought realizes, when he is in love, that he is one of so many millions of men who are in love at this moment, that not more than one of all the millions can be right in thinking his love supreme, and that it is not likely that that one is oneself. He perceives that the state of being in love in those whose instinct is unaffected by thought or spirit, is a state of illusion, serving the ends of Nature and making a man a slave to the life of the species, not a willing minister to the impersonal ends which he sees to be good. Thought rejects this slavery; for no end that Nature may have in view will thought abdicate, or forgo its right to think truly. 'Better the world should perish than that I or any other human being should believe a lie' – this is the religion of thought, in whose scorching flames the dross of the world is being burnt away. It is a good religion, and its work of destruction must be completed. But it is not all that man has need of. New growth must come after the destruction, and new growth can come only through the spirit.

Both patriotism and love of man and woman, when they are merely instinctive, have the same defects: their exclusions, their enclosing walls, their indifference or hostility to the outside world. It is through this that thought is led to satire, that comedy has infected what men used to consider their holiest feelings. The satire and the comedy are justified, but not the death of instinct which they may produce if they remain in supreme command. They are justified, not as the last word of wisdom, but as the gateway of pain through which men pass to a new life, where instinct is purified and yet nourished by the deeper desires and insight of spirit.

The man who has the life of the spirit within him views the love of man and woman, both in himself and in others, quite differently from the man who is exclusively dominated by mind. He sees, in his moments of insight, that in all human beings there is something deserving of love, something mysterious, something appealing, a cry out of the night, a groping journey, and a possible victory. When his instinct loves, he welcomes its help in seeing and feeling the value of the human being whom he loves. Instinct becomes a reinforcement to spiritual insight. What instinct tells him spiritual insight confirms, however much the mind may be aware of littlenesses, limitations, and enclosing walls that prevent the spirit from shining forth. His spirit divines in all men what his instinct shows him in the object of his love.

The love of parents for children has need of the same transformation. The purely instinctive love, unchecked by thought, uninformed by spirit, is exclusive, ruthless, and unjust. No benefit to others is felt, by the purely instinctive parent, to be worth an injury to one's own children. Honour and conventional morality place certain important practical limitations on the vicarious selfishness of parents, since a civilized community exacts a certain minimum before it will give respect. But within the limits allowed by public opinion, parental affection, when it is merely instinctive, will seek the advantage of children without regard to others. Mind can weaken the impulse to injustice, and diminish the force of instinctive love, but it cannot keep the whole force of instinctive love and turn it to more universal ends. Spirit can do this. It can leave the instinctive love of children undimmed, and extend the poignant devotion of a parent, in imagination, to the whole world. And parental love itself will prompt the parent who has the life of the spirit to give to his children the sense of justice, the readiness for service, the reverence, the will that controls self-seeking, which he feels to be a greater good than any personal success.

The life of the spirit has suffered in recent times by its association with traditional religion, by its apparent hostility to the life of the mind, and by the fact that it has seemed to centre in renunciation. The life of the spirit demands readiness for renunciation when the occasion arises, but is in its essence as positive and as capable of enriching individual existence as mind and instinct are. It brings with it the joy of vision, of the mystery and profundity of the world, of the contemplation of life, and above all the joy of universal love. It liberates those who have it from the prison-house of insistent personal passion and mundane cares. It gives freedom and breadth and beauty to men's thoughts and feelings, and to all their relations with others. It brings the solution of doubts, the end of the feeling that all is vanity. It restores harmony between mind and instinct, and leads the separated unit back into his place in the life of mankind. For those who have once entered the world of thought, it is only through spirit that happiness and peace can return.

15

INHERENT TENDENCIES OF INDUSTRIALISM

Religion, in its traditional forms, appears to be difficult to combine with industrialism, although it is by no means obvious why this should be the case. Of course the successful capitalists remain religious, partly because they have every reason to thank God for their blessings, and partly because religion is a conservative force, tending to repress the rebelliousness of wage-earners. But industrial wage-earners everywhere tend to lose their religious beliefs. I think this is partly for the merely accidental reason that the teachers of religion derive their incomes either from endowments or from the bounty of the rich, and therefore often take the side of the rich, and represent religion itself as being on this side. But this cannot be the sole reason, since, if it were, wage-earners would invent democratic variants of the traditional religion, as was done by the English Independents in the seventeenth century and by the peasants who revolted against agrarian oppression in the Middle Ages and in the time of Luther. It is singularly easy to adapt Christianity to the needs of the poor, since it is only necessary to revert to the teachings of Christ. Yet that is not the course which industrial populations take; on the contrary, they tend everywhere to atheism and materialism. Their rebellion against traditional religion must, therefore, have some deeper cause than the mere accidents of present-day politics.

The chief reason is, I believe, that the welfare of industrial wage-earners is more dependent upon human agency, and less upon natural causes, than is the case with people whose manner of life is more primitive. People who depend upon the weather are always apt to be religious, because the weather is capricious and non-human, and is therefore regarded as of divine origin. On the rock-bound coast of Brittany, where Atlantic storms make sea-faring a constant and imminent peril, the fishermen are more religious than any other population of Europe; churches crowd the coast, particularly its most dangerous portions, while every headland has its Calvary, with the lofty crucifix so placed as to be visible from many miles out to sea. While the fisherman is at sea, he and his wife pray for his safe return; as soon as he lands, his relief finds expression in drunkenness. A life of this kind, exposed constantly to non-human dangers, is the most favourable to traditional religion. Indeed, the whole of traditional religion may be regarded as an attempt to mitigate the terror inspired by destructive natural forces. Sir J.G. Frazer, in his *Golden Bough*, has shown that most of the elements in Christianity are derived from worship of the spirit of vegetation, the religion invented in the infancy of agriculture to insure the fertility of the soil. Harvest Thanksgiving, prayers for rain or fair weather, and so on, illustrate what has been really vital in religion. To the peasant, fertility and famine are sent by God, and religious rites exist to secure the one and avert the other.

The industrial worker is not dependent upon the weather or the seasons, except in a very minor degree. The causes which make his prosperity or misfortune seem to him, in the main, to be purely human and easily ascertainable. It is true that natural causes affect him, but they are not such as we are accustomed to attribute to supernatural agency. God may send rain in answer to prayer, because the need of rain was felt while religion was still young and creative. But although a population may be ruined by the exhaustion of its coal-fields, no one supposes that God would create new seams, however earnestly the miners were to pray. Petroleum may bring prosperity, but if Moses had brought petroleum out of the rock instead of water, we should have regarded the occurrence as a fact of geology, not as a miracle. The fact is that religion is no longer sufficiently vital to take hold of anything new; it was formed long ago to suit certain ancient needs, and has subsisted by the force of tradition, but is no longer able to assimilate anything that cannot be viewed traditionally. Hence the alteration of daily habits and interests resulting from industrialism has proved fatal to the religious outlook, which has grown dim even among those who have not explicitly rejected it. This is, I believe, the fundamental reason for the decay of religion in modern communities. The lessened vitality of religion, which has made it unable to survive new conditions, is in the main attributable to science. It remains to be seen whether science will prove strong enough to prevent the growth of a wholly new religion, such as Marxism, adapted to the habits and aspirations of industrial communities.

16

HAS RELIGION MADE
USEFUL CONTRIBUTIONS
TO CIVILIZATION?

My own view on religion is that of Lucretius. I regard it as a disease born of fear and as a source of untold misery to the human race. I cannot, however, deny that it has made *some* contributions to civilization. It helped in early days to fix the calendar, and it caused Egyptian priests to chronicle eclipses with such care that in time they became able to predict them. These two services I am prepared to acknowledge, but I do not know of any others.

The word 'religion' is used nowadays in a very loose sense. Some people, under the influence of extreme Protestantism, employ the word to denote any serious personal convictions as to morals or the nature of the universe. This use of the word is quite unhistorical. Religion is primarily a social phenomenon. Churches may owe their origin to teachers with strong individual convictions, but these teachers have seldom had much influence upon the Churches that they founded, whereas Churches have had enormous influence upon the communities in which they flourished. To take the case that is of most interest to members of Western civilization: the teaching of Christ, as it appears in the Gospels, has had extraordinarily little to do with the ethics of Christians. The most important thing about Christianity, from a social and historical point of view, is not Christ, but the Church, and if we are to judge of Christianity as a social force, we must not go to the Gospels for our material. Christ taught that you should give your goods to the poor, that you should not fight, that you should not go to church, and that you should not punish adultery. Neither Catholics nor Protestants have shown any strong desire to follow his teaching in any of these respects. Some of the Franciscans, it is true, attempted to teach the doctrine of apostolic poverty, but the Pope condemned them, and their doctrine was declared heretical. Or, again, consider such a text as 'Judge not, that ye be not judged', and ask yourself what influence such a text has had upon the Inquisition and the Ku Klux Klan.

What is true of Christianity is equally true of Buddhism. The Buddha was amiable and enlightened; on his death-bed he laughed at his disciples for supposing that he was immortal. But the Buddhist priesthood, as it exists, for example, in Tibet, has been obscurantist, tyrannous, and cruel in the highest degree.

There is nothing accidental about this difference between a Church and its Founder. As soon as absolute truth is supposed to be contained in the sayings of a certain man, there is a body of experts to interpret his sayings, and these experts infallibly acquire power, since they hold the key to truth. Like any other privileged caste, they use their power for their own advantage. They are, however, in one respect worse than any other privileged caste, since it is their business to expound an unchanging truth, revealed once for all in utter perfection, so that they become necessarily opponents of all intellectual and moral progress. The Church opposed Galileo and Darwin; in our own day it opposes Freud. In the days of its greatest power it went further in its opposition to the intellectual life. Pope Gregory the Great wrote to a certain bishop a letter beginning: 'A report has reached us, which we cannot mention without a blush, that thou expoundest grammar to certain friends.' The bishop was compelled by pontifical authority to desist from this wicked labour, and Latinity did not recover until the Renaissance. It is not only intellectually, but also morally, that religion is pernicious. I mean by this that it teaches ethical codes which are not conducive to human happiness. When, a few years ago, a plebiscite was taken in Germany as to whether the deposed royal houses should still be allowed to enjoy their private property, the Churches in Germany officially stated that it would be contrary to the teaching of Christianity to deprive them of it. The Churches, as everyone knows, opposed the abolition of slavery as long as they dared, and with a few well-advertised exceptions they oppose at the present day every movement towards economic justice. The Pope has officially condemned Socialism.

Christianity and sex

The worst feature of the Christian religion, however, is its attitude towards sex – an attitude so morbid and so unnatural that it can only be understood when taken in relation to the sickness of the civilized world at the time when the Roman Empire was decaying.

We sometimes hear talk to the effect that Christianity improved the status of women. This is one of the grossest perversions of history that it is possible to make. Women cannot enjoy a tolerable position in society where it is considered of the utmost importance that they should not infringe a very rigid moral code. Monks have always regarded Woman primarily as the Temptress; they have thought of her mainly as the inspirer of impure lusts. The teaching of the Church has been, and still is, that virginity is best, but that for those who find this impossible marriage is permissible. 'It is better to marry than to burn', as St Paul brutally puts it. By making marriage indissoluble, and by stamping out all knowledge of the *ars amandi*, the Church did what it could to secure that the only form of sex which it permitted should involve very little pleasure and a great deal of pain. The opposition to birth control has in fact the same motive: if a woman has a child a year until she dies worn out, it is not to be supposed that she will derive much pleasure from her married life; therefore birth control must be discouraged.

The conception of Sin which is bound up with Christian ethics is one that does an extraordinary amount of harm, since it affords people an outlet for their sadism which they believe to be legitimate, and even noble. Take, for example, the question of the prevention of syphilis. It is known that, by precautions taken in advance, the danger of contracting this disease can be made negligible. Christians, however, object to the dissemination of knowledge of this fact, since they hold it good that sinners should be punished. They hold this so good that they are even willing that punishment should extend to the wives and children of sinners. There are in the world at the present moment many thousands of children suffering from congenital syphilis who would never have been born but for the desire of Christians to see sinners punished. I cannot understand how doctrines leading to this fiendish cruelty can be considered to have any good effect upon morals.

It is not only in regard to sexual behaviour, but also in regard to knowledge on sex subjects, that the attitude of Christians is dangerous to human welfare. Every person who has taken the trouble to study the question in an unbiased spirit knows that the artificial ignorance on sex subjects which orthodox Christians attempt to enforce upon the young is extremely dangerous to mental and physical health, and causes in those who pick up their knowledge by the way of 'improper' talk, as most children do, an attitude that sex is in itself indecent and ridiculous. I do not think there can be any defence for the view that knowledge is ever undesirable. I should not put barriers in the way of the acquisition of knowledge by anybody at any age. But in the particular case of sex knowledge there are much weightier arguments in its favour than in the case of most other knowledge. A person is much less likely to act wisely when he is ignorant than when he is instructed, and it is ridiculous to give young people a sense of sin because they have a natural curiosity about an important matter.

Every boy is interested in trains. Suppose we told him that an interest in trains is wicked; suppose we kept his eyes bandaged whenever he is in a train or on a railway station; suppose we never allowed the word 'train' to be mentioned in his presence and preserved an impenetrable mystery as to the means by which he is transported from one place to another. The result would not be that he would cease to be interested in trains; on the contrary, he would become more interested than ever, but would have a morbid sense of sin, because this interest had been represented to him as improper. Every boy of active intelligence could by this means be rendered in a greater or less degree neurasthenic. This is precisely what is done in the matter of sex; but, as sex is more interesting than trains, the results are worse. Almost every adult in a Christian community is more or less diseased nervously as a result of the taboo on sex knowledge when he or she was young. And the sense of sin which is thus artificially implanted is one of the causes of cruelty, timidity, and stupidity in later life. There is no rational ground of any sort or kind for keeping a child ignorant of anything that he may wish to know, whether on sex or on any other matter. And we shall never get a sane population until this fact is recognized in early education, which is impossible so long as the Churches are able to control educational politics.

Leaving these comparatively detailed objections on one side, it is clear that the fundamental doctrines of Christianity demand a great deal of ethical perversion before they can be accepted. The world, we are told, was created by a God who is both good and omnipotent. Before He created the world He foresaw all the pain and misery that it would contain; He is therefore responsible for all of it. It is useless to argue that the pain in the world is due to sin. In the first place, this is not true; it is not sin that causes rivers to overflow their banks or volcanoes to erupt. But even if it were true, it would make no difference. If I were to beget a child knowing that the child was going to be a homicidal maniac, I should be responsible for his crimes. If God knew in advance the sins of which man would be guilty, He was clearly responsible for all the consequences of those

172

sins when He decided to create man. The usual Christian argument is that the suffering in the world is a purification for sin, and is therefore a good thing. This argument is, of course, only a rationalization of sadism; but in any case it is a very poor argument. I would invite any Christian to accompany me to the children's ward of a hospital, to watch the suffering that is there being endured, and then to persist in the assertion that those children are so morally abandoned as to deserve what they are suffering. In order to bring himself to say this, a man must destroy in himself all feelings of mercy and compassion. He must, in short, make himself as cruel as the God in whom he believes. No man who believes that all is for the best in this suffering world can keep his ethical values unimpaired, since he is always having to find excuses for pain and misery.

The objections to religion

The objections to religion are of two sorts – intellectual and moral. The intellectual objection is that there is no reason to suppose any religion true; the moral objection is that religious precepts date from a time when men were more cruel than they are today, and therefore tend to perpetuate inhumanities which the moral conscience of the age would otherwise outgrow.

To take the intellectual objections first: there is a certain tendency in our practical age to consider that it does not much matter whether religious teaching is true or not, since the important question is whether it is useful. One question cannot, however, well be decided without the other. If we believe the Christian religion, our notions of what is good will be different from what they will be if we do not believe it. Therefore to Christians the effects of Christianity may seem good, while to unbelievers they may seem bad. Moreover, the attitude that one ought to believe such and such a proposition, independently of the question whether there is evidence in its favour, is an attitude which produces hostility to evidence and causes us to close our minds to every fact that does not suit our prejudices.

A certain kind of scientific candour is a very important quality, and it is one which can hardly exist in a man who imagines that there are things which it is his duty to believe. We cannot therefore really decide whether religion does good without investigating the question whether religion is true. To Christians, Mohammedans, and Jews the most fundamental question involved in the truth of religion is the existence of God. In the days when religion was still triumphant the word 'God' had a perfectly definite meaning; but as a result of the onslaughts of Rationalists the word has become paler and paler, until it is difficult to see what people mean when they assert that they believe in God. Let us take for purposes of argument Matthew Arnold's definition: 'A power not ourselves that makes for righteousness'. Perhaps we might make this even more vague, and ask ourselves whether we have any evidence of purpose in the universe apart from the purposes of living beings on the surface of this planet.

The usual argument of religious people on this subject is roughly as follows: 'I and my friends are persons of amazing intelligence and virtue. It is hardly conceivable that so much intelligence and virtue could have come about by chance. There must therefore be some one at least as intelligent and virtuous as we are, who set the cosmic machinery in motion with a view to producing Us.' I am sorry to say that I do not find this argument so impressive as it is found by those who use it. The universe is large; yet, if we are to believe Eddington, there are probably nowhere else in the universe beings as intelligent as men. If you consider the total amount of matter in the world and compare it with the amount forming the bodies of intelligent beings, you will see that the latter bears an almost infinitesimal proportion to the former. Consequently, even if it is enormously improbable that the laws of chance will produce an organism capable of intelligence out of a casual selection of atoms, it is nevertheless probable that there will be in the universe that very small number of such organisms that we do in fact find.

Then again, considered as the climax to such a vast process, we do not really seem to me sufficiently marvellous. Of course I am aware that many divines are far more marvellous than I am, and that I cannot wholly appreciate merits so far transcending my own. Nevertheless, even after making allowances under this head, I cannot but think that Omnipotence operating through all eternity might have produced something better. And then we have to reflect that even this result is only a flash in the pan. The earth will not always remain habitable; the human race will die out; and if the cosmic process is to justify itself hereafter, it will have to do so elsewhere than on the surface of our planet. And even if this should occur, it must stop sooner or later. The second law of thermodynamics makes it scarcely possible to doubt that the universe is running down, and that ultimately nothing of the slightest interest will be possible anywhere. Of course it is open to us to say that when that time comes, God will wind up the machinery again; but, if we do say this, we can base our assertion only upon faith, not upon one shred of scientific evidence. So far as scientific evidence goes, the universe has crawled by slow stages to a somewhat pitiful result on this earth, and is going to crawl by still more pitiful stages to a condition of universal death. If this is to be taken as evidence of purpose, I can only say that the purpose is one that does not appeal to me. I see no reason therefore to believe in any sort of God, however vague and however attenuated. I leave on one side the old metaphysical arguments, since religious apologists themselves have thrown them over.

The soul and immortality

The Christian emphasis on the individual soul has had a profound influence upon the ethics of Christian communities. It is a doctrine fundamentally akin to that of the Stoics, arising as theirs did in communities that could no longer cherish political hopes. The natural impulse of the vigorous person of decent character is to attempt to *do* good, but if he is deprived of all political power and of all opportunity to influence events, he will be deflected from his natural course and will decide that the important thing is to *be* good. This is what happened to the early Christians; it led to a conception of personal holiness as something quite independent of beneficent action, since holiness had to be something that could be achieved by people who were impotent in action. Social virtue came therefore to be excluded from Christian ethics. To this day conventional Christians think an adulterer more wicked than a politician who takes bribes, although the latter probably does a thousand times as much harm. The mediaeval conception of virtue, as one sees in their pictures, was of something wishy-washy, feeble, and sentimental. The most virtuous man was the man who retired from the world; the only men of action who were regarded as saints were those who wasted the lives and substance of their subjects in fighting the Turks, like St Louis. The Church would never regard a man as a saint because he reformed the finances, or the criminal law, or the judiciary. Such mere contributions to human welfare would be regarded as of no importance. I do not believe there is a single saint in the whole calendar whose saintship is due to work of public utility.

With this separation between the social and the moral person there went an increasing separation between soul and body, which has survived in Christian metaphysics and in the systems derived from Descartes. One may say, broadly speaking, that the body represents the social and public part of a man, whereas the soul represents the private part. In emphasizing the soul Christian ethics has made itself completely individualistic. I think it is clear that the net result of all the centuries of Christianity has been to make men more egotistic, more shut up in themselves, than nature made them; for the impulses that naturally take a man outside the walls of his ego are those of sex, parenthood, and patriotism or herd instinct. Sex the Church did everything it could to decry and degrade; family affection was decried by Christ himself and by the bulk of his followers; and patriotism could find no place among the subject populations of the Roman Empire. The polemic against the family in the Gospels is a matter that has not received the attention it deserves. The Church treats the Mother of Christ with reverence, but he himself showed little of this attitude. 'Woman, what have I to do with thee?' (John, ii, 4) is his way of speaking to her. He says also that he has come to set a man at variance against his father, the daughter against her mother, and the daughter-in-law against her mother-in-law, and that he that loveth father and mother more than him is not worthy of him (Matthew, x, 35, 37). All this means the break-up of the biological family tie for the sake of creed – an attitude which had a great deal to do with the intolerance that came into the world with the spread of Christianity.

This individualism culminated in the doctrine of the immortality of the individual soul, which was to enjoy hereafter endless bliss or endless woe according to circumstances. The circumstances upon which this momentous difference depended were somewhat curious. For example, if you died immediately after a priest had sprinkled water upon you while pronouncing certain words, you inherited eternal bliss; whereas, if after a long and virtuous life you happened to be struck by lightning at a moment when you were using bad language because you had broken a bootlace, you would inherit eternal torment. I do not say that the modern Protestant Christian believes this, nor even perhaps the modern Catholic Christian who has not been adequately instructed in theology; but I do say that this is the orthodox doctrine and was firmly believed until recent times. The Spaniards in Mexico and Peru used to baptize Indian infants, and then immediately dash their brains out: by this means they secured that these infants went to heaven. No orthodox Christian can find any logical reason for condemning their action, although all nowadays do so. In countless ways the doctrine of personal immortality in its Christian form has had disastrous effects upon morals, and the metaphysical separation of soul and body has had disastrous effects upon philosophy.

Sources of intolerance

The intolerance that spread over the world with the advent of Christianity is one of its most curious features, due I think to the Jewish belief in righteousness and in the exclusive reality of the Jewish God. Why the Jews should have had these peculiarities I do not know. They seem to have developed during the captivity as a reaction against the attempt to absorb the Jews into alien populations. However that may be, the Jews, and more especially the prophets, invented emphasis upon personal righteousness and the idea that it is wicked to tolerate any religion except one. These two ideas have had an extraordinarily disastrous effect upon occidental history.

The Church has made much of the persecution of Christians by the Roman state before the time of Constantine. This persecution, however, was slight and intermittent and wholly political. At all times, from the age of Constantine to the end of the seventeenth century, Christians were far more fiercely persecuted by other Christians than they ever were by the Roman emperors. Before the rise of Christianity this persecuting attitude was unknown to the ancient world except among the Jews. If you read, for example, Herodotus, you find a bland and tolerant account of the habits of the foreign nations he has visited. Sometimes, it is true, a peculiarly barbarous custom may shock him, but in general he is hospitable to foreign gods and foreign customs. He is not anxious to prove that people who call Zeus by some other name will suffer eternal perdition and ought to be put to death in order that their punishment may begin as soon as possible. This attitude has been reserved for Christians. It is true that the modern Christian is less robust, but that is not thanks to Christianity; it is thanks to the generations of freethinkers, who from the Renaissance to the present day have made Christians ashamed of many of their traditional beliefs. It is amusing to hear the modern Christian telling you how mild and rationalistic Christianity really is, and ignoring the fact that all its mildness and rationalism is due to the teaching of men who in their own day were persecuted by all orthodox Christians.

Nobody nowadays believes that the world was created in 4004 BC; but not so very long ago scepticism on this point was thought an abominable crime. My great-great-grandfather, after observing the depth of the lava on the slopes of Etna, came to the conclusion that the world must be older than the orthodox supposed, and published this opinion in a book. For this offence he was cut by the County and ostracized from society. Had he been a man in humbler circumstances, his punishment would doubtless have been more severe. It is no credit to the orthodox that they do not now believe all the absurdities that were believed 150 years ago. The gradual emasculation of the Christian doctrine has been effected in spite of the most vigorous resistance, and solely as the result of the onslaughts of freethinkers.

The doctrine of free will

The attitude of the Christians on the subject of natural law has been curiously vacillating and uncertain. There was, on the one hand, the doctrine of free will, in which the great majority of Christians believed; and this doctrine required that the acts of human beings at least should not be subject to natural law. There was, on the other hand, especially in the eighteenth and nineteenth centuries, a belief in God as the Lawgiver and in natural law as one of the main evidences of the existence of a Creator. In recent times the objection to the reign of law in the interests of free will has begun to be felt more strongly than the belief in natural law as affording evidence for a Lawgiver. Materialists used the laws of physics to show, or attempt to show, that the movements of human bodies are mechanically determined, and that consequently everything that we say and every change of position that we effect fall outside the sphere of any possible free will. If this be so, whatever may be left for our unfettered volitions is of little value. If, when a man writes a poem or commits a murder, the bodily movements involved in his act result solely from physical causes, it would seem absurd to put up a statue to him in the one case and to hang him in the other. There might in certain metaphysical systems remain a region of pure thought in which the will would be free; but, since that can only be communicated to others by means of bodily movement, the realm of freedom would be one that could never be the subject of communication, and could never have any social importance.

Then, again, evolution has had a considerable influence upon those Christians who have accepted it. They have seen that it will not do to make claims on behalf of Man which are totally different from those which are made on behalf of other forms of life. Therefore, in order to safeguard free will in Man, they have objected to every attempt at explaining the behaviour of living matter in terms of physical and chemical laws. The position of Descartes, to the effect that all lower animals are automata, no longer finds favour with liberal theologians. The doctrine of continuity makes them inclined to go a step further still and maintain that even what is called dead matter is not rigidly governed in its behaviour by unalterable laws. They seem to have overlooked the fact that, if you abolish the reign of law, you also abolish the possibility of miracles, since miracles are acts of God which contravene the laws governing ordinary phenomena. I can, however, imagine the modern liberal theologian maintaining with an air of profundity that all creation is miraculous, so that he no longer needs to fasten upon certain occurrences as special evidence of Divine intervention.

Under the influence of this reaction against natural law, some Christian apologists have seized upon the latest doctrines of the atom, which tend to show that the physical laws in which we have hitherto believed have only an approximate and average truth as applied to large numbers of atoms, while the individual electron behaves pretty much as it likes. My own belief is that this is a temporary phase, and that the physicists will in time discover laws governing minute phenomena, although these laws may differ very considerably from those of traditional physics. However that may be, it is worth while to observe that the modern doctrines as to minute phenomena have no bearing upon anything that is of practical importance. Visible motions, and indeed all motions that make any difference to anybody, involve such large numbers of atoms that they come well within the scope of the old laws. To write a poem or commit a murder (reverting to our previous illustration), it is necessary to move an appreciable mass of ink or lead. The electrons composing the ink may be dancing freely round their little ballroom, but the ballroom as a whole is moving according to the old laws of physics, and this alone is what concerns the poet and his publisher. The modern doctrines, therefore, have no appreciable bearing upon any of those problems of human interest with which the theologian is concerned.

The free-will question consequently remains just where it was. Whatever may be thought about it as a matter of ultimate metaphysics, it is quite clear that nobody believes in it in practice. Everyone has always believed that it is possible to train character; everyone has always known that alcohol or opium will have a certain effect upon behaviour. The apostle of free will maintains that a man can by will-power avoid getting drunk, but he does not maintain that when drunk a man can say 'British Constitution' as clearly as if he were sober. And everybody who has ever had to do with children knows that a suitable diet does more to make them virtuous than the most eloquent preaching in the world. The one effect that the free-will doctrine has in practice is to prevent people from following out such common-sense knowledge to its rational conclusion. When a man acts in ways that annoy us we wish to think him wicked, and we refuse to face the fact that his annoying behaviour is a result of antecedent causes which, if you follow them long enough, will take you beyond the moment of his birth, and therefore to events for which he cannot be held responsible by any stretch of imagination.

No man treats a motor car as foolishly as he treats another human being. When the car will not go, he does not attribute its annoying behaviour to sin; he does not say: 'You are a wicked motor car, and I shall not give you any more petrol until you go.' He attempts to find out what is wrong, and to set it right. An analogous way of treating human beings is, however, considered to be contrary to the truths of our holy religion. And this applies even in the treatment of little children. Many children have bad habits which are perpetuated by punishment, but will probably pass away of themselves if left unnoticed. Nevertheless, nurses with very few exceptions consider it right to inflict punishment, although by so doing they run the risk of causing insanity. When insanity has been caused it is cited in courts of law as a proof of the harmfulness of the habit, not of the punishment. (I am alluding to a recent prosecution for obscenity in the State of New York.)

Reforms in education have come very largely through the study of the insane and feeble-minded, because *they* have not been held morally responsible for their failures, and have therefore been treated more scientifically than normal children. Until very recently it was held that, if a boy could not learn his lessons, the proper cure was caning or flogging. This view is nearly extinct in the treatment of children, but it survives in the criminal law. It is evident that a man with a propensity to crime must be stopped, but so must a man who has hydrophobia and wants to bite people, although nobody considers *him* morally responsible. A man who is suffering from plague has to be imprisoned until he is cured, although nobody thinks him wicked. The same thing should be done with a man who suffers from a propensity to commit forgery; but there should be no more idea of guilt in the one case than in the other. And this is only common sense, though it is a form of common sense to which Christian ethics and metaphysics are opposed.

To judge of the moral influence of any institution upon a community, we have to consider the kind of impulse which is embodied in the institution, and the degree to which the institution increases the efficacy of the impulse in that community. Sometimes the impulse concerned is quite obvious, sometimes it is more hidden. An Alpine club, for example, obviously embodies the impulse to adventure, and a learned society embodies the impulse towards knowledge. The family as an institution embodies jealousy and parental feeling; a football club or a political party embodies the impulse towards competitive play; but the two greatest social institutions – namely, the Church and the State – are more complex in their psychological motivation. The primary purpose of the State is clearly security against both internal criminals and external enemies. It is rooted in the tendency of children to huddle together when they are frightened, and to look for a grown-up person who will give them a sense of security. The Church has more complex origins. Undoubtedly the most important source of religion is fear; this can be seen at the present day, since anything that causes alarm is apt to turn people's thoughts to God. Battle, pestilence, and shipwreck all tend to make people religious. Religion has, however, other appeals besides that of terror; it appeals especially to our human self-esteem. If Christianity is true, mankind are not such pitiful worms as they seem to be; they are of interest to the Creator of the universe, who takes the trouble to be pleased with them when they behave well and displeased when they behave badly. This is a great compliment. We should not think of studying an ants' nest to find out which of the ants performed their formicular duty, and we should certainly not think of picking out those individual ants who were remiss and putting them into a bonfire. If God does this for us, it is a compliment to our importance; and it is an even pleasanter compliment if He awards to the good among us everlasting happiness in heaven. Then there is the comparatively modern idea that cosmic evolution is all designed to bring about the sort of results which we call 'good' – that is to say, the sort of results that give us pleasure. Here again it is flattering to suppose that the universe is controlled by a Being who shares our tastes and prejudices.

The idea of righteousness

The third psychological impulse which is embodied in religion is that which has led to the conception of righteousness. I am aware that many freethinkers treat this conception with great respect, and hold that it should be preserved in spite of the decay of dogmatic religion. I cannot agree with them on this point. The psychological analysis of the idea of righteousness seems to me to show that it is rooted in undesirable passions, and ought not to be strengthened by the *imprimatur* of reason. Righteousness and unrighteousness must be taken together; it is impossible to stress the one without stressing the other also. Now, what is 'unrighteousness' in practice? It is in practice behaviour of a kind disliked by the herd. By calling it unrighteousness, and by arranging an elaborate system of ethics round this conception, the herd justifies itself in wreaking punishment upon the objects of its own dislike, while at the same time, since the herd is righteous by definition, it enhances its own self-esteem at the very moment when it lets loose its impulse to cruelty. This is the psychology of lynching, and of the other ways in which criminals are punished. The essence of the conception of righteousness, therefore, is to afford an outlet for sadism by cloaking cruelty as justice.

But, it will be said, the account you have been giving of right-eousness is wholly inapplicable to the Hebrew prophets, who, after all, on your own showing, invented the idea. There is truth in this: righteousness in the mouths of the Hebrew prophets meant what was approved by them and Yahweh. One finds the same attitude expressed in the Acts of the Apostles, where the Apostles began a pronouncement with the words: 'For it seemed good to the Holy Ghost, and to us' (Acts, xv, 28). This kind of individual certainty as to God's tastes and opinions cannot, however, be made the basis of any institution. That has always been the difficulty with which Protestantism has had to contend: a new prophet could maintain that his revelation was more authentic than those of his predecessors, and there was nothing in the general outlook of Protestantism to show that this claim was invalid. Consequently Protestantism split into innumerable sects, which weakened each other; and there is reason to suppose that a hundred years hence Catholicism will be the only effective representative of the Christian faith. In the Catholic Church inspiration such as the prophets enjoyed has its place; but it is recognized that phenomena which look rather like genuine divine inspiration may be inspired by the Devil, and it is the business of the Church to discriminate, just as it is the business of an art connoisseur to know a genuine Leonardo from a forgery. In this way revelation becomes institutionalized, and fitted into the framework of the Church. Obviously righteousness becomes institutionalized at the same time. Righteousness is what the Church approves, and unrighteousness is what it disapproves. Thus the effective part of the conception of righteousness is a justification of herd antipathy.

It would seem, therefore, that the three human impulses embodied in religion are fear, conceit, and hatred. The purpose of religion, one may say, is to give an air of respectability to these passions, provided they run in certain channels. It is because these passions make on the whole for human misery that religion is a force for evil, since it permits men to indulge these passions without restraint, where but for its sanction they might, at least to a certain degree, control them.

I can imagine at this point an objection, not likely to be urged perhaps by most orthodox believers, but nevertheless worthy to be examined. Hatred and fear, it may be said, are essential human characteristics; mankind always has felt them and always will. The best that you can do with them, I may be told, is to direct them into certain channels in which they are less harmful than they would be in certain other channels. A Christian theologian might say that their treatment by the Church is analogous to its treatment of the sex impulse, which it deplores. It attempts to render concupiscence innocuous by confining it within the bounds of matrimony. So, it may be said, if mankind must inevitably feel hatred, it is better to direct this hatred against those who are really harmful, and this is precisely what the Church does by its conception of righteousness.

To this contention there are two replies – one comparatively superficial; the other going to the root of the matter. The superficial reply is that the Church's conception of righteousness is not the best possible; the fundamental reply is that hatred and fear can, with our present psychological knowledge and our present industrial technique, be eliminated altogether from human life.

To take the first point first. The Church's conception of righteousness is socially undesirable in various ways – first and foremost in its depreciation of intelligence and science. This defect is inherited from the Gospels. Christ tells us to become as little children, but little children cannot understand the differential calculus, or the principles of currency, or the modern methods of combating disease. To acquire such knowledge is no part of our duty according to the Church. The Church no longer contends that knowledge is in itself sinful, though it did so in its palmy days; but the acquisition of knowledge, even though not sinful, is dangerous, since it may lead to pride of intellect, and hence to a questioning of the Christian dogma. Take, for example, two men, one of whom has stamped out yellow fever throughout some large region in the tropics, but has in the course of his labours had occasional relations with women to whom he was not married; while the other has been lazy and shiftless, begetting a child a year until his wife died of exhaustion, and taking so little care of his children that half of them died from preventable causes, but never indulging in illicit sexual intercourse. Every good Christian must maintain that the second of these men is more virtuous than the first. Such an attitude is, of course, superstitious and totally contrary to reason. Yet something of this absurdity is inevitable so long as avoidance of sin is thought more important than positive merit, and so long as the importance of knowledge as a help to a useful life is not recognized.

The second and more fundamental objection to the utilization of fear and hatred in the way practised by the Church is that these emotions can now be almost wholly eliminated from human nature by educational, economic, and political reforms. The educational reforms must be the basis, since men who feel hate and fear will also admire these emotions and wish to perpetuate them, although this admiration and this wish will be probably unconscious, as it is in the ordinary Christian. An education designed to eliminate fear is by no means difficult to create. It is only necessary to treat a child with kindness, to put him in an environment where initiative is possible without disastrous results, and to save him from contact with adults who have irrational terrors, whether of the dark, of mice, or of social revolution. A child must also not be subject to severe punishment, or to threats, or to grave and excessive reproof. To save a child from hatred is a somewhat more elaborate business. Situations arousing jealousy must be very carefully avoided by means of scrupulous and exact justice as between different children. A child must feel himself the object of warm affection on the part of some at least of the adults with whom he has to do, and he must not be thwarted in his natural activities and curiosities except when danger to life or health is concerned. In particular, there must be no taboo on sex knowledge, or on conversation about matters which conventional people consider improper. If these simple precepts are observed from the start, the child will be fearless and friendly.

On entering adult life, however, a young person so educated will find himself or herself plunged into a world full of injustice, full of cruelty, full of preventable misery. The injustice, the cruelty, and the misery that exist in the modern world are an inheritance from the past, and their ultimate source is economic, since life-and-death competition for the means of subsistence was in former days inevitable. It is not inevitable in our age. With our present industrial technique we can, if we choose, provide a tolerable subsistence for everybody. We could also secure that the world's population should be stationary if we were not prevented by the political influence of Churches which prefer war, pestilence, and famine to contraception. The knowledge exists by which universal happiness can be secured; the chief obstacle to its utilization for that purpose is the teaching of religion. Religion prevents our children from having a rational education; religion prevents us from removing the fundamental causes of war; religion prevents us from teaching the ethic of scientific co-operation in place of the old fierce doctrines of sin and punishment. It is possible that mankind is on the threshold of a golden age; but, if so, it will be necessary first to slay the dragon that guards the door, and this dragon is religion.

17

THE SENSE OF SIN

Concerning the sense of sin we have already had occasion to say something, but we must now go into it more fully, since it is one of the most important of the underlying psychological causes of unhappiness in adult life.

There is a traditional religious psychology of sin which no modern psychologist can accept. It was supposed, especially by Protestants, that conscience reveals to every man when an act to which he is tempted is sinful, and that after committing such an act he may experience either of two painful feelings, one called remorse, in which there is no merit, and the other called repentance, which is capable of wiping out his guilt. In Protestant countries even many of those who lost their faith continued for a time to accept with greater or smaller modifications the orthodox view of sin. In our own day, partly owing to psychoanalysis, we have the opposite state of affairs: not only do the unorthodox reject the old doctrine of sin, but many of those who still consider themselves orthodox do so likewise. Conscience has ceased to be something mysterious which, because it was mysterious, could be regarded as the voice of God. We know that conscience enjoins different acts in different parts of the world, and that broadly speaking it is everywhere in agreement with tribal custom. What then is really happening when a man's conscience pricks him?

The word 'conscience' covers as a matter of fact several different feelings; the simplest of these is the fear of being found out. You, reader, have, I am sure, lived a completely blameless life, but if you will ask some one who has at some time acted in a manner for which he would be punished if it became known you will find that when discovery seemed imminent, the person in question repented of his crime. I do not say that this would apply to the professional thief who expects a certain amount of prison as a trade risk, but it applies to what may be called the respectable offender, such as the bank manager who has embezzled in a moment of stress, or the clergyman who has been tempted by passion into some sensual irregularity. Such men can forget their crime when there seems little chance of detection, but when they are found out or in grave danger of being so, they wish they had been more virtuous, and this wish may give them a lively sense of the enormity of their sin. Closely allied with this feeling is the fear of becoming an outcast from the herd. A man who cheats at cards or fails to pay his debts of honour has nothing within himself by which to stand up against the disapproval of the herd when he is found out. In this he is unlike the religious innovator, the anarchist, and the revolutionary, who all feel that, whatever may be their fate in the present, the future is with them and will honour them as much as they are execrated in the present. These men, in spite of the hostility of the herd, do not feel sinful, but the man who entirely accepts the morality of the herd while acting against it suffers great unhappiness when he loses caste, and the fear of this disaster or the pain of it when it has happened may easily cause him to regard his acts themselves as sinful.

But the sense of sin in its most important forms is something which goes deeper. It is something which has its roots in the unconscious, and does not appear in consciousness as fear of other people's disapproval. In consciousness certain kinds of acts are labelled Sin for no reason visible to introspection. When a man commits these acts he feels uncomfortable without quite knowing why. He wishes he were the kind of man who could abstain from what he believes to be sin. He gives moral admiration only to those whom he believes to be pure in heart. He recognizes with a greater or less degree of regret that it is not for him to be a saint; indeed his conception of saintship is probably one which it is nearly impossible to carry out in an ordinary everyday life. Consequently he goes through life with a sense of guilt, feeling that the best is not for him and that his highest moments are those of maudlin penitence.

The source of all this in practically every case is the moral teaching which the man received before he was six years old at the hands of his mother or his nurse. He learned before that age that it is wicked to swear and not quite nice to use any but the most ladylike language, that only bad men drink, and that tobacco is incompatible with the highest virtue. He learned that one should never tell a lie. And above all he learned that any interest in the sexual parts is an abomination. He knew these to be the view of his mother, and believed them to be those of his Creator. To be affectionately treated by his mother, or, if she was neglectful, by his nurse, was the greatest pleasure of his life, and was only obtainable when he had not been known to sin against the moral code. He therefore came to associate something vaguely awful with any conduct of which his mother or nurse would disapprove. Gradually as he grew older he forgot where his moral code had come from and what had originally been the penalty for disobeying it, but he did not throw off the moral code or cease to feel that something dreadful was liable to happen to him if he infringed it.

Now very large parts of this infantile moral teaching are devoid of all rational foundation and such as cannot be applied to the ordinary behaviour of ordinary men. A man who uses what is called 'bad language', for example, is not from a rational point of view any worse than a man who does not. Nevertheless practically everybody in trying to imagine a saint would consider abstinence from swearing as essential. Considered in the light of reason this is simply silly. The same applies to alcohol and tobacco. With regard to alcohol the feeling does not exist in southern countries, and indeed there is an element of impiety about it, since it is known that Our Lord and the Apostles drank wine. With regard to tobacco it is easier to maintain a negative position, since all the greatest saints lived before its use was known. But here also no rational argument is possible. The view that no saint would smoke is based in the last analysis upon the view that no saint would do anything solely because it gave him pleasure. This ascetic element in ordinary morality has become almost unconscious, but it operates in all kinds of ways that make our moral code irrational. In a rational ethic it will be held laudable to give pleasure to any one, even to oneself, provided there is no counterbalancing pain to oneself or to others. The ideally virtuous man, if we had got rid of asceticism, would be the man who permits the enjoyment of all good things whenever there is no evil consequence to outweigh the enjoyment. Take again the question of lying. I do not deny that there is a great deal too much lying in the world and that we should all be the better for an increase of truthfulness; but I do deny, as I think every rational person must, that lying is in no circumstances justified. I once in the course of a country walk saw a tired fox at the last stages of exhaustion still forcing himself to run. A few minutes afterwards I saw the hunt. They asked me if I had seen the fox, and I said I had. They asked me which way he had gone, and I lied to them. I do not think I should have been a better man if I had told the truth.

But it is above all in the realm of sex that early moral teaching does harm. If a child has been conventionally educated by somewhat stern parents or nurses, the association between sin and the sex organs is so firmly established by the time he is six years old that it is unlikely ever to be completely undone throughout the rest of his life. This feeling is of course reinforced by the Oedipus complex, since the woman most loved in childhood is one with whom all sexual freedoms are impossible. The result is that adult men feel women to be degraded by sex, and cannot respect their wives unless their wives hate sexual intercourse. But the man whose wife is cold will be driven by instinct to seek instinctive satisfaction elsewhere. His instinctive satisfaction, however, even if he momentarily finds it, will be poisoned by the sense of guilt, so that he cannot be happy in any relation with a woman, whether in marriage or outside it. On the woman's side the same sort of thing happens if she has been very emphatically taught to be what is called 'pure'. She instinctively holds herself back in her sexual relations with her husband, and is afraid of deriving any pleasure from them. In the present day, however, there is very much less of this on the part of women than there was fifty years ago. I should say that at present among educated people the sex life of men is more contorted and more poisoned by the sense of sin than that of women.

There is beginning to be widespread awareness, though not of course on the part of public authorities, of the evils of traditional sex education in regard to the very young. The right rule is simple: until a child is nearing the age of puberty teach him or her no sexual morality whatever, and avoid carefully instilling the idea that there is anything disgusting in the natural bodily functions. As the time approaches when it becomes necessary to give moral instruction, be sure that it is rational, and that at every point you can give good grounds for what you say. But it is not on education that I wish to speak in this book. In this book I am concerned rather with what the adult can do to minimize the evil effects of unwise education in causing an irrational sense of sin.

The problem here is the same as has confronted us in earlier chapters, namely that of compelling the unconscious to take note of the rational beliefs that govern our conscious thought. Men must not allow themselves to be swayed by their moods, believing one thing at one moment and another at another. The sense of sin is especially prominent at moments when the conscious will is weakened by fatigue, by illness, by drink, or by any other cause. What a man feels at these moments (unless caused by drink) is supposed to be a revelation from his higher self. 'The devil was sick, the devil a saint would be.' But it is absurd to suppose that moments of weakness give more insight than moments of strength. In moments of weakness it is difficult to resist infantile suggestions, but there is no reason whatsoever for regarding such suggestions as preferable to the beliefs of the adult man when in full possession of his faculties. On the contrary, what a man deliberately believes with his whole reason when he is vigorous ought to be to him the norm as to what he had better believe at all times. It is quite possible to overcome infantile suggestions of the unconscious, and even to change the contents of the unconscious, by employing the right kind of technique. Whenever you begin to feel remorse for an act which your reason tells you is not wicked, examine the causes of your feeling of remorse, and convince yourself in detail of their absurdity. Let your conscious beliefs be so vivid and emphatic that they make an impression upon your unconscious strong enough to cope with the impressions made by your nurse or your mother when you were an infant. Do not be content with an alternation between moments of rationality and moments of irrationality. Look into the irrationality closely with a determination not to respect it, and not to let it dominate you. Whenever it thrusts foolish thoughts or feelings into your consciousness, pull them up by the roots, examine them, and reject them. Do not allow yourself to remain a vacillating creature, swayed half by reason and half by infantile folly. Do not be afraid of irreverence towards the memory of those who controlled your childhood. They seemed to you then strong and wise because you were weak and foolish; now that you are neither, it is your business to examine their apparent strength and wisdom, to consider whether they deserve that reverence that from force of habit you still bestow upon them. Ask yourself seriously whether the world is the better for the moral teaching traditionally given to the young. Consider how much of unadulterated superstition goes into the make-up of the conventionally virtuous man, and reflect that, while all kinds of imaginary moral dangers were guarded against by incredibly foolish prohibitions, the real moral dangers to which an adult is exposed were practically unmentioned. What are the really harmful acts to which the average man is tempted? Sharp practice in business of the sort not punished by law, harshness towards employees, cruelty towards wife and children, malevolence towards competitors, ferocity in political conflicts – these are the really harmful sins that are common among respectable and respected citizens. By means of these sins a man spreads misery in his immediate circle and does his bit towards destroying civilization. Yet these are not the things that make him, when he is ill, regard himself as an outcast who has forfeited all claim to divine favour. These are not the things that cause him in nightmares to see visions of his mother bending reproachful glances upon him. Why is his subconscious morality thus divorced from reason? Because the ethic believed in by those who had charge of his infancy was silly; because it was not derived from any study of the individual's duty to the community; because it was made up of old scraps of irrational taboos; and because it contained within itself elements of morbidness derived from the spiritual sickness that troubled the dying Roman Empire. Our nominal morality has been formulated by priests and mentally enslaved women. It is time that men who have to take a normal part in the normal life of the world learned to rebel against this sickly nonsense.

But if the rebellion is to be successful in bringing individual happiness and in enabling a man to live consistently by one standard, not to vacillate between two, it is necessary that he should think and feel deeply about what his reason tells him. Most men, when they have thrown off superficially the superstitions of their childhood, think that there is no more to be done. They do not realize that these superstitions are still lurking underground. When a rational conviction has been arrived at, it is necessary to dwell upon it, to follow out its consequences, to search out in oneself whatever beliefs inconsistent with the new conviction might otherwise survive, and when the sense of sin grows strong, as from time to time it will, to treat it not as a revelation and a call to higher things, but as a disease and a weakness, unless of course it is caused by some act which a rational ethic would condemn. I am not suggesting that a man should be destitute of morality, I am only suggesting that he should be destitute of superstitious morality, which is a very different thing.

But even when a man has offended against his own rational code, I doubt whether a sense of sin is the best method of arriving at a better way of life. There is in the sense of sin something abject, something lacking in self-respect. No good was ever done to any one by the loss of self-respect. The rational man will regard his own undesirable acts as he regards those of others, as acts produced by certain circumstances, and to be avoided either by a fuller realization that they are undesirable, or, where this is possible, by avoidance of the circumstances that caused them.

As a matter of fact the sense of sin, so far from being a cause of a good life, is quite the reverse. It makes a man unhappy and it makes him feel inferior. Being unhappy, he is likely to make claims upon other people which are excessive and which prevent him from enjoying happiness in personal relations. Feeling inferior, he will have a grudge against those who seem superior. He will find admiration difficult and envy easy. He will become a generally disagreeable person and will find himself more and more solitary. An expansive and generous attitude towards other people not only gives happiness to others, but is an immense source of happiness to its possessor, since it causes him to be generally liked. But such an attitude is scarcely possible to the man haunted by a sense of sin. It is an outcome of poise and self-reliance; it demands what may be called mental integration, by which I mean that the various layers of a man's nature, conscious, subconscious, and unconscious, work together harmoniously and are not engaged in perpetual battle. To produce such harmony is possible in most cases by wise education, but where education has been unwise it is a more difficult process. It is the process which the psychoanalysts attempt, but I believe that in a very great many cases the patient can himself perform the work which in more extreme cases requires the help of the expert. Do not say, 'I have no time for such psychological labours, my life is a busy one filled with affairs, and I must leave my unconscious to its tricks.' Nothing so much diminishes not only happiness but efficiency as a personality divided against itself. The time spent in producing harmony between the different parts of one's personality is time usefully employed. I do not suggest that a man should set apart, say, an hour a day for self-examination. This is to my mind by no means the best method, since it increases self-absorption, which is part of the disease to be cured, for a harmonious personality is directed outward. What I suggest is that a man should make up his mind with emphasis as to what he rationally believes, and should never allow contrary irrational beliefs to pass unchallenged or obtain a hold over him, however brief. This is a question of reasoning with himself in those moments in which he is tempted to become infantile, but the reasoning, if it is sufficiently emphatic, may be very brief. The time involved, therefore, should be negligible.

There is in many people a dislike of rationality, and where this exists the kind of thing that I have been saying will seem irrelevant and unimportant. There is an idea that rationality, if allowed free play, will kill all the deeper emotions. This belief appears to me to be due to an entirely erroneous conception of the function of reason in human life. It is not the business of reason to generate emotions, though it may be part of its function to discover ways of preventing such emotions as are an obstacle to well-being. To find ways of minimizing hatred and envy is no doubt part of the function of a rational psychology. But it is a mistake to suppose that in minimizing these passions we shall at the same time diminish the strength of those passions which reason does not condemn. In passionate love, in parental affection, in friendship, in benevolence, in devotion to science or art, there is nothing that reason should wish to diminish. The rational man, when he feels any or all of these emotions, will be glad that he feels them and will do nothing to lessen their strength, for all these emotions are parts of the good life, the life, that is, that makes for happiness both in oneself and in others. There is nothing irrational in the passions as such, and many irrational people feel only the most trivial passions. No man need fear that by making himself rational he will make his life dull. On the contrary, since rationality consists in the main of internal harmony, the man who achieves it is freer in his contemplation of the world and in the use of his energies to achieve external purposes than is the man who is perpetually hampered by inward conflicts. Nothing is so dull as to be encased in self, nothing so exhilarating as to have attention and energy directed outwards.

Our traditional morality has been unduly self-centred, and the conception of sin is part of this unwise focusing of attention upon self. To those who have never passed through the subjective moods induced by this faulty morality, reason may be unnecessary. But to those who have once acquired the sickness, reason is necessary in effecting a cure. And perhaps the sickness is a necessary stage in mental development. I am inclined to think that the man who has passed beyond it by the help of reason has reached a higher level than the man who has never experienced either the sickness or the cure. The hatred of reason which is common in our time is very largely due to the fact that the operations of reason are not conceived in a sufficiently fundamental way. The man divided against himself looks for excitement and distraction; he loves strong passions, not for sound reasons, but because for the moment they take him outside himself and prevent the painful necessity of thought. Any passion is to him a form of intoxication, and since he cannot conceive of fundamental happiness, all relief from pain appears to him solely possible in the form of intoxication. This, however, is the symptom of a deep-seated malady. Where there is no such malady, the greatest happiness comes with the most complete possession of one's faculties. It is in the moments when the mind is most active and the fewest things are forgotten that the most intense joys are experienced. This indeed is one of the best touchstones of happiness. The happiness that requires intoxication of no matter what sort is a spurious and unsatisfying kind. The happiness that is genuinely satisfying is accompanied by the fullest exercise of our faculties, and the fullest realization of the world in which we live.

Part V

RELIGION AND HISTORY

In this collection we have included segments of Russell's historical accounts of the Western religions. These segments are taken from the *History of Western Philosophy*, Russell's most comprehensive account of the role of religion in the history of Western civilization. Historians of religion will object to much of this material. Many of Russell's judgments are based on flawed secondary sources, and others are controversial and even dogmatic. On the other hand Russell's approach to the contribution of Judaism and Christianity, for good and for ill, to the development of the West is more complex and more balanced than much of his polemic and still worth considering.

Russell's approach to the role of Christianity as the source of Western civilization steers a course between those who, at the end of World War II, argued that the Judeo-Christian tradition was the source of all that was best in Western civilization – including science – and those who today conclude that the Judeo-Christian tradition is the source of all that is worst – also including science, meaning the technology that gave us imperialism and environmental disaster. The former, shaken by the devastation caused by the ideologies of the right and the left in the 1930s and 1940s, argued that neglect of the values and treasures of the Judeo-Christian tradition had undermined Western civilization and made it vulnerable to the 'paganism' of Nazism and Bolshevism. Theologians such as Reinhold Niebuhr and Paul Tillich became popular, as did the views of historians and philosophers such as Herbert Butterfield and Michael Foster, who traced the biblical origins of Western science. Today, philosophers inspired by Nietzsche and Foucault argue that science does indeed arise out of Christianity and is the source of the intellectual imperialism of the

West. Environmentalists trace the destruction of the environment to the commandment in Genesis to take dominion over nature.

Russell's account of the interaction of philosophy of religion and of science in the West is more complex than the accounts of either of these contending schools of thought. According to Russell science and religion are independent of one another and have both claimed custody over philosophy. His narrative of the history of Western philosophy is as follows: science as well as philosophy inspired by science began independently in ancient Greece among the pre-Socratics. In the course of this development science was submerged and philosophy co-opted by a rising tide of religion that originated in the cults of the Orphics. Orphism became the source of much of classical metaphysics, notably that of Plato. When classical paganism went into decline philosophy was handed over to Christianity and remained its handmaiden until the early modern period, when once again science emerged independently. Russell argues for the alliance between science and philosophy but fears that in the modern world this alliance is threatened by a deadly combination of Humean scepticism (and its attendant relativism), subjectivism and Romanticism. Russell rejects totally the claims of both schools cited above about the dependence of science on religion; he has partial agreements and disagreement with each concerning the role of religion. He agrees with contemporary critics that Western religion is the source of much that is to be condemned in the West – moral arrogance and imperialism. But he also concedes to the celebrants of Western civilization that it is the source of much that is best.

Thus Russell cites Judaism as the source of exclusivism, nationalism and the spiritual pride of the West. He acknowledges the role of both Judaism and Christianity for preserving philosophy but cites Christianity for its contribution to fanaticism and persecution in making conformity of belief crucial to salvation. One other consequence of Russell's dim view of Western religion is that in spite of the fact that he praises the scientific revolution he does not extol the superiority of European civilization. He rejected the claim of Butterfield and others, that Christian theology, because it stressed the doctrine of creation and one universe ruled by God, had prepared the way for a unified scientific universe ruled by causality. Russell proposed that Christianity unwittingly paved the way to science because of its failure to maintain conformity of belief gave rise to schisms so consuming and so bloody that by the end of the Middle Ages thinkers sought more humane and valid procedures for arriving at truth. Ironically, today Russell might be praised for one of those themes in his thought that was either ignored or was a source of dismay when it was originally published: readiness to emphasize the defects of his Western civilization. 'To us it seems that Western European civilization is civilization, this is a narrow view....There is an imperialism of culture that is harder to overcome than the imperialism of power.'

In another work based on his history, 'The Unity of Western Culture' (1949) Russell finds much to praise in the religions of the West.

> The Moral ideas that are more or less distinctive to the West, have their origin in Christianity. There is a belief, however inadequately embodied in practice, that no human being should be treated merely as a means but that each human soul is an end in itself. From this source has sprung the abolition of judicial torture and slavery, and, on our day the move against economic injustice.
>
> ('Unity of Western Culture' in *World Review*, n.s. 2 (April 1949), p. 5)

In this work he praises Judaism for introducing the idea of selfless philanthropy and brotherly love. He pays tribute to the moral integrity of early Christianity and to the fact that the call for obedience to the City of God negated the claims of the state to absolute authority over believers. Russell's account of Protestantism is the most arresting of his accounts of the contributions of religion to modernity. In this account Protestantism seems to supersede science as the moral and intellectual source of modernity. Because of Protestantism, he writes, 'Truth was no longer to be ascertained by consulting authority', a consequence that Russell must have warmly approved. But he is also candid about the problems that this gave rise to, the growth of individual anarchy, the struggle to find ways to limit subjectivism without destroying the self, all leaving us with the continuing problem of finding a formula whereby we can combine the need for social cohesion with the need for liberty.

Much that Russell writes as an historian about Western religion may not survive the careful scrutiny of the historian of Western civilization, but it provides an irreplaceable account of the complexity of his view of religion, of the relationship of philosophy to science and of the strengths and shortcomings of civilization in the West.

18

INTRODUCTION TO
HISTORY OF WESTERN PHILOSOPHY

From the sixteenth century onward, the history of European thought is dominated by the Reformation. The Reformation was a complex many-sided movement, and owed its success to a variety of causes. In the main, it was a revolt of the northern nations against the renewed dominion of Rome. Religion was the force that had subdued the North, but religion in Italy had decayed: the papacy remained as an institution, and extracted a huge tribute from Germany and England, but these nations, which were still pious, could feel no reverence for the Borgias and Medicis, who professed to save souls from purgatory in return for cash which they squandered on luxury and immorality. National motives, economic motives, and moral motives all combined to strengthen the revolt against Rome. Moreover the Princes soon perceived that, if the Church in their territories became merely national, they would be able to dominate it, and would thus become much more powerful at home than they had been while sharing dominion with the Pope. For all these reasons, Luther's theological innovations were welcomed by rulers and peoples alike throughout the greater part of northern Europe.

The Catholic Church was derived from three sources. Its sacred history was Jewish, its theology was Greek, its government and canon law were, at least indirectly, Roman. The Reformation rejected the Roman elements, softened the Greek elements, and greatly strengthened the Judaic elements. It thus co-operated with the nationalist forces which were undoing the work of social cohesion which had been effected first by the Roman Empire and then by the Roman Church. In Catholic doctrine, divine revelation did not end with the scriptures, but continued from age to age through the medium of the Church, to which, therefore, it was the duty of the individual to submit his private opinions. Protestants, on the contrary, rejected the Church as a vehicle of revelation; truth was to be sought only in the Bible, which each man could interpret for himself. If men differed in their interpretation, there was no divinely appointed authority to decide the dispute. In practice, the State claimed the right that had formerly belonged to the Church, but this was a usurpation. In Protestant theory, there should be no earthly intermediary between the soul and God.

The effects of this change were momentous. Truth was no longer to be ascertained by consulting authority, but by inward meditation. There was a tendency, quickly developed, towards anarchism in politics, and, in religion, towards mysticism, which had always fitted with difficulty into the framework of Catholic orthodoxy. There came to be not one Protestantism, but a multitude of sects; not one philosophy opposed to scholasticism, but as many as there were philosophers; not, as in the thirteenth century, one Emperor opposed to the Pope, but a large number of heretical kings. The result, in thought as in literature, was a continually deepening subjectivism, operating at first as a wholesome liberation from spiritual slavery, but advancing steadily towards a personal isolation inimical to social sanity.

Modern philosophy begins with Descartes, whose fundamental certainty is the existence of himself and his thought, from which the external world is to be inferred. This was only the first stage in a development, through Berkeley and Kant, to Fichte, for whom everything is only an emanation of the ego. This was insanity, and, from this extreme, philosophy has been attempting, ever since, to escape into the world of everyday common sense.

With subjectivism in philosophy, anarchism in politics goes hand in hand. Already during Luther's lifetime, unwelcome and unacknowledged disciples had developed the doctrine of Anabaptism, which, for a time, dominated the city of Münster. The Anabaptists repudiated all law, since they held that the good man will be guided at every moment by the Holy Spirit, who cannot be bound by formulas. From this premiss they arrive at communism and sexual promiscuity; they were therefore exterminated after a heroic resistance. But their doctrine, in softened forms, spread to Holland, England and America; historically, it is the source of Quakerism. A fiercer form of anarchism, no longer connected with religion, arose in the nineteenth century. In Russia, in Spain, and to a lesser degree in Italy, it had considerable success, and to this day it remains a bugbear of the American immigration authorities. This modern form, though anti-religious, has still much of the spirit of early Protestantism; it differs mainly in directing against secular governments the hostility that Luther directed against popes.

Subjectivity, once let loose, could not be confined within limits until it had run its course. In morals, the Protestant emphasis on the individual conscience was essentially anarchic. Habit and custom were so strong that, except in occasional outbreaks such as that of Münster, the disciples of individualism in ethics continued to act in a manner which was conventionally virtuous. But this was a precarious equilibrium. The eighteenth-century cult of 'sensibility' began to break it down: an act was admired, not for its good consequences, or for its conformity to a moral code, but for the emotion that inspired it. Out of this attitude developed the cult of the hero, as it is expressed by Carlyle and Nietzsche, and the Byronic cult of violent passion of no matter what kind.

The romantic movement, in art, in literature, and in politics, is bound up with this subjective way of judging men, not as members of a community, but as aesthetically delightful objects of contemplation. Tigers are more beautiful than sheep, but we prefer them behind bars. The typical romantic removes the bars and enjoys the magnificent leaps with which the tiger annihilates the sheep. He exhorts men to imagine themselves tigers, and when he succeeds the results are not wholly pleasant.

Against the more insane forms of subjectivism in modern times there have been various reactions. First, a halfway compromise philosophy, the doctrine of liberalism, which attempted to assign the respective spheres of government and the individual. This begins, in its modern form, with Locke, who is as much opposed to 'enthusiasm' – the individualism of the Anabaptists – as to absolute authority and blind subservience to tradition. A more thoroughgoing revolt leads to the doctrine of State worship, which assigns to the State the position that Catholicism gave to the Church, or even sometimes, to God. Hobbes, Rousseau, and Hegel represent different phases of this theory, and their doctrines are embodied practically in Cromwell, Napoleon, and modern Germany. Communism, in theory, is far removed from such philosophies, but is driven, in practice, to a type of community very similar to that which results from State worship.

Throughout this long development, from 600 BC to the present day, philosophers have been divided into those who wished to tighten social bonds and those who wished to relax them. With this difference others have been associated. The disciplinarians have advocated some system of dogma, either old or new, and have therefore been compelled to be, in a greater or less degree, hostile to science, since their dogmas could not be proved empirically. They have almost invariably taught that happiness is not the good, but that 'nobility' or 'heroism' is to be preferred. They have had a sympathy with the irrational parts of human nature, since they have felt reason to be inimical to social cohesion. The libertarians, on the other hand, with the exception of the extreme anarchists, have tended to scientific, utilitarian, rationalistic, hostile to violent passion, and enemies of all the more profound forms of religion. This conflict existed in Greece before the rise of what we recognize as philosophy, and is already quite explicit in the earliest Greek thought. In changing forms, it has persisted down to the present day, and no doubt will persist for many ages to come.

It is clear that each party to this dispute – as to all that persist through long periods of time – is partly right and partly wrong. Social cohesion is a necessity, and mankind has never yet succeeded in enforcing cohesion by merely rational arguments. Every community is exposed to two opposite dangers; ossification through too much discipline and reverence for tradition, on the one hand; on the other hand, dissolution, or subjection to foreign conquest, through the growth of an individualism and personal independence that makes co-operation impossible. In general, important civilizations start with a rigid and superstitious system, gradually relaxed, and leading, at a certain stage, to a period of brilliant genius, while the good of the old tradition remains and the evil inherent in its dissolution has not yet developed. But as the evil unfolds, it leads to anarchy, thence, inevitably, to a new tyranny, producing a new synthesis secured by a new system of dogma. The doctrine of liberalism is an attempt to escape from this endless oscillation. The essence of liberalism is an attempt to secure a social order not based on irrational dogma, and insuring stability without involving more restraints than are necessary for the preservation of the community. Whether this attempt can succeed only the future can determine.

19

THE RELIGIOUS DEVELOPMENT OF THE JEWS

The Christian religion, as it was handed over by the late Roman Empire to the barbarians, consisted of three elements: first, certain philosophical beliefs, derived mainly from Plato and the Neoplatonists, but also in part from the Stoics; second, a conception of morals and history derived from the Jews; and third, certain theories, more especially as to salvation, which were on the whole new in Christianity, though in part traceable to Orphism, and to kindred cults of the Near East.

The most important Jewish elements in Christianity appear to me to be the following:

1   A sacred history, beginning with the creation, leading to a consummation in the future, and justifying the ways of God to man.
2   The existence of a small section of mankind whom God specially loves. For Jews, this section was the Chosen People; for Christians, the elect.
3   A new conception of 'righteousness'. The virtue of almsgiving, for example, was taken over by Christianity from later Judaism. The importance attached to baptism might be derived from Orphism or from oriental pagan mystery religions, but practical philanthropy, as an element in the Christian conception of virtue, seems to have come from the Jews.
4   The Law. Christians kept part of the Hebrew Law, for instance the decalogue, while they rejected its ceremonial and ritual parts. But in practice they attached to the Creed much the same feelings that the Jews attached to the Law. This involved the doctrine that correct belief is at least as important as virtuous action, a doctrine which is essentially Hellenic. What is Jewish in origin is the exclusiveness of the elect.

5   The Messiah. The Jews believed that the Messiah would bring
    them temporal prosperity, and victory over their enemies here
    on earth; moreover, he remained in the future. For Christians,
    the Messiah was the historical Jesus, who was also identified
    with the Logos of Greek philosophy; and it was not on earth,
    but in heaven, that the Messiah was to enable his followers to
    triumph over their enemies.

6   The Kingdom of Heaven. Other-worldliness is a conception
    which Jews and Christians, in a sense, share with later Plato-
    nism, but it takes, with them, a much more concrete form than
    with Greek philosophers. The Greek doctrine – which is to be
    found in much Christian philosophy, but not in popular Chris-
    tianity – was that the sensible world, in space and time, is an
    illusion, and that, by intellectual and moral discipline, a man
    can learn to live in the eternal world, which alone is real. The
    Jewish and Christian doctrine, on the other hand, conceived the
    Other World as not *metaphysically* different from this world, but
    as in the future, when the virtuous would enjoy everlasting
    bliss and the wicked would suffer everlasting torment. This
    belief embodied revenge psychology, and was intelligible to all
    and sundry, as the doctrines of Greek philosophers were not.

To understand the origin of these beliefs, we must take account of
certain facts in Jewish history, to which we will now turn our
attention.

   The early history of the Israelites cannot be confirmed from any
source outside the Old Testament, and it is impossible to know at
what point it ceases to be purely legendary. David and Solomon
may be accepted as kings who probably had a real existence, but at
the earliest points at which we come to something certainly
historical there are already two kingdoms of Israel and Judah. The
first person mentioned in the Old Testament of whom there is an
independent record is Ahab, King of Israel, who is spoken of in an
Assyrian letter of 853 BC. The Assyrians finally conquered the
Northern kingdom in 722 BC, and removed a great part of the
population. After this time, the kingdom of Judah alone preserved
the Israelite religion and tradition. The kingdom of Judah just
survived the Assyrians, whose power came to an end with the
capture of Nineveh by the Babylonians and Medes in 606 BC. But
in 586 BC Nebuchadrezzar captured Jerusalem, destroyed the
Temple, and removed a large part of the population to Babylon.
The Babylonian kingdom fell in 538 BC, when Babylon was taken

by Cyrus, king of the Medes and Persians. Cyrus, in 537 BC, issued an edict allowing the Jews to return to Palestine. Many of them did so, under the leadership of Nehemiah and Ezra; the Temple was rebuilt, and Jewish orthodoxy began to be crystallized.

In the period of the captivity, and for some time before and after this period, Jewish religion went through a very important development. Originally, there appears to have been not very much difference, from a religious point of view, between the Israelites and surrounding tribes. Yahweh was, at first, only a tribal god who favoured the children of Israel, but it was not denied that there were other gods, and their worship was habitual. When the first Commandment says, 'Thou shalt have none other gods but me,' it is saying something which was an innovation in the time immediately preceding the captivity. This is made evident by various texts in the earlier prophets. It was the prophets at this time who first taught that the worship of heathen gods was sin. To win the victory in the constant wars of that time, they proclaimed, the favour of Yahweh was essential; and Yahweh would withdraw his favour if other gods were also honoured. Jeremiah and Ezekiel, especially, seem to have invented the idea that all religions except one are false, and that the Lord punishes idolatry.

Some quotations will illustrate their teachings, and the prevalence of the heathen practices against which they protested.

> Seest Thou not what they do in the cities of Judah and in the streets of Jerusalem? The children gather wood, and the fathers kindle the fire, and the women knead their dough, to make cakes to the queen of heaven [Ishtar], and pour out drink offerings unto other gods, that they may provoke me to anger.[1]

The Lord is angry about it. 'And they have built the high places of Tophet, which is in the valley of the son of Hinnom, to burn their sons and their daughters in the fire; which I commanded them not, neither came it into my heart.'[2]

There is a very interesting passage in Jeremiah in which he denounces the Jews in Egypt for their idolatry. He himself had lived among them for a time. The prophet tells the Jewish refugees in Egypt that Yahweh will destroy them all because their wives have burnt incense to other gods. But they refuse to listen to him, saying:

> We will certainly do whatsoever thing goeth forth out of
> our own mouth, to burn incense unto the queen of heaven,
> and to pour out drink offerings unto her, as we have done,
> we and our fathers, our kings and our princes, in the cities
> of Judah, and in the streets of Jerusalem; for then had we
> plenty of victuals, and were well, and saw no evil.

But Jeremiah assures them that Yahweh noticed these idolatrous
practices, and that misfortune has come because of them.

> Behold, I have sworn by my great name, saith the Lord,
> that my name shall no more be named in the mouth of any
> man of Judah in all the land of Egypt....I will watch over
> them for evil, and not for good; and all the men of Judah
> that are in the land of Egypt shall be consumed by the
> sword and by the famine, until there be an end of them.[3]

Ezekiel is equally shocked by the idolatrous practices of the Jews.
The Lord in a vision shows him women at the north gate of the
temple weeping for Tammuz (a Babylonian deity); then he shows
him 'greater abominations', five and twenty men at the door of the
temple worshipping the sun. The Lord declares: 'Therefore will I
also deal in fury: mine eye shall not spare, neither will I have pity:
and though they cry in mine ears with a loud voice, yet will I not
hear them.'[4]

The idea that all religions but one are wicked, and that the Lord
punishes idolatry, was apparently invented by these prophets. The
prophets, on the whole, were fiercely nationalistic, and looked
forward to the day when the Lord would utterly destroy the
gentiles.

The captivity was taken to justify the denunciations of the prophets. If Yahweh was all-powerful, and the Jews were his Chosen
People, their sufferings could only be explained by their wickedness.
The psychology is that of paternal correction: the Jews are to be
purified by punishment. Under the influence of this belief, they
developed, in exile, an orthodoxy much more rigid and much more
nationally exclusive than that which had prevailed while they were
independent. The Jews who remained behind and were not
transplanted to Babylon did not undergo this development to
anything like the same extent. When Ezra and Nehemiah came back

to Jerusalem after the captivity, they were shocked to find that mixed marriages had been common, and they dissolved all such marriages.[5]

The Jews were distinguished from the other nations of antiquity by their stubborn national pride. All the others, when conquered, acquiesced inwardly as well as outwardly; the Jews alone retained the belief in their own pre-eminence, and the conviction that their misfortunes were due to God's anger, because they had failed to preserve the purity of their faith and ritual. The historical books of the Old Testament, which were mostly compiled after the captivity, give a misleading impression, since they suggest that the idolatrous practices against which the prophets protested were a falling-off from earlier strictness, whereas in fact the earlier strictness had never existed. The prophets were innovators to a much greater extent than appears in the Bible when read unhistorically.

Some things which were afterwards characteristic of Jewish religion were developed, though in part from previously existing sources, during the captivity. Owing to the destruction of the Temple, where alone sacrifices could be offered, the Jewish ritual perforce became non-sacrificial. Synagogues began at this time, with readings from such portions of the Scriptures as already existed. The importance of the Sabbath was first emphasized at this time, and so was circumcision as the mark of the Jew. As we have already seen, it was only during the exile that marriage with gentiles came to be forbidden. There was a growth of every form of exclusiveness, 'I am the Lord your God, which have separated you from other people.'[6] 'Ye shall be holy, for I the Lord your God am holy.'[7] The Law is a product of this period. It was one of the chief forces in preserving national unity.

What we have as the Book of Isaiah is the work of two different prophets, one before the exile and one after. The second of these, who is called by biblical students Deutero-Isaiah, is the most remarkable of the prophets. He is the first who reports the Lord as saying, 'There is no God but I.' He believes in the resurrection of the body, perhaps as a result of Persian influence. His prophecies of the Messiah were, later, the chief Old Testament texts used to show that the prophets foresaw the coming of Christ.

In Christian arguments with both pagans and Jews, these texts from Deutero-Isaiah played a very important part, and for this reason I shall quote the most noteworthy of them. All nations are to be converted in the end:

They shall beat their swords into ploughshares, and their spears into pruning-hooks: nation shall not lift up sword against nation, neither shall they learn war any more.

(Is. ii, 4)

Behold a virgin shall conceive and bear a son, and shall call his name Immanuel.[8]

(As to this text there was a controversy between Jews and Christians; the Jews said that the correct translation is 'a young woman shall conceive', but the Christians thought the Jews were lying.)

The people that walked in darkness have seen a great light; they that dwell in the land of the shadow of death, upon them hath the light shined....For unto us a child is born, unto us a son is given: and the government shall be upon his shoulder: and his name shall be called Wonderful, Counsellor, the mighty God, the everlasting Father, the Prince of Peace.[9]

The most apparently prophetic of these passages is the fifty-third chapter, which contains the familiar texts:

He is despised and rejected of men; a man of sorrows and acquainted with grief....Surely he hath borne our griefs, and carried our sorrows....But he was wounded for our transgressions, he was bruised for our iniquities: the chastisement of our peace was upon him; and with his stripes we are healed....He was oppressed, and he was afflicted, yet he opened not his mouth: he is brought as a lamb to the slaughter, and as a sheep before her shearers is dumb, so he openeth not his mouth.

The inclusion of the gentiles in the ultimate salvation is explicit: 'And the gentiles shall come to thy light, and kings to the brightness of thy rising.'[10]

After Ezra and Nehemiah, the Jews for a while disappear from history. The Jewish State survived as a theocracy, but its territory was very small – only the region of ten to fifteen miles around Jerusalem, according to E. Bevan.[11] After Alexander, it became a disputed territory between the Ptolemies and Seleucids. This, however, seldom involved fighting in actual Jewish territory, and left the Jews, for a long time, to the free exercise of their religion.

Their moral maxims, at this time, are set forth in Ecclesiasticus, probably written about 200 BC. Until recently, this book was only known in a Greek version; this is the reason for its being banished to the Apocrypha. But a Hebrew manuscript has lately been discovered, in some respects different from the Greek text translated in our version of the Apocrypha. The morality taught is very mundane. Reputation among neighbours is highly prized. Honesty is the best policy, because it is useful to have Yahweh on your side. Almsgiving is recommended. The only sign of Greek influence is in the praise of medicine.

Slaves must not be treated too kindly. 'Fodder, a wand, and burdens, are for the ass: and bread, correction, and work, for a servant....Set him to work, as is fit for him: if he be not obedient, put on more heavy fetters' (xxiii, 24, 28). At the same time, remember that you have paid a price for him, and that if he runs away you will lose your money; this sets a limit to profitable severity (Ibid., 30, 31). Daughters are a great source of anxiety; apparently in the writer's day they were much addicted to immorality (xlii, 9–11). He has a low opinion of women: 'From garments cometh a moth, and from women wickedness' (Ibid., 13). It is a mistake to be cheerful with your children; the right course is to 'bow down their neck from their youth' (vii. 23, 24).

Altogether, like the elder Cato, he represents the morality of the virtuous businessman in a very unattractive light.

This tranquil existence of comfortable self-righteousness was rudely interrupted by the Seleucid king Antiochus IV, who was determined to hellenize all his dominions. In 175 BC he established a gymnasium in Jerusalem, and taught young men to wear Greek hats and practise athletics. In this he was helped by a hellenizing Jew named Jason, whom he made high priest. The priestly aristocracy had become lax, and had felt the attraction of Greek civilization; but they were vehemently opposed by a party called the 'Hasidim' (meaning 'Holy'), who were strong among the rural population.[12] When, in 170 BC, Antiochus became involved in war with Egypt, the Jews rebelled. Thereupon Antiochus took the holy vessels from the Temple, and placed in it the image of the God. He identified Yahweh with Zeus, following a practice which had been successful everywhere else.[13] He resolved to extirpate the Jewish religion, and to stop circumcision and the observance of the laws relating to food. To all this Jerusalem submitted, but outside Jerusalem the Jews resisted with the utmost stubbornness.

The history of this period is told in the first Book of Maccabees. The first chapter tells how Antiochus decreed that all the inhabitants of his kingdom should be one people, and abandon their separate laws. All the heathen obeyed, and many of the Israelites, although the king commanded that they should profane the Sabbath, sacrifice swine's flesh, and leave their children uncircumcised. All who disobeyed were to suffer death. Many, nevertheless, resisted.

> They put to death certain women, that had caused their children to be circumcised. And they hanged the infants about their necks, and rifled their houses, and slew them that had circumcised them. Howbeit many in Israel were fully resolved and confirmed in themselves not to eat any unclean thing. Wherefore they chose rather to die, that they might not be defiled with meats, and that they might not profane the holy covenant: so then they died.[14]

It was at this time that the doctrine of immortality came to be widely believed among the Jews. It had been thought that virtue would be rewarded here on earth; but persecution, which fell upon the most virtuous, made it evident that this was not the case. In order to safeguard divine justice, therefore, it was necessary to believe in rewards and punishments hereafter. This doctrine was not universally accepted among the Jews; in the time of Christ, the Sadducees still rejected it. But by that time they were a small party, and in later times all Jews believed in immortality.

The revolt against Antiochus was led by Judas Maccabaeus, an able military commander, who first recaptured Jerusalem (164 BC), and then embarked upon aggression. Sometimes he killed all the males, sometimes he circumcised them by force. His brother Jonathan was made high priest, was allowed to occupy Jerusalem with a garrison, and conquered part of Samaria, acquiring Joppa and Akra. He negotiated with Rome, and was successful in securing complete autonomy. His family were high priests until Herod, and are known as the Hasmonean dynasts.

In enduring and resisting persecution the Jews of this time showed immense heroism, although in defence of things that do not strike us as important, such as circumcision and the wickedness of eating pork.

The time of the persecution by Antiochus IV was crucial in Jewish history. The Jews of the Dispersion were, at this time, becoming more and more hellenized; the Jews of Judea were few; and even among them the rich and powerful were inclined to acquiesce in Greek innovations. But for the heroic resistance of the Hasidim, the Jewish religion might easily have died out. If this had happened, neither Christianity nor Islam could have existed in anything like the form they actually took. Townsend, in his Introduction to the translation of the Fourth Book of Maccabees, says:

> It has been finely said that if Judaism as a religion had perished under Antiochus, the seed-bed of Christianity would have been lacking; and thus the blood of the Maccabean martyrs, who saved Judaism, ultimately became the seed of the Church. Therefore as not only Christendom but also Islam derive their monotheism from a Jewish source, it may well be that the world to-day owes the very existence of monotheism both in the East and in the West to the Maccabees.[15]

The Maccabees themselves, however, were not admired by later Jews, because their family, as high priests, adopted, after their successes, a worldly and temporizing policy. Admiration was for the martyrs. The Fourth Book of Maccabees, written probably in Alexandria about the time of Christ, illustrates this as well as some other interesting points. In spite of its title, it nowhere mentions the Maccabees, but relates the amazing fortitude, first of an old man, and then of seven young brothers, all of whom were first tortured and then burnt by Antiochus, while their mother, who was present, exhorted them to stand firm. The king, at first, tried to win them by friendliness, telling them that, if they would only consent to eat pork, he would take them into his favour, and secure successful careers for them. When they refused, he showed them the instruments of torture. but they remained unshakeable, telling him that he would suffer eternal torment after death, while they would inherit everlasting bliss. One by one, in each other's presence, and in that of their mother, they were first exhorted to eat pork, then, when they refused, tortured and killed. At the end, the king turned round to his soldiers and told them he hoped they would profit by such an example of courage. The account is of course embellished by legend, but it is historically true that the persecution was severe and was endured heroically; also that the main points at issue were circumcision and eating pork.

This book is interesting in another respect. Although the writer is obviously an orthodox Jew, he uses the language of the Stoic philosophy, and is concerned to prove that the Jews live most completely in accordance with its precepts. The book opens with the sentence: 'Philosophical in the highest degree is the question I propose to discuss, namely whether the Inspired Reason is supreme ruler over the passions; and to the philosophy of it I would seriously entreat your earnest attention.'

Alexandrian Jews were willing, in philosophy, to learn from the Greeks, but they adhered with extraordinary tenacity to the Law, especially circumcision, observance of the Sabbath, and abstinence from pork and other unclean meats. From the time of Nehemiah till after the fall of Jerusalem in AD 70, the importance that they attached to the Law steadily increased. They no longer tolerated prophets who had anything new to say. Those among them who felt impelled to write in the style of the prophets pretended that they had discovered an old book, by Daniel or Solomon or some other ancient of impeccable respectability. Their ritual peculiarities held them together as a nation, but emphasis on the Law gradually destroyed originality and made them intensely conservative. This rigidity makes the revolt of St Paul against the domination of the Law very remarkable.

The New Testament, however, is not such a completely new beginning as it is apt to seem to those who know nothing of Jewish literature in the times just before the birth of Christ. Prophetic fervour was by no means dead, though it had to adopt the device of pseudonymity, in order to obtain a hearing. Of the greatest interest, in this respect, is the Book of Enoch,[16] a composite work, due to various authors, the earliest being slightly before the time of the Maccabees, and the latest about 64 BC. Most of it professes to relate apocalyptic visions of the patriarch Enoch. It is very important for the side of Judaism which turned to Christianity. The New Testament writers are familiar with it; St Jude considers it to be actually by Enoch. Early Christian Fathers, for instance Clement of Alexandria and Tertullian, treated it as canonical, but Jerome and Augustine rejected it. It fell, consequently, into oblivion, and was lost until, early in the nineteenth century, three manuscripts of it, in Ethiopic, were found in Abyssinia. Since then, manuscripts of parts of it have been found in Greek and Latin versions. It appears to have been originally written partly in Hebrew, partly in Aramaic. Its authors were members of the Hasidim, and their successors, the Pharisees. It denounces kings and princes, meaning the Hasmonean dynasty and the Sadducees. It influenced New Testament doctrine, particularly as regards the Messiah, Sheol (hell), and demonology.

The book consists mainly of 'parables', which are more cosmic than those of the New Testament. There are visions of heaven and hell, of the Last Judgment, and so on; one is reminded of the first two Books of *Paradise Lost* where the literary quality is good, and of Blake's Prophetic Books where it is inferior.

There is an expansion of Genesis vi. 2, 4, which is curious and Promethean. The angels taught men metallurgy, and were punished for revealing 'eternal secrets'. They were also cannibals. The angels that had sinned became pagan gods, and their women became sirens; but at the last, they were punished with everlasting torments.

There are descriptions of heaven and hell which have considerable literary merit. The Last Judgment is performed by 'the Son of Man, who hath righteousness' and who sits on the throne of his glory. Some of the gentiles, at the last, will repent and be forgiven; but most gentiles, and all hellenizing Jews, will suffer eternal damnation, for the righteous will pray for vengeance, and their prayer will be granted.

There is a section on astronomy, where we learn that the sun and moon have chariots driven by the wind, that the year consists of 364 days, that human sin causes the heavenly bodies to depart from their courses, and that only the virtuous can know astronomy. Falling stars are falling angels, and are punished by the seven archangels.

Next comes sacred history. Up to the Maccabees, this pursues the course known from the Bible in its earlier portions, and from history in the later parts. Then the author goes on into the future: the New Jerusalem, the conversion of the remnant of the gentiles, the resurrection of the righteous, and the Messiah.

There is a great deal about the punishment of sinners and the reward of the righteous, who never display an attitude of Christian forgiveness towards sinners. 'What will ye do, ye sinners, and whither will ye flee on that day of judgment, when ye hear the voice of the prayer of the righteous?' 'Sin has not been sent upon the earth, but man of himself has created it.' Sins are recorded in heaven. 'Ye sinners shall be cursed for ever, and ye shall have no peace.' Sinners may be happy all their lives, and even in dying, but their souls descend into Sheol, where they shall suffer 'darkness and chains and a burning flame'. But as for the righteous, 'I and my Son will be united with them for ever.'

The last words of the book are:

> To the faithful he will give faithfulness in the habitation of upright paths. And they shall see those who were born in darkness led into darkness, while the righteous shall be resplendent. And the sinners shall cry aloud and see them resplendent, and they indeed will go where days and seasons are prescribed for them.

Jews, like Christians, thought much about sin, but few of them thought of *themselves* as sinners. This was, in the main, a Christian innovation, introduced by the parable of the Pharisee and the publican, and taught as a virtue in Christ's denunciations of the Scribes and Pharisees. The Christians endeavoured to practise Christian humility; the Jews, in general, did not.

There are, however, important exceptions among orthodox Jews just before the time of Christ. Take, for instance, 'The Testaments of the Twelve Patriarchs,' written between 109 and 107 BC by a Pharisee who admired John Hyrcanus, a high priest of the Hasmonean dynasty. This book, in the form in which we have it, contains Christian interpolations, but these are all concerned with dogma. When they are excised, the ethical teaching remains closely similar to that of the Gospels. As the Rev. Dr R.H. Charles says:

> The Sermon on the Mount reflects in several instances the spirit and even reproduces the very phrases of our text: many passages in the Gospels exhibit traces of the same, and St Paul seems to have used the book as a vade mecum.
>
> (op. cit., pp. 291–292)

We find in this book such precepts as the following:

> Love ye one another from the heart; and if a man sin against thee, speak peaceably to him, and in thy soul hold not guile; and if he repent and confess, forgive him. But if he deny it, do not get into a passion with him, lest catching the poison from thee he take to swearing, and so then

214

sin doubly....And if he be shameless and persist in wrong-doing, even so forgive him from the heart, and leave to God the avenging.

Dr Charles is of opinion that Christ must have been acquainted with this passage. Again we find:

Love the Lord and your neighbour.

Love the Lord through all your life, and one another with a true heart.

I love the Lord; likewise also every man with all my heart.

These are to be compared with Matthew xxii, 37–39. There is a reprobation of all hatred in 'The Testaments of the Twelve Patriarchs'; for instance:

Anger is blindness, and does not suffer one to see the face of any man with truth.

Hatred, therefore, is evil; for it constantly mateth with lying.

The author of this book, as might be expected, holds that not only the Jews, but all the gentiles, will be saved.

Christians have learnt from the Gospels to think ill of Pharisees, yet the author of this book was a Pharisee, and he taught, as we have seen, those very ethical maxims which we think of as most distinctive of Christ's preaching. The explanation, however, is not difficult. In the first place, he must have been, even in his own day, an exceptional Pharisee; the more usual doctrine was, no doubt, that of the Book of Enoch. In the second place, we know that all movements tend to ossify; who could infer the principles of Jefferson from those of the Daughters of the American Revolution? In the third place, we know, as regards the Pharisees in particular, that their devotion to the law, as the absolute and final truth, soon put an end to all fresh and living thought and feeling among them. As Dr Charles says:

When Pharisaism, breaking with the ancient ideals of its party, committed itself to political interests and movements, and concurrently therewith surrendered itself more and more wholly to the study of the letter of the Law, it soon ceased to offer scope for the development of such a lofty system of ethics as the Testaments [of the Patriarchs] attest, and so the true successors of the early Hasids and their teaching quitted Judaism and found their natural home in the bosom of primitive Christianity.

After a period of rule by the High Priests, Mark Antony made his friend Herod King of the Jews. Herod was a gay adventurer, often on the verge of bankruptcy, accustomed to Roman society, and very far removed from Jewish piety. His wife was of the family of the high priests, but he was an Idumaean, which alone would suffice to make him an object of suspicion to the Jews. He was a skilful time-server, and deserted Antony promptly when it became evident that Octavius was going to be victorious. However, he made strenuous attempts to reconcile the Jews to his rule. He rebuilt the Temple, though in a hellenistic style, with rows of Corinthian pillars; but he placed over the main gate a large golden eagle, thereby infringing the second Commandment. When it was rumoured that he was dying, the Pharisees pulled down the eagle, but he, in revenge, caused a number of them to be put to death. He died in 4 BC, and soon after his death the Romans abolished the kingship, putting Judea under a procurator. Pontius Pilate, who became procurator in AD 26, was tactless, and was soon retired.

In AD 66, the Jews, led by the party of the Zealots, rebelled against Rome. They were defeated, and Jerusalem was captured in AD 70. The Temple was destroyed, and few Jews were left in Judea.

The Jews of the Dispersion had become important centuries before this time. The Jews had been originally an almost wholly agricultural people, but they learnt trading from the Babylonians during the captivity. Many of them remained in Babylon after the time of Ezra and Nehemiah, and among these some were very rich. After the foundation of Alexandria, great numbers of Jews settled in that city; they had a special quarter assigned to them, not as a ghetto, but to keep them from danger of pollution by contact with gentiles. The Alexandrian Jews became much more hellenized than those of Judea, and forgot Hebrew. For this reason it became necessary to translate the Old Testament into Greek; the result was the Septuagint. The Pentateuch was translated in the middle of the third century BC; the other parts somewhat later.

Legends arose about the Septuagint, so called because it was the work of seventy translators. It was said that each of the seventy translated the whole independently, and that when the versions were compared they were found to be identical down to the smallest detail, having all been divinely inspired. Nevertheless, later scholarship showed that the Septuagint was gravely defective. The Jews, after the rise of Christianity, made little use of it, but reverted to reading the Old Testament in Hebrew. The early Christians, on the contrary, few of whom knew Hebrew, depended upon the Septuagint, or upon translations from it into Latin. A better text was produced by the labours of Origen in the third century, but those who only knew Latin had very defective versions until Jerome, in the fifth century, produced the Vulgate. This was, at first, received with much criticism, because he had been helped by Jews in establishing the text, and many Christians thought that Jews had deliberately falsified the prophets in order that they should not seem to foretell Christ. Gradually, however, the work of St Jerome was accepted, and it remains to this day authoritative in the Catholic Church.

The philosopher Philo, who was a contemporary of Christ, is the best illustration of Greek influence on the Jews in the sphere of thought. While orthodox in religion, Philo is, in philosophy, primarily a Platonist; other important influences are those of the Stoics and Neo-pythagoreans. While his influences among the Jews ceased after the fall of Jerusalem, the Christian Fathers found that he had shown the way to reconcile Greek philosophy with acceptance of the Hebrew scriptures.

In every important city of antiquity there came to be considerable colonies of Jews, who shared with the representatives of other Eastern religions an influence upon those who were not content either with scepticism or with the official religions of Greece and Rome. Many converts were made to Judaism, not only in the Empire, but also in South Russia. It was probably to Jewish and semi-Jewish circles that Christianity first appealed. Orthodox Judaism, however, became more orthodox and more narrow after the fall of Jerusalem, just as it had done after the earlier fall due to Nebuchadrezzar. After the first century, Christianity also crystallized, and the relations of Judaism and Christianity were wholly hostile and external; as we shall see, Christianity powerfully stimulated anti-Semitism. Throughout the Middle Ages, Jews had no part in the culture of Christian countries, and were too severely persecuted to be able to make contributions to civilization, beyond supplying capital for the building of cathedrals and such enterprises. It was only among the Mohammedans, at that period, that Jews were treated humanely, and were able to pursue philosophy and enlightened speculation.

Throughout the Middle Ages, the Mohammedans were more civilized and more humane than the Christians. Christians persecuted Jews, especially at times of religious excitement; the Crusades were associated with appalling pogroms. In Mohammedan countries, on the contrary, Jews at most times were not in any way ill treated. Especially in Moorish Spain, they contributed to learning; Maimonides (1135–1204), who was born at Cordova, is regarded by some as the source of much of Spinoza's philosophy. When the Christians reconquered Spain, it was largely the Jews who transmitted to them the learning of the Moors. Learned Jews, who knew Hebrew, Greek, and Arabic, and were acquainted with the philosophy of Aristotle, imparted their knowledge to less learned schoolmen. They transmitted also less desirable things, such as alchemy and astrology.

After the Middle Ages, the Jews still contributed largely to civilization as individuals, but no longer as a race.

20

CHRISTIANITY DURING THE FIRST FOUR CENTURIES

Christianity, at first, was preached by Jews to Jews, as a reformed Judaism. St James, and to a lesser extent St Peter, wished it to remain no more than this, and they might have prevailed but for St Paul, who was determined to admit gentiles without demanding circumcision or submission to the Mosaic Law. The contention between the two factions is related in the Acts of the Apostles, from a Pauline point of view. The communities of Christians that St Paul established in many places were, no doubt, composed partly of converts from among the Jews, partly of gentiles seeking a new religion. The certainties of Judaism made it attractive in that age of dissolving faiths, but circumcision was an obstacle to the conversion of men. The ritual laws in regard to food were also inconvenient. These two obstacles, even if there had been no others, would have made it almost impossible for the Hebrew religion to become universal. Christianity, owing to St Paul, retained what was attractive in the doctrines of the Jews, without the features that gentiles found hardest to assimilate.

The view that the Jews were the Chosen People remained, however, obnoxious to Greek pride. This view was radically rejected by the Gnostics. They, or at least some of them, held that the sensible world had been created by an inferior deity named Ialdabaoth, the rebellious son of Sophia (heavenly wisdom). He, they said, is the Yahweh of the Old Testament, while the serpent, so far from being wicked, was engaged in warning Eve against his deceptions. For a long time, the supreme Deity allowed Ialdabaoth free play; at last He sent His Son to inhabit temporarily the body of the man Jesus, and to liberate the world from the false teaching of Moses. Those who held this view, or something like it, combined it, as a rule, with a Platonic philosophy; Plotinus, as we saw, found some difficulty in refuting it. Gnosticism afforded a halfway house between philosophic paganism and Christianity, for, while it honoured Christ, it thought ill of the Jews. The same was true, later, of Manichaeism, through which St Augustine came to the Catholic faith. Manichaeism combined Christian and Zoroastrian elements, teaching that evil is a positive principle, embodied in matter, while the good principle is embodied in spirit. It condemned meat-eating, and all sex, even in marriage. Such intermediate doctrines helped much in the gradual conversion of cultivated men of Greek speech; but the New Testament warns true believers against them: 'O Timothy, keep that which is committed to thy trust, avoiding profane and vain babblings, and oppositions of science [Gnosis] falsely so called: which some professing have erred concerning the faith.'[1]

Gnostics and Manichaeans continued to flourish until the government became Christian. After that time they were led to conceal their beliefs, but they still had a subterranean influence. One of the doctrines of a certain sect of Gnostics was adopted by Mohammed. They taught that Jesus was a mere man, and that the Son of God descended upon him at the baptism, and abandoned him at the time of the Passion. In support of this view they appealed to the text: 'My God, my God, why hast thou forsaken me?'[2] – a text which, it must be confessed, Christians have always found difficult. The Gnostics considered it unworthy of the Son of God to be born, to be an infant, and, above all, to die on the cross; they said that these things had befallen the man Jesus, but not the divine Son of God. Mohammed, who recognized Jesus as a prophet, though not as divine, had a strong class feeling that prophets ought not to come to a bad end. He therefore adopted the view of the Docetics (a Gnostic sect), according to which it was a mere phantom that hung upon the cross, upon which, impotently and ignorantly, Jews and Romans wreaked their ineffectual vengeance. In this way, something of Gnosticism passed over into the orthodox doctrine of Islam.

The attitude of Christians to contemporary Jews early became hostile. The received view was that God had spoken to the patriarchs and prophets, who were holy men, and had foretold the coming of Christ; but when Christ came, the Jews failed to recognize him, and were thenceforth to be accounted wicked. Moreover Christ had abrogated the Mosaic Law, substituting the two commandments to love God and our neighbour; this, also, the Jews perversely failed to recognize. As soon as the State became Christian, anti-Semitism, in its medieval form, began, nominally as a manifestation of Christian zeal. How far the economic motives, by which it was inflamed in later times, operated in the Christian Empire, it seems impossible to ascertain.

In proportion as Christianity became hellenized, it became theological. Jewish theology was always simple. Yahweh developed from a tribal deity into the sole omnipotent God who created heaven and earth; divine justice, when it was seen not to confer earthly prosperity upon the virtuous, was transferred to heaven, which entailed belief in immortality. But throughout its evolution the Jewish creed involved nothing complicated and metaphysical; it had no mysteries, and every Jew could understand it.

This Jewish simplicity, on the whole, still characterizes the synoptic Gospels (Matthew, Mark, and Luke), but has already disappeared in St John, where Christ is identified with the Platonic-Stoic Logos. It is less Christ the Man than Christ the theological figure that interests the fourth evangelist. This is still more true of the Fathers; you will find, in their writings, many more allusions to St John than to the other three gospels put together. The Pauline epistles also contain much theology, especially as regards salvation; at the same time they show a considerable acquaintance with Greek culture – a quotation from Menander, an allusion to Epimenides the Cretan who said that all Cretans are liars, and so on. Nevertheless St Paul[3] says: 'Beware lest any man spoil you through philosophy and vain deceit.'

The synthesis of Greek philosophy and Hebrew scriptures remained more or less haphazard and fragmentary until the time of Origen (AD 185–254). Origen, like Philo, lived in Alexandria, which, owing to commerce and the university, was, from its foundation to its fall, the chief centre of learned syncretism. Like his contemporary Plotinus, he was a pupil of Ammonius Saccas, whom many regard as the founder of Neoplatonism. His doctrines, as set forth in his work *De Principiis*, have much affinity to those of Plotinus – more, in fact, than is compatible with orthodoxy.

There is, Origen says, nothing wholly incorporeal except God – Father, Son, and Holy Ghost. The stars are living rational beings, to whom God has given souls that were already in existence. The sun, he thinks, can sin. The souls of men, as Plato taught, come to them at birth from elsewhere, having existed even since the Creation. *Nous* and soul are distinguished more or less as in Plotinus. When *Nous* falls away, it becomes soul; soul, when virtuous, becomes *Nous*. Ultimately all spirits will become wholly submissive to Christ, and will then be bodiless. Even the Devil will be saved at the last.

Origen, in spite of being recognized as one of the Fathers, was, in later times, condemned as having maintained four heresies:

1   The pre-existence of souls, as taught by Plato.
2   That the human nature of Christ, and not only his divine nature, existed before the Incarnation.
3   That, at the resurrection, our bodies will be transformed into absolutely ethereal bodies.
4   That all men, and even devils, shall be saved at the last.

St Jerome, who had expressed a somewhat unguarded admiration of Origen for his work in establishing the text of the Old Testament, found it prudent, subsequently, to expend much time and vehemence in repudiating his theological errors.

Origen's aberrations were not only theological; in his youth he was guilty of an irreparable error through a too literal interpretation of the text: 'There be eunuchs, which have made themselves eunuchs for the kingdom of heaven's sake.'[4] This method of escaping the temptations of the flesh, which Origen rashly adopted, had been condemned by the Church; moreover it made him ineligible for holy orders, although some ecclesiastics seem to have thought otherwise, thereby giving rise to unedifying controversies.

Origen's longest work is a book entitled *Against Celsus*. Celsus was the author of a book (now lost) against Christianity, and Origen set to work to answer him point by point. Celsus begins by objecting to Christians because they belong to illegal associations; this Origen does not deny, but claims to be a virtue, like tyrannicide. He then comes to what is no doubt the real basis for the dislike of Christianity: Christianity, says Celsus, comes from the Jews, who are barbarians; and only Greeks can extract sense out of the teachings of barbarians. Origen replies that any one coming from Greek philosophy to the Gospels would conclude that they are true, and supply a demonstration satisfying to the Greek intellect. But further,

> The Gospel has a demonstration of its own, more divine than any established by Grecian dialectics. And this diviner method is called by the apostle the 'manifestation of the Spirit and of power'; of 'the Spirit', on account of the prophecies, which are sufficient to produce faith in any one who reads them, especially in those things which relate to Christ; and of 'power', because of the signs and wonders

which we must believe to have been performed, both on many other grounds, and on this, that traces of them are still preserved among those who regulate their lives by the precepts of the Gospel.[5]

This passage is interesting, as showing already the twofold argument for belief which is characteristic of Christian philosophy. On the one hand, pure reason, rightly exercised, suffices to establish the essentials of the Christian faith, more especially God, immortality, and free will. But on the other hand the Scriptures prove not only these bare essentials, but much more; and the divine inspiration of the Scriptures is proved by the fact that the prophets foretold the coming of the Messiah, by the miracles, and by the beneficent effects of belief on the lives of the faithful. Some of these arguments are now considered out of date, but the last of them was still employed by William James. All of them, until the Renaissance, were accepted by every Christian philosopher.

Some of Origen's arguments are curious. He says that magicians invoke the 'God of Abraham', often without knowing who He is; but apparently this invocation is specially potent. Names are essential in magic; it is not indifferent whether God is called by His Jewish, Egyptian, Babylonian, Greek, or Brahman name. Magic formulae lose their efficacy when translated. One is led to suppose that the magicians of the time used formulae from all known religions, but if Origen is right, those derived from Hebrew sources were the most effective. The argument is the more curious as he points out that Moses forbade sorcery.[6]

Christians, we are told, should not take part in the government of the State, but only of the 'divine nation', i.e., the Church.[7] This doctrine, of course, was somewhat modified after the time of Constantine, but something of it survived. It is implicit in St Augustine's *City of God*. It led churchmen, at the time of the fall of the Western Empire, to look on passively at secular disasters, while they exercised their very great talents in church discipline, theological controversy, and the spread of monasticism. Some trace of it still exists: most people regard politics as 'worldly' and unworthy of any really holy man.

Church government developed slowly during the first three centuries, and rapidly after the conversion of Constantine. Bishops were popularly elected; gradually they acquired considerable power over Christians in their own dioceses, but before Constantine there was hardly any form of central government over the whole Church.

The power of bishops in great cities was enhanced by the practice of almsgiving: the offerings of the faithful were administered by the bishop, who could give or withhold charity to the poor. There came thus to be a mob of the destitute, ready to do the bishop's judicial and administrative functions. There came also to be a central government, at least in matters of doctrine. Constantine was annoyed by the quarrel between Catholics and Arians; having thrown in his lot with the Christians, he wanted them to be a united party. For the purpose of healing dissensions, he caused the convening of the oecumenical Council of Nicaea, which drew up the Nicene Creed,[8] and, so far as the Arian controversy was concerned, determined for all time the standard of orthodoxy. Other later controversies were similarly decided by oecumenical councils, until the division between East and West and the Eastern refusal to admit the authority of the Pope made them impossible.

The Pope, though officially the most important individual in the Church, had no authority over the Church as a whole until a much later period. The gradual growth of the papal power is a very interesting subject, which I shall deal with in later chapters.

The growth of Christianity before Constantine, as well as the motives of his conversion, has been variously explained by various authors. Gibbon[9] assigns five causes:

1 The inflexible, and, if we may use the expression, the intolerant zeal of the Christians, derived, it is true, from the Jewish religion, but purified from the narrow and unsocial spirit which, instead of inviting, had deterred the Gentiles from embracing the Law of Moses.
2 The doctrine of a future life, improved by every additional circumstance which could give weight and efficacy to that important truth.
3 The miraculous powers ascribed to the primitive Church.
4 The pure and austere morals of the Christians.
5 The union and discipline of the Christian republic, which gradually formed an independent and increasing State in the heart of the Roman empire.

Broadly speaking, this analysis may be accepted, but with some comments. The first cause – the inflexibility and intolerance derived from the Jews – may be wholly accepted. We have seen in our own day the advantages of intolerance in propaganda. The Christians, for the most part, believed that they alone would go to heaven, and that the most awful punishments would, in the next world, fall upon the heathen. The other religions which competed for favour during the third century had not this threatening character. The worshippers of the Great Mother, for example, while they had a ceremony – the Taurobolium – which was analogous to baptism, did teach that those who omitted it would go to hell. It may be remarked, incidentally, that the Taurobolium was expensive: a bull had to be killed, and its blood allowed to trickle over the convert. A rite of this sort is aristocratic, and cannot be the basis of a religion which is to embrace the great bulk of the population, rich and poor, free and slave. In such respects, Christianity had an advantage over all its rivals.

As regards the doctrine of a future life, in the West it was first taught by the Orphics and thence adopted by Greek philosophers. The Hebrew prophets, some of them, taught the resurrection of the body, but it seems to have been from the Greeks that the Jews learnt to believe in the resurrection of the spirit.[10] The doctrine of immortality, in Greece, had a popular form in Orphism and a learned form in Platonism. The latter, being based upon difficult arguments, could not become widely popular; the Orphic form, however, probably had a great influence on the general opinions of later antiquity, not only among pagans, but also among Jews and Christians. Elements of mystery religions, both Orphic and Asiatic, enter largely into Christian theology; in all of them, the central myth is that of the dying god who rises again.[11] I think, therefore, that the doctrine of immortality must have had less to do with the spread of Christianity than Gibbon thought.

Miracles certainly played a very large part in Christian propaganda. But miracles, in later antiquity, were very common, and were not the prerogative of any one religion. It is not altogether easy to see why, in this competition, the Christian miracles came to be more widely believed than those of other sects. I think Gibbon omits one very important matter, namely the possession of a Sacred Book. The miracles to which Christians appealed had begun in a remote antiquity, among a nation which the ancients felt to be mysterious; there was a consistent history, from the Creation onwards, according to which Providence had always worked wonders, first for the Jews, then for the Christians. To a modern historical student it is obvious that the early history of the Israelites is in the main legendary, but not so to the ancients. They believed in the Homeric account of the siege of Troy, in Romulus and Remus, and so on; why, asks Origen, should you accept these traditions and reject those of the Jews? To this argument there was no logical answer. It was therefore natural to accept Old Testament miracles, and, when they had been admitted, those of more recent date became credible, especially in view of the Christian interpretation of the prophets.

The morals of the Christians, before Constantine, were undoubtedly very superior to those of average pagans. The Christians were persecuted at times, and were almost always at a disadvantage in competition with pagans. They believed firmly that virtue would be rewarded in heaven and sin punished in hell. Their sexual ethics had a strictness that was rare in antiquity. Pliny, whose official duty it was to persecute them, testifies to their high moral character. After the conversion of Constantine, there were, of course, time-servers among Christians; but prominent ecclesiastics, with some exceptions, continued to be men of inflexible moral principles. I think Gibbon is right in attributing great importance to this high moral level as one of the causes of the spread of Christianity.

Gibbon puts last 'the union and discipline of the Christian republic'. I think that, from a political point of view, this was the most important of his five causes. In the modern world, we are accustomed to political organization; every politician has to reckon with the Catholic vote, but it is balanced by the vote of other organized groups. A Catholic candidate for the American Presidency is at a disadvantage, because of Protestant prejudice. But, if there were no such thing as Protestant prejudice, a Catholic candidate would stand a better chance than any other. This seems to have been Constantine's calculation. The support of the Christians, as a single organized bloc, was to be obtained by favouring them. Whatever dislike of the Christians existed was unorganized and politically ineffective. Probably Rostovtseff is right in holding that a large part of the army was Christian, and that this was what most influenced Constantine. However that may be, the Christians, while still a minority, had a kind of organization which was then new, though now common, and which gave them all the political influence of a pressure group to which no other pressure groups are opposed. This was the natural consequence of their virtual monopoly of zeal, and their zeal was an inheritance from the Jews.

Unfortunately, as soon as the Christians acquired political power, they turned their zeal against each other. There had been heresies, not a few, before Constantine, but the orthodox had had no means of punishing them. When the State became Christian, great prizes, in the shape of power and wealth, became open to ecclesiastics;

there were disputed elections, and theological quarrels were also quarrels for worldly advantages. Constantine himself preserved a certain degree of neutrality in the disputes of theologians, but after his death (337) his successors (except for Julian the Apostate) were, in a greater or less degree, favourable to the Arians, until the accession of Theodosius in 379.

The hero of this period is Athanasius (*ca.* 297–373), who was throughout his long life the most intrepid champion of Nicene orthodoxy.

The period from Constantine to the Council of Chalcedon (451) is peculiar owing to the political importance of theology. Two questions successively agitated the Christian world: first, the nature of the Trinity, and then the doctrine of the Incarnation. Only the first of these was to the fore in the time of Athanasius. Arius, a cultivated Alexandrian priest, maintained that the Son is not the equal of the Father, but created by Him. At an earlier period, this view might not have aroused much antagonism, but in the fourth century most theologians rejected it. The view which finally prevailed was that the Father and the Son were equal, and of the same substance; they were, however, distinct Persons. The view that they were not distinct, but only different aspects of one Being, was the Sabellian heresy, called after its found Sabellius. Orthodoxy thus had to tread a narrow line: those who unduly emphasized the distinctness of the Father and the Son were in danger of Arianism, and those who unduly emphasized their oneness were in danger of Sabellianism.

The doctrines of Arius were condemned by the Council of Nicaea (325) by an overwhelming majority. But various modifications were suggested by various theologians, and favoured by Emperors. Athanasius, who was Bishop of Alexandria from 328 till his death, was constantly in exile because of his zeal for Nicene orthodoxy. He had immense popularity in Egypt, which, throughout the controversy, followed him unwaveringly. It is curious that, in the course of theological controversy, national (or at least regional) feeling, which had seemed extinct since the Roman conquest, revived. Constantinople and Asia inclined to Arianism; Egypt was fanatically Athanasian; the West steadfastly adhered to the decrees of the Council of Nicaea. After the Arian controversy was ended, new controversies, of a more or less kindred sort, arose, in which Egypt became heretical in one direction and Syria in another. These heresies, which were persecuted by the orthodox, impaired the unity of the Eastern Empire, and facilitated the Mohammedan conquest.

The separatist movements, in themselves, are not surprising, but it is curious that they should have been associated with very subtle and abstruse theological questions.

The Emperors, from 335 to 378, favoured more or less Arian opinions as far as they dared, except for Julian the Apostate (361–363), who, as a pagan, was neutral as regards the internal disputes of the Christians. At last, in 379, the Emperor Theodosius gave his full support to the Catholics, and their victory throughout the Empire was complete. St Ambrose, St Jerome, and St Augustine lived most of their lives during this period of Catholic triumph. It was succeeded, however, in the West, by another Arian domination, that of the Goths and Vandals, who, between them, conquered most of the Western Empire. Their power lasted for about a century, at the end of which it was destroyed by Justinian, the Lombards, and the Franks, of whom Justinian and the Franks, and ultimately the Lombards also, were orthodox. Thus at last the Catholic faith achieved definitive success.

21

MOHAMMEDAN CULTURE
AND PHILOSOPHY

The attacks upon the Eastern Empire, Africa, and Spain, differed from those of Northern barbarians on the West in two respects: first, the Eastern Empire survived till 1453, nearly a thousand years longer than the Western; second, the main attacks upon the Eastern Empire were made by Mohammedans, who did not become Christians after conquest, but developed an important civilization of their own.

The Hegira,[1] with which the Mohammedan era begins, took place in AD 622; Mohammed died ten years later. Immediately after his death the Arab conquests began, and they proceeded with extraordinary rapidity. In the East, Syria was invaded in 634, and completely subdued within two years. In 637 Persia was invaded; in 650 its conquest was completed. India was invaded in 664; Constantinople was besieged in 669 (and again in 716–717). The westward movement was not quite so sudden. Egypt was conquered in 642, Carthage not till 697. Spain, except for a small corner in the northwest, was acquired in 711–712. Westward expansion (except in Sicily and southern Italy) was brought to a standstill by the defeat of the Mohammedans at the battle of Tours in 732, just one hundred years after the death of the prophet. (The Ottoman Turks, who finally conquered Constantinople, belong to a later period than that with which we are now concerned.)

Various circumstances facilitated this expansion. Persia and the Eastern Empire were exhausted by their long wars. The Syrians, who were largely Nestorian, suffered persecution at the hands of the Catholics, whereas Mohammedans tolerated all sects of Christians in return for the payment of tribute. Similarly in Egypt the Monophysites, who were the bulk of the population, welcomed the invaders. In Africa, the Arabs allied themselves with the Berbers, whom the Romans had never thoroughly subdued. Arabs and

229

Berbers together invaded Spain, where they were helped by the Jews, whom the Visigoths had severely persecuted.

The religion of the Prophet was a simple monotheism, uncomplicated by the elaborate theology of the Trinity and the Incarnation. The Prophet made no claim to be divine, nor did his followers make such a claim on his behalf. He revived the Jewish prohibition of graven images, and forbade the use of wine. It was the duty of the faithful to conquer as much of the world as possible for Islam, but there was to be no persecution of Christians, Jews, or Zoroastrians – the 'people of the Book', as the Koran calls them, i.e. those who followed the teaching of a Scripture.

Arabia was largely desert, and was growing less and less capable of supporting its population. The first conquests of the Arabs began as mere raids for plunder, and only turned into permanent occupation after experience had shown the weakness of the enemy. Suddenly, in the course of some twenty years, men accustomed to all the hardships of a meagre existence on the fringe of the desert found themselves masters of some of the richest regions of the world, able to enjoy every luxury and to acquire all the refinements of an ancient civilization. They withstood the temptations of this transformation better than most of the Northern barbarians had done. As they had acquired their empire without much severe fighting, there had been little destruction, and the civil administration was kept on almost unchanged. Both in Persia and in the Byzantine Empire, the civil government had been highly organized. The Arab tribesmen, at first, understood nothing of its complications, and perforce accepted the services of the trained men whom they found in charge. These men, for the most part, showed no reluctance to serve under their new masters. Indeed, the change made their work easier, since taxation was lightened very considerably. The populations, moreover, in order to escape the tribute, very largely abandoned Christianity for Islam.

The Arab Empire was an absolute monarchy, under the caliph, who was the successor of the Prophet, and inherited much of his holiness. The caliphate was nominally elective, but soon became hereditary. The first dynasty, that of the Umayyads, who lasted till 750, was founded by men whose acceptance of Mohammed was purely political, and it remained always opposed to the more fanatical among the faithful. The Arabs, although they conquered a great part of the world in the name of a new religion, were not a very religious race; the motive of their conquests was plunder and wealth rather than religion. It was only in virtue of their lack of fanaticism that a handful of warriors were able to govern, without much difficulty, vast populations of higher civilization and alien religion.

The Persians, on the contrary, have been, from the earliest times, deeply religious and highly speculative. After their conversion, they made out of Islam something much more interesting, more religious, and more philosophical, than had been imagined by the Prophet and his kinsmen. Ever since the death of Mohammed's son-in-law Ali in 661, Mohammedans have been divided into two sects, the Sunni and the Shiah. The former is the larger; the latter follows Ali, and considers the Umayyad dynasty to have been usurpers. The Persians have long belonged to the Shiah sect. Largely by Persian influence, the Umayyads were at last overthrown, and succeeded by the Abbasids, who represented Persian interests. The change was marked by the removal of the capital from Damascus to Baghdad.

The Abbasids were, politically, more in favour of the fanatics than the Umayyads had been. They did not, however, acquire the whole of the empire. One member of the Umayyad family escaped the general massacre, fled to Spain, and was there acknowledged as the legitimate ruler. From that time on, Spain was independent of the rest of the Mohammedan world.

Under the early Abbasids the caliphate attained its greatest splendour. The best known of them is Harun-al-Rashid (d. 809), who was a contemporary of Charlemagne and the Empress Irene, and is known to everyone in legendary form through the *Arabian Nights*. His court was a brilliant centre of luxury, poetry, and learning; his revenue was enormous; his empire stretched from the Straits of Gibraltar to the Indus. His will was absolute; he was habitually accompanied by the executioner, who performed his office at a nod from the caliph. This splendour, however, was short-lived. His successor made the mistake of composing his army mainly of Turks, who were insubordinate, and soon reduced the caliph to a cipher to be blinded or murdered whenever the soldiery grew tired of him. Nevertheless, the caliphate lingered on; the last caliph of the Abbasid dynasty was put to death by the Mongols in 1256, along with 800,000 of the inhabitants of Baghdad.

The political and social system of the Arabs had defects similar to those of the Roman Empire, together with some others. Absolute monarchy combined with polygamy led, as it usually does, to dynastic wars whenever a ruler died, ending with the victory of one of the ruler's sons and the death of all the rest. There were immense numbers of slaves, largely as a result of successful wars; at times there were dangerous servile insurrections. Commerce was greatly developed, the more so as the caliphate occupied a central position between East and West.

Not only did the possession of enormous wealth create a demand for costly articles, such as silks from China, and furs from Northern Europe, but trade was promoted by certain special conditions, such as the vast extent of the Muslim Empire, the spread of Arabic as a world-language, and the exalted status assigned to the merchant in the Muslim system of ethics; it was remembered that the Prophet himself had been a merchant and had commended trading during the pilgrimage to Mecca.[2]

This commerce, like military cohesion, depended on the great roads which the Arabs inherited from the Romans and Persians, and which they, unlike the Northern conquerors, did not allow to fall into disrepair. Gradually, however, the empire broke up into fractions – Spain, Persia, North Africa, and Egypt successively split off and acquired complete or almost complete independence.

One of the best features of the Arab economy was agriculture, particularly the skilful use of irrigation, which they learnt from living where water is scarce. To this day Spanish agriculture profits by Arab irrigation works.

The distinctive culture of the Muslim world, though it began in Syria, soon came to flourish most in the Eastern and Western extremities, Persia and Spain. The Syrians, at the time of the conquest, were admirers of Aristotle, whom Nestorians preferred to Plato, the philosopher favoured by Catholics. The Arabs first acquired their knowledge of Greek philosophy from the Syrians, and thus, from the beginning, they thought Aristotle more important than Plato. Nevertheless, their Aristotle wore a Neoplatonic dress. Kindi (d. *ca.* 873), the first to write philosophy in Arabic, and the only philosopher of note who was himself an Arab, translated parts of the *Enneads* of Plotinus, and published his translation under the title *The Theology of Aristotle*. This introduced great confusion into Arabic ideas of Aristotle, from which it took centuries to recover.

Meanwhile, in Persia, Muslims came in contact with India. It was from Sanskrit writings that they acquired, during the eighth century, their first knowledge of astronomy. About 830, Muhammad ibn Musa al-Khwarazmi, a translator of mathematical and astronomical books from the Sanskrit, published a book which was translated into Latin in the twelfth century, under the title *Algoritmi de numero Indrum*. It was from this book that the West first learnt of what we call 'Arabic' numerals, which ought to be called 'Indian'. The same author wrote a book on algebra which was used in the West as a text-book until the sixteenth century.

Persian civilization remained both intellectually and artistically admirable, though it was seriously damaged by the invasion of the Mongols in the thirteenth century. Omar Khayyám, the only man known to me who was both a poet and a mathematician, reformed the calendar in 1079. His best friend, oddly enough, was the founder of the sect of the Assassins, the 'Old Man of the Mountain', of legendary fame. The Persians were great poets: Firdousi (*ca.* 941), author of the *Shahnama*, is said by those who have read him to be comparable to Homer. They were also remarkable as mystics, which other Mohammedans were not. The Sufi sect, which still exists, allowed itself great latitude in the mystical and allegorical interpretation of orthodox dogma; it was more or less Neoplatonic.

The Nestorians, through whom, at first, Greek influences came into the Muslim world, were by no means purely Greek in their outlook. Their school at Edessa had been closed by the Emperor Zeno in 481; its learned men thereupon migrated to Persia, where they continued their work, but not without suffering Persian influences. The Nestorians valued Aristotle only for his logic, and it was above all his logic that the Arabic philosophers thought important at first. Later, however, they studied also his *Metaphysics* and his *De Anima*. Arabic philosophers, in general, are encyclopaedic: they are interested in alchemy, astrology, astronomy, and zoology, as much as in what we should call philosophy. They were looked upon with suspicion by the populace, which was fanatical and bigoted; they owed their safety (when they were safe) to the protection of comparatively free-thinking princes.

Two Mohammedan philosophers, one of Persia, one of Spain, demand special notice; they are Avicenna and Averroes. Of these the former is the more famous among Mohammedans, the latter among Christians.

Avicenna (Ibn Sina) (980–1037) spent his life in the sort of places that one used to think only exist in poetry. He was born in the province of Bohara; at the age of twenty-four he went to Khiva – 'lone Khiva in the waste' – then to Khorassan – 'the lone Chorasmian shore'. For a while he taught medicine and philosophy at Ispahan; then he settled at Teheran. He was even more famous in medicine than in philosophy, though he added little to Galen. From the twelfth to the seventeenth century, he was used in Europe as a guide to medicine. He was not a saintly character, in fact he had a passion for wine and women. He was suspect to the orthodox, but was befriended by princes on account of his medical skill. At times he got into trouble owing to the hostility of Turkish mercenaries; sometimes he was in hiding, sometimes in prison. He was the author of an encyclopaedia, almost unknown to the East because of the hostility of theologians, but influential in the West through Latin translations. His psychology has an empirical tendency.

His philosophy is nearer to Aristotle, and less Neoplatonic, than that of his Muslim predecessors. Like the Christian scholastics later, he is occupied with the problem of universals. Plato said they were anterior to things. Aristotle has two views, one when he is thinking, the other when he is combating Plato. This makes him ideal material for the commentator.

Avicenna invented a formula, which was repeated by Averroes and Albertus Magnus: 'Thought brings about the generality in forms.' From this it might be supposed that he did not believe in universals apart from thought. This, however, would be an unduly simple view. Genera – that is, universals – are, he says, at once before things, in things, and after things. He explains this as follows. They are *before* things in God's understanding. (God decides, for instance, to create cats. This requires that He should have the idea 'cat', which is thus, in this respect, anterior to particular cats.) Genera are *in* things in natural objects. (When cats have been created, felinity is in each of them.) Genera are *after* things in our thought. (When we have seen many cats, we notice their likeness to each other, and arrive at the general idea 'cat'.) This view is obviously intended to reconcile different theories.

Averroes (Ibn Rushd) (1126–1198) lived at the opposite end of the Muslim world from Avicenna. He was born at Cordova, where his father and grandfather had been cadis; he himself was a cadi, first in Seville, then in Cordova. He studied, first, theology and jurisprudence, then medicine, mathematics, and philosophy. He was recommended to the 'Caliph' Abu Yaqub Yusuf as a man capable of making an analysis of the works of Aristotle. (It seems, however, that he did not know Greek.) This ruler took him into favour; in 1184 he made him his physician, but unfortunately the patient died two years later. His successor, Yaqub Al-Mansur, for eleven years continued his father's patronage; then, alarmed by the opposition of the orthodox to the philosopher, he deprived him of his position, and exiled him, first to a small place near Cordova, and then to Morocco. He was accused of cultivating the philosophy of the ancients at the expense of the true faith. Al-Mansur published an edict to the effect that God had decreed hell-fire for those who thought that truth could be found by the unaided reason. All the books that could be found on logic and metaphysics were given to the flames.[3]

Shortly after this time the Moorish territory in Spain was greatly diminished by Christian conquests. Muslim philosophy in Spain ended with Averroes; and in the rest of the Mohammedan world a rigid orthodoxy put an end to speculation.

Ueberweg, rather amusingly, undertakes to defend Averroes against the charge of unorthodoxy – a matter, one would say, for Muslims to decide. Ueberweg points out that, according to the mystics, every text of the Koran had 7 or 70 or 700 layers of interpretation, the literal meaning being only for the ignorant vulgar. It would seem to follow that a philosopher's teaching could not possibly conflict with the Koran; for among 700 interpretations there would surely be at least one that would fit what the philosopher had to say. In the Mohammedan world, however, the ignorant seem to have objected to all learning that went beyond a knowledge of the Holy Book; it was dangerous, even if no specific heresy could be demonstrated. The view of the mystics, that the populace should take the Koran literally but wise people need not do so, was hardly likely to win wide popular acceptance.

Averroes was concerned to improve the Arabic interpretation of Aristotle, which had been unduly influenced by Neoplatonism. He gave to Aristotle the sort of reverence that is given to the founder of a religion – much more than was given even by Avicenna. He holds that the existence of God can be proved by reason independently of revelation, a view also held by Thomas Aquinas. As regards immortality, he seems to have adhered closely to Aristotle, maintaining that the soul is not immortal, but intellect (*nous*) is. This, however, does not secure *personal* immortality, since intellect is one and the same when manifested in different persons. This view, naturally, was combated by Christian philosophers.

Averroes, like most of the later Mohammedan philosophers, though a believer, was not rigidly orthodox. There was a sect of completely orthodox theologians, who objected to all philosophy as deleterious to the faith. One of these, named Algazel, wrote a book called *Destruction of the Philosophers*, pointing out that, since all necessary truth is in the Koran, there is no need of speculation independent of revelation. Averroes replied by a book called *Destruction of the Destruction*. The religious dogmas that Algazel specially upheld against the philosophers were the creation of the world in time out of nothing, the reality of the divine attributes, and the resurrection of the body. Averroes regards religion as containing philosophic truth in allegorical form. This applies in particular to creation, which he, in his philosophic capacity, interprets in an Aristotelian fashion.

Averroes is more important in Christian than in Mohammedan philosophy. In the latter he was a dead end; in the former, a beginning. He was translated into Latin early in the thirteenth century by Michael Scott; as his works belong to the latter half of the twelfth century, this is surprising. His influence in Europe was very great, not only on the scholastics, but also on a large body of unprofessional freethinkers, who denied immortality and were called Averroists. Among professional philosophers, his admirers were at first especially among the Franciscans and at the University of Paris.

Arabic philosophy is not important as original thought. Men like Avicenna and Averroes are essentially commentators. Speaking generally, the views of the more scientific philosophers come from Aristotle and the Neoplatonists in logic and metaphysics, from Galen in medicine, from Greek and Indian sources in mathematics and astronomy, and among mystics religious philosophy has also an admixture of old Persian beliefs. Writers in Arabic showed some originality in mathematics and in chemistry – in the latter case, as an incidental result of alchemical researches. Mohammedan civilization in its great days was admirable in the arts and in many technical ways, but it showed no capacity for independent speculation in theoretical matters. Its importance, which must not be underrated, is as a transmitter. Between ancient and modern European civilization, the dark ages intervened. The Mohammedans and the Byzantines, while lacking the intellectual energy required for innovation, preserved the apparatus of civilization – education, books, and learned leisure. Both stimulated the West when it emerged from barbarism – the Mohammedans chiefly in the thirteenth century, the Byzantines chiefly in the fifteenth. In each case the stimulus produced new thought better than any produced by the transmitters – in the one case scholasticism, in the other the Renaissance (which however had other causes also).

Between the Spanish Moors and the Christians, the Jews formed a useful link. There were many Jews in Spain, who remained when the country was reconquered by the Christians. Since they knew Arabic, and perforce acquired the language of the Christians, they were able to supply translations. Another means of transfusion arose through Mohammedan persecution of Aristotelians in the thirteenth century, which led Moorish philosophers to take refuge with Jews, especially in Provence.

The Spanish Jews produced one philosopher of importance, Maimonides. He was born in Cordova in 1135, but went to Cairo at the age of thirty, and stayed there for the rest of his life. He wrote in Arabic, but was immediately translated into Hebrew. A few decades after his death, he was translated into Latin, probably at the request of the Emperor Frederick II. He wrote a book called *Guide to Wanderers*, addressed to philosophers who have lost their faith. Its purpose is to reconcile Aristotle with Jewish theology. Aristotle is the authority on the sublunary world, revelation on the heavenly. But philosophy and revelation come together in the knowledge of God. The pursuit of truth is a religious duty. Astrology is rejected. The Pentateuch is not always to be taken literally; when the literal sense conflicts with reason, we must seek an allegorical interpretation. As against Aristotle, he maintains that God created not only form, but matter, out of nothing. He gives a summary of the *Timaeus* (which he knew in Arabic), preferring it on some points to Aristotle. The essence of God is unknowable, being above all predicated perfections. The Jews considered him heretical, and went so far as to invoke the Christian ecclesiastical authorities against him. Some think that he influenced Spinoza, but this is very questionable.

22

THE REFORMATION AND
COUNTER-REFORMATION

The Reformation and Counter-Reformation, alike, represent the rebellion of less civilized nations against the intellectual domination of Italy. In the case of the Reformation, the revolt was also political and theological: the authority of the Pope was rejected, and the tribute which he had obtained from the power of the keys ceased to be paid. In the case of the Counter-Reformation, there was only revolt against the intellectual and moral freedom of Renaissance Italy; the power of the Pope was not diminished, but enhanced, while at the same time it was made clear that his authority was incompatible with the easy-going laxity of the Borgias and Medici. Roughly speaking, the Reformation was German, the Counter-Reformation Spanish; the wars of religion were at the same time wars between Spain and its enemies, coinciding in date with the period when Spanish power was at its height.

The attitude of public opinion in northern nations towards Renaissance Italy is illustrated in the English saying of that time:

An Englishman Italianate
Is a devil incarnate.

It will be observed how many of the villains in Shakespeare are Italians. Iago is perhaps the most prominent instance, but an even more illustrative one is Iachimo in *Cymbeline*, who leads astray the virtuous Briton travelling in Italy, and comes to England to practise his wicked wiles upon unsuspecting natives. Moral indignation against Italians had much to do with the Reformation. Unfortunately it involved also intellectual repudiation of what Italy had done for civilization.

The three great men of the Reformation and Counter-Reformation are Luther, Calvin and Loyola. All three, intellectually, are mediaeval in philosophy, as compared either to the Italians who immediately preceded them, or to such men as Erasmus and More. Philosophically, the century following the beginning of the Reformation is a barren one. Luther and Calvin reverted to St Augustine, retaining, however, only that part of his teaching which deals with the relation of the soul to God, not the part which is concerned which the Church. Their theology was such as to diminish the power of the Church. They abolished purgatory, from which the souls of the dead could be delivered by masses. They rejected the doctrine of Indulgences, upon which a large part of the papal revenue depended. By the doctrine of predestination, the fate of the soul after death was made wholly independent of the actions of priests. These innovations, while they helped in the struggle with the Pope, prevented the Protestant Churches from becoming as powerful in Protestant countries as the Catholic Church was in Catholic countries. Protestant divines were (at least at first) just as bigoted as Catholic theologians, but they had less power, and were therefore less able to do harm.

Almost from the very beginning, there was a division among Protestants as to the power of the State in religious matters. Luther was willing, wherever the prince was Protestant, to recognize him as head of the Church in his own country. In England, Henry VIII and Elizabeth vigorously asserted their claims in this respect, and so did the Protestant princes of Germany, Scandinavia, and (after the revolt from Spain) Holland. This accelerated the already existing tendency to increase in the power of kings.

But those Protestants who took seriously the individualistic aspects of the Reformation were as unwilling to submit to the king as to the Pope. The Anabaptists in Germany were suppressed, but their doctrine spread to Holland and England. The conflict between Cromwell and the Long Parliament had many aspects; in its theological aspect, it was in part a conflict between those who rejected and those who accepted the view that the State should decide in religious matters. Gradually weariness resulting from the wars of religion led to the growth of belief in religious toleration, which was one of the sources of the movement which developed into eighteenth- and nineteenth-century liberalism.

Protestant success, at first amazingly rapid, was checked mainly as a resultant of Loyola's creation of the Jesuit order. Loyola had been a soldier, and his order was founded on military models; there must be unquestioning obedience to the General, and every Jesuit was to consider himself engaged in warfare against heresy. As early as the Council of Trent, the Jesuits began to be influential. They were disciplined, able, completely devoted to the cause, and skilful propagandists. Their theology was the opposite of that of the Protestants; they rejected those elements of St Augustine's teaching which the Protestants emphasized. They believed in free will, and opposed predestination. Salvation was not by faith alone, but by both faith and works. The Jesuits acquired prestige by their missionary zeal, especially in the Far East. They became popular as confessors, because (if Pascal is to be believed) they were more lenient, except towards heresy, than other ecclesiastics. They concentrated on education, and thus acquired a firm hold on the minds of the young. Whenever theology did not interfere, the education they gave was the best obtainable; we shall see that they taught Descartes more mathematics than he would have learnt elsewhere. Politically, they were a single united disciplined body, shrinking from no dangers and no exertions; they urged Catholic princes to practise relentless persecution, and, following in the wake of conquering Spanish armies, re-established the terror of the Inquisition, even in Italy, which had had nearly a century of free-thought.

The results of the Reformation and Counter-Reformation, in the intellectual sphere, were at first wholly bad, but ultimately beneficial. The Thirty Years' War persuaded everybody that neither Protestants nor Catholics could be completely victorious; it became necessary to abandon the mediaeval hope of doctrinal unity, and this increased men's freedom to think for themselves, even about fundamentals. The diversity of creeds in different countries made it possible to escape persecution by living abroad. Disgust with theological warfare turned the attention of able men increasingly to secular learning, especially mathematics and science. These are among the reasons for the fact that, while the sixteenth century, after the rise of Luther, is philosophically barren, the seventeenth contains the greatest names and makes the most notable advance since Greek times. This advance began in science.

NOTES

INTRODUCTION

1 This volume p. 169.
2 K. Tait, *My Father Bertrand Russell* (London: Harcourt Brace, 1975), p. 184.
3 A.C. Grayling, *Russell* (Oxford: Oxford University Press, 1996), p. 83.
4 R. Monk, *Bertrand Russell: The Spirit is Solitude* (New York: Free Press, 1996), p. xix.
5 Barry Feinberg, Ronald Kasrils, eds, *Dear Bertrand Russell* (Boston: Houghton Mifflin, 1964).
6 M. Griffin, 'Bertrand Russell as a Critic of Religion' in *Studies in Religion Sciences/Sciences Religieuses*, vol. 24, no. 1, pp. 47–58.
7 Ibid.
8 This volume p. 28.
9 This volume p. 28.
10 This volume p. 57.
11 J. Burnet, *Early Greek Philosophy* (New York: Meridian Books, 1957), pp. 112–129
12 E. Gibbon, *The Decline and Fall of the Roman Empire* (abridged by Dero A. Saunders, Middlesex: Penguin, 1982), p. 53.
13 J. Slater, ed., PBR, vol. 10, p.22.
14 S. Andersson, *In Quest of Certainty* (Stockholm: Almquist, 1994).
15 This volume p. 27.
16 This volume p. 80.
17 This volume p. 80.
18 B. Russell, *The Scientific Outlook* (London: George Allen & Unwin), p. 105.
19 John H. Brooke, *Science and Religion* (Cambridge: Cambridge University Press, 1995), p. 51.
20 Bertrand Russell, 'Scientific Certainty' in John G. Slater (ed.) with the assistance of Peter Kollner, *Collected Papers of Bertrand Russell: A Fresh Look at Empiricism, 1927–42* (London: Routledge, 1996), vol. 11, p.61.
21 *Scientific* (1931) p.125.
22 This volume p. 82.
23 This volume p. 183.

24 This volume p. 84.
25 This volume p. 183.
26 This volume p. 171.
27 William James, *Varieties of Religious Experience* (New York: Image Books, 1978), p. 48.
28 B. Russell, *Religion and Science* (New York: Oxford University Press, 1961).
29 James, p. 49.
30 Ibid., p. 57.
31 B. Russell, *Religion and Science* (New York: Oxford University Press, 1961).
32 E.S. Brightman, 'Russell's Philosophy of Religion' in Paul Arthur Schilpp, *The Philosophy of Bertrand Russell* (New York: Tudor, 1951), pp. 537–557.
33 R. Jaeger, *The Development of Bertrand Russell's Philosophy* (London: Allen and Unwin, 1972).
34 John Lynden, *Enduring Issues in Religion* (San Diego: Greenhave Press, 1995), p. 51.
35 K. Blackwell, *The Spinozistic Ethics of Bertrand Russell* (London: Allen and Unwin, 1985).
36 Ibid., p. 127.
37 This volume, see p. 39.
38 B. Russell, *Principles of Social Reconstruction* (London: George Allen & Unwin, 1915).
39 This volume p. 158.
40 This volume p. 110.
41 B. Russell, 'In Place of Science in a Liberal Education' in R. Rempel, A. Brink, M. Moran, eds, *Collected Papers of Bertrand Russell*, vol. 12, *Contemplation and Action* (London: Allen and Unwin, 1985), p. 395.
42 B. Russell, *History of Western Philosophy* (London: Allen and Unwin, 1946), p. 782.
43 B. Russell, *The Impact of Science on Society* (London: Allen and Unwin, 1952), p. 114.

1 FROM 'MY MENTAL DEVELOPMENT' AND 'REPLY TO CRITICISMS'

† Source *CPBR*, vol. 11.

2 THE FREE MAN'S WORSHIP

† Source *CPBR*, vol. 12.

3 AUTOBIOGRAPHY: MYSTIC ILLUMINATION

† Source *Autobiography*, vol. 1.

4 WHAT IS AN AGNOSTIC?

† Source *CPBR*, vol. 11.

PART II: RELIGION AND PHILOSOPHY

1 For a quick overview of Russell's definitions of religion, philosophy and science, see *The Wit and Wisdom of Bertrand Russell* (Boston: 1951) edited, with an introduction, by Lester E. Dennon, *Bertrand Russell's Dictionary of Mind, Matter and Morals* (New York: 1952) edited, with an introduction, by Lester E. Dennon, and *Bertrand Russell's Best* (London: 1958) edited, with an introduction, by Robert E. Egner.

2 The relationship between Russell and Wittgenstein is a very interesting one, particularly their different understandings of religion and mysticism, which are exemplified by Wittgenstein's reaction to Russell's essay, 'The Essence of Religion'. When Russell met Wittgenstein again after the First World War, he had, according to Russell, turned into a complete mystic. But it was not the kind of mysticism that originated from Pythagoras, Parmenides and Plato, which Russell appreciated, but a kind of mysticism that puts emphasis on the submission to the will of an incomprehensible God. For information about their relationship, see Kenneth Blackwell, 'The Middle Russell and the Early Wittgenstein' in *Perspectives on Wittgenstein*, edited by Irving Block (Oxford: 1981). See also Ray Monk's biographies of Wittgenstein and Russell, *Ludwig Wittgenstein: The Duty of Genius* (London: 1990) and *Bertrand Russell: The Spirit of Solitude* (London: 1996).

5 THE ESSENCE OF RELIGION

† Source *CPBR*, vol. 12.

6 THE ESSENCE AND EFFECT OF RELIGION

† Source *CPBR*, vol. 15.
1 A church practises persecution when it uses oppressive methods against a heretic and arrests him.

7 WHY I AM NOT A CHRISTIAN

† Source *CPBR*, vol. 10.
1 Stanley Baldwin.

8 THE EXISTENCE AND NATURE OF GOD

† Source *CPBR*, vol. 10.

9 MYSTICISM AND LOGIC

† Source *CPBR*, vol. 12.
1 All the above quotations are from Burnet's *Early Greek Philosophy* (2nd edn 1908), pp. 146–156.
2 *Republic*, 514, translated by Davies and Vaughan.

3 This section, and also one or two pages in later sections, have been printed in a course of Lowell lectures on *Our Knowledge of the External World*, published by the Open Court Publishing Company. But I have left them here, as this is the context for which they were originally written.
4 *Introduction to Metaphysics*, p. i.
5 Whinfield's translation of the *Masnavi* (Trübner, 1887), p. 34.
6 *Ethics*, Book iv, Prop. lxii.
7 Ibid., Part ii, Df. vi.
8 Ibid., Part vi, Df. i.

10 SCIENCE AND RELIGION

† Source *CPBR*, vol. 10.
1 'The principle of natural selection is absolutely incompatible with the Word of God.'
2 Editors' note: the (now Royal) Society for the Prevention of Cruelty to Animals.
3 Exodus xxii: 18.

11 REVIEW OF SIR ARTHUR EDDINGTON *THE NATURE OF THE PHYSICAL WORLD*

† Source *CPBR*, vol. 10.

12 REVIEW OF JAMES JEANS, *THE MYSTE-RIOUS UNIVERSE*

† Source *CPBR*, vol. 10.

13 DO SCIENCE AND RELIGION CONFLICT?

† Source *CPBR*, vol. 11. *Some Aspects of the Conflict between Science & Religion* by H.H. Price. The Seventh Arthur Stanley Eddington Memorial Lecture, 3 November 1953. Cambridge at the University Press, 1953, Pp. v, 54.

14 RELIGION AND THE CHURCHES

† Source *Principles of Social Reconstruction*.
1 I should add artists, but for the fact that most modern artists seem to find much greater difficulty in creation than men of science usually find.

15 INHERENT TENDENCIES OF INDUSTRI-ALISM

† Source *Prospects of Industrial Civilization*.

16 HAS RELIGION MADE USEFUL CONTRI-
BUTIONS TO CIVILIZATION

† Source *CPBR*, vol. 10.

17 THE SENSE OF SIN

† Source *Conquest of Happiness.*

19 THE RELIGIOUS DEVELOPMENT OF THE
JEWS

1 Jeremiah vii, 17–18.
2 *Ibid.*, vii, 31.
3 Jeremiah xliv, 11–end.
4 Ezekiel vii, 11–end.
5 Ezra ix–x, 5.
6 Leviticus xx, 24.
7 Ibid., xix, 2.
8 Isaiah vii, 14.
9 Ibid., x, 2, 6.
10 Ibid., lx, 3.
11 *Jerusalem under the High Priests*, p. 12.
12 From them, probably, developed the sect of the Essenes, whose doctrines seem to have influenced primitive Christianity. See Oesterley and Robinson, *History of Israel*, vol. II, p. 323ff. The Pharisees also descended from them.
13 Some Alexandrian Jews did not object to this identification. See *Letter of Aristeas*, 15, 16.
14 I Maccabees i, 60–63.
15 *The Apocrypha and Pseudepigrapha of the Old Testament in English*. Edited by R.H. Charles, vol. II, p. 659.
16 For the text of this book, in English, see Charles, op. cit., whose introduction also is valuable.

20 CHRISTIANITY DURING THE FIRST
FOUR CENTURIES

1 I Timothy vi, 20, 21.
2 Mark xxv, 34.
3 Or rather the author of an Epistle attributed to St Paul – Colossians ii, 8.
4 Matthew xix, 12.
5 Origen, *Contra Celsum*, Book I, chap. ii.
6 Ibid., Book I, chap. xxvi.
7 Ibid., Book VIII, chap. lxxv.
8 Not exactly in its present form, which was decided upon in 362.
9 *The Decline and Fall of the Roman Empire*, chap. xv.
10 See Oesterley and Robinson, *Hebrew Religion*.
11 See Angus, *The Mystery Religions and Christianity*.

21 MOHAMMEDAN CULTURE AND PHILOSOPHY

1 The Hegira was Mohammed's flight from Mecca to Medina.
2 *Cambridge Medieval History*, IV, 286.
3 It is said that Averroes was taken back into favour shortly before his death.

SELECTED BIBLIOGRAPHY

This is a selected bibliography of the books and articles that are mentioned in the text. For full information about what Russell wrote about religion, we refer the reader to *A Bibliography of Bertrand Russell* in three volumes edited by Kenneth Blackwell and Harry Ruja. For information about what had been written about Russell and religion up to 1987, see Stefan Andersson's article 'A secondary religious bibliography of Bertrand Russell' in *Russell: the Journal of the Bertrand Russell Archives*, New Series, Vol. 7, no. 2, Winter 1987–8, pp. 147–161. The most important works on Russell's views on religion published in the last decade are: Andersson (1994), Griffin (1995) and Larry Harwood 'Russell's Reticence with Religion' in *Russell: the Journal of the Bertrand Russell Archives*, New Series, Vol. 17, no. 1, Summer 1997.

Andersson, Stefan (1994) *In Quest of Certainty. Bertrand Russell's Search for Certainty in Religion and Mathematics up to 'The Principles of Mathematics'* (1903), Stockholm: Almqvist & Wiksell International.

Blackwell, Kenneth (1985) *The Spinozistic Ethics of Bertrand Russell*, London: Allen & Unwin.

Brightman, Edgar Sheffield (1944) 'Russell's Philosophy of Religion' in *The Philosophy of Bertrand Russell*, Library of Living Philosophers, ed. P. A. Schilpp, Evanston and Chicago, Ill.

Grayling, Anthony (1996) *Russell*, Oxford: Oxford University Press.

Griffin, Nicholas (1995) 'Bertrand Russell as a Critic of Religion' in *Studies in Religion/Sciences Religieuses*, Volume 24, Number 1, pp. 47–58.

Jager, Ronald (1972) *The Development of Bertrand Russell's Philosophy*, London: Allen & Unwin. (Chapter 10: Ethics and Religion.)

—— (1972) 'Russell and Religion' in *Russell in Review*, eds, J. E. Thomas and K. Blackwell, Toronto: Samuel Stevens, Hakkert & Company, pp. 91–113.

James, William (1978) *The Varieties of Religious Experience*, New York: Image Books.

Monk, Ray (1996) *Bertrand Russell: The Spirit of Solitude*, New York: Free Press.

Bertrand, Russell (1910) *Philosophical Essays*, London: Longmans, Green and Co.

—— (1912) *The Problems of Philosophy*, London: Williams and Norgate.

—— (1916) *Principles of Social Reconstruction*, London: Allen & Unwin.

—— (1918) *Mysticism and Logic*, London: Longmans, Green and Co.

—— (1918) *Roads to Freedom*, London: Allen & Unwin.

—— (1923) *Prospects of Industrial Civilization*, London: Allen & Unwin.

—— (1930) *The Conquest of Happiness*, New York: Horace Liveright.

—— (1935) *Religion and Science*, London: Thornton Butterworth Ltd.

—— (1946) *History of Western Philosophy*, London: Allen & Unwin.

—— (1952) *The Impact of Science on Society*, London: Allen & Unwin.

—— (1956) *Portraits From Memory*, London: Allen & Unwin.

—— (1998) *Autobiography* (in one volume), London: Routledge.

Tait, Katharine (1996) *My Father Bertrand Russell*, Bristol: Thoemmes Press.

INDEX